RETHINKING LAW, SOCIETY

Titles in this Series

Rethinking Law, Society and Governance
Foucault's Bequest

Edited by
GARY WICKHAM
Murdoch University
and
GEORGE PAVLICH
University of Alberta

OÑATI INTERNATIONAL SERIES IN LAW AND SOCIETY

A SERIES PUBLISHED FOR THE OÑATI INSTITUTE
FOR THE SOCIOLOGY OF LAW

·HART·
PUBLISHING
OXFORD – PORTLAND OREGON
2001

Hart Publishing
Oxford and Portland, Oregon

Published in North America (US and Canada) by
Hart Publishing c/o
International Specialized Book Services
5804 NE Hassalo Street
Portland, Oregon
97213-3644
USA

Distributed in the Netherlands, Belgium and Luxembourg by
Intersentia, Churchillaan 108
B2900 Schoten
Antwerpen
Belgium

Hart Publishing is a specialist legal publisher based in Oxford, England.
To order further copies of this book or to request a list of other
publications please write to:

Hart Publishing, Salter's Boatyard, Folly Bridge,
Abingdon Road, Oxford OX1 4LB
Telephone: +44 (0)1865 245533 or Fax: +44 (0)1865 794882
e-mail: mail@hartpub.co.uk
WEBSITE: http//www.hartpub.co.uk

British Library Cataloguing in Publication Data
Data Available
ISBN 1–84113–293–4 (hardback)
1–84113–294–2 (paperback)

Typeset by Hope Services (Abingdon) Ltd.
Printed and bound in Great Britain on acid-free paper by
Biddles Ltd, www.biddles.co.uk

Contents

Series Editors' Foreword

In this book, governmentality, most often associated with the theoretical work of Michel Foucault, is re-explored to measure its relevance to contemporary sociolegal issues. Building on a vast range of social and legal theory, governmentalilty is posited against pressing issues of space and landscape, art and architecture, new forms of regulation and management, and new grounds of legal context. The book considers whether political involvement, and specifically progressive political involvement, should be a necessary component of a governmentality approach. This analysis directly challenges many governmentality theorists who have been content to analyse grand conceptual practices without demanding that they be applied to local political systems. The book also raises pertinent and innovative questions regarding methodology, and suggests how a governmentality approach may undermine our assumed methodological objectivity. Throughout the essays the contributors to this book, all scholars at the forefront of their fields, engage in a variety of exciting ways and creative perspectives with issues of power and resistance as they rethink the value of a governmentality approach and its application to ever-widening boundaries of sociolegal scholarship and politicised activities.

The book is the product of a workshop held at the International Institute for the Sociology of Law (IISL) in Onati, Spain. The IISL is a partnership between the Research Committee on the Sociology of Law and the Basque Government. For more than a decade it has conducted an international master's programme in the sociology of law and hosted hundreds of workshops devoted to sociolegal studies. It maintains an extensive sociolegal library open to scholars from any country and any relevant discipline. Detailed information about the IISL can be found at <www.iisj.es>. This book is the most recent publication in the Onati International Series in Law and Society, a series that publishes the best manuscripts produced from Onati workshops conducted in English. A similar series, Coleccion Onati: Derecho Y Sociedad, is published in Spanish.

William L F Felstiner
Eve Darian-Smith

List of Contributors

David Brown is Professor of Law at the University of New South Wales, Sydney.

Kerry Carrington is a member of the Critical Social Sciences Research Group and Associate Professor in the School of Sociology and Justice Studies at the University of Western Sydney, Hawkesbury.

Russell Hogg is a member of the Critical Social Sciences Research Group in the School of Sociology and Justice Studies at the University of Western Sydney, Hawkesbury.

Jo Goodie is a Lecturer in Law at Murdoch University, Perth.

Jeff Malpas is Professor of Philosophy at the University of Tasmania. His contribution to this volume was completed while a Humboldt Research Fellow at the University of Heidelberg.

Pat O'Malley is Professor at the School of Law and Legal Studies, La Trobe University, Victoria.

George Pavlich is Professor of Sociology and Associate Chair at the University of Alberta, Edmonton.

Annette Pedersen works in the School of Architecture and Fine Arts at the University of Western Australia, Perth.

Kevin Stenson is Director of the Social Policy Research Group and Professor of Social Policy and Criminology at Buckinghamshire Chilterns University College, High Wycombe.

William Walters is Assistant Professor in Political Science at Carleton University, Ottawa.

Introduction

Transforming Images:
Society, Law and Critique

GEORGE PAVLICH

For MUCH OF the twentieth century, a popular but nebulous concept held considerable sway over many Western nation states' images of how to regulate subjects—namely, the "social". Under the guise of society, social welfare, social order, social defence, social need, social security, social insurance and the like, these states relied on disciplinary technologies of *social* control to complement the visibly coercive elements of their laws (Donzelot 1979; 1991; Foucault, 1977). The ensuing regulatory horizons were indelibly marked with the ink of a discourse centred on the social, and this shaped the mentalities of dominant ruling practices (Hacking 1999). As such, and evoking Foucault's (1991) neologism, prevalent "governmentalities" relied upon images of the social to enunciate visions of governors (e.g., social experts), subjects of governance (e.g., normal and abnormal individuals in society), governmental techniques (e.g., disciplinary correction and social rehabilitation, ordering) and so on (see Bauman 1987; 1997). Looking back, one would not be amiss to conclude that the "social", and its derivative variants, reigned supreme in many regulatory contexts for much of the last century.

Not surprisingly, the privilege granted to social welfare governmentalities profoundly affected the identity of associated legal institutions, at all levels. Even academic debates devoted to law's basic ontology did not escape the omniscience of social thinking. One could, for example, point to an influential *social* theme underlying many approaches to the sociology of law, jurisprudence and legal anthropology. Whilst appropriated variously in different contexts, the theme declared law to derive from a social basis (e.g., Milovanovic 1988; Cotterrell 1984). In the more daring of these formulations, law was depicted as nothing other than a social construction; but most legal analyses defined parts of the law's identity as recursively related to wider *social* norms. Even here, though, the social theme was treated as a privileged idea, and many adherents accepted—

[handwritten margin notes: "2change", "Social-uprising/revolution-law pressured", "more formulation of disciplining concepts - law + society", reproduced as marginalia]

as Comack and Brickey point out—the following image as an almost canonical assumption: "Law can be said to have a distinctly *social basis*; it both shapes—and is shaped by—the society in which it operates" (1991: 15). Although we shall return to the idea later, it is perhaps useful to mention this in passing: as older images of social order faced attack, so predicated identities of law confronted significant pressure to change.

By the early 1970s, the auspices of social control within liberal welfare states were jolted by the successful assaults of diverse neo-liberal, public choice, free market, neo-conservative political ideas and programmes. The assaults spread across national and conventional party political boundaries, and included the much publicised (neo-liberal?) Labo(u)r experiments in New Zealand and Australia, the new conservatisms of 1980s Britain, the United States, Canada, Europe and elsewhere. Despite vast contextual differences, most reflected more or less sustained attacks on aspects of Keynesian (and other) social governance (e.g., Keynes 1936). Allied neo-liberal programmes sought to roll back social welfare provisions, cut back state functions, privatise and corporatise public services, revise social taxation schemes, and so on (e.g., Kelsey 1993). Directly related to the concerns of this book, several analysts drew attention to the effects of such attacks on the underlying rationales and techniques of social governance. These thinkers described key shifts in how collective formations used new images and tools to create, control, regulate, shape and organise compliant subjects (see, generally, Dean 1999; O'Malley 1994; 1996a; 2000; Rose 1989; 1996b; 1999). This body of work developed out of Foucault's (1977; 1980; 1991) conceptions of power-knowledge, and his ambiguous sketches of "governmentality", in an effort to diagnose the budding mentalities of contemporary governance.

THE COLLECTED ESSAYS

The present collection taps into the noted governmentality debates as it grapples with the legacy of social governance in contexts seeking to regulate subjects beyond welfare "societies" (often ambiguously labelled neo-liberal, neo-social, advanced liberal and neo-conservative regulatory terrains). Overall, its essays examine the emergence of "law" and "society" as key concepts of disciplinary social governance (with particular reference to Australia), the ways in which both concepts are being redeployed in current regulatory arenas and how to address this changing political climate. One could argue that all implicitly work from the following notion:

> "During the last two decades the social has been increasingly challenged and extensively displaced by political rationalities of rule . . . that seek to govern through individuals, families and a multitude of quasi contractual, quasi voluntary collectivities such as the 'community' " (O'Malley 1996c: 27).

Signalling this shift, disciplinary power-knowledge relations attending to social institutions have been prized loose from the stability of earlier (social welfare) political moorings (Bauman 1997; 1992; Pavlich 1995). Some commentators see in this the grounds for asserting a "post-disciplinary" ethos in which quite different power relations colonise the ruins of erstwhile disciplinary power-knowledge formations (Readings 1996). Allied arguments proffer the view that for all intents and purposes the social is now dead (Baudrillard 1983; Rose 1996c). These point out how different regulatory concepts (e.g., community) have usurped the place once accorded to the "social". In turn, one can see how this might have important consequences for the identity of the legal edifices bound to images of the social in welfare state formations.

But what lies behind the "death of the social" claim? Baudrillard (1983: 86 *et seq*) presents various arguments to signal the changing ways in which key hyper-real images (simulacra, like the "social") are produced. He argues that changes to ways simulacra are produced involve concomitant changes to the ensuing hyper-real images. As such, he argues that older hyper-real images of an amorphous social are now obsolete. Along related lines, Rose (1996c; 1999) challenges the view that the social is a basic and inevitable construct:

> "the 'social' does not refer to an inescapable fact about human beings—that they are social creatures—but to a way in which human intellectual, political and moral authorities, within a limited geographical territory, thought about and acted upon the collective experience for about a century" (1999: 101).

Moreover, he contends that the social as a basis for thinking and acting "upon the collective experience" is now dead; new imaginings have taken its place in various "advanced liberal" arenas (Rose 1996b). Not all accept Baudrillard's or Rose's "death of the social" arguments, and their critics might point to various degrees of social governance that still loom relatively large in most Western contexts (i.e., substantial sums are still spent on social services, social policy is still very much in focus, etc.). However, few would contest the claim that several cornerstones of social welfare governance have been eroded, displaced, modified and even partly overthrown.

But the dissolutions indicated are not meant to imply a neat, clean or decisive break from socially ordered regulatory arenas to an environment absolutely beyond social governance. Indeed, gradual, haphazard and complex moves away from diverse discipline-based forms of welfare liberalism have, perhaps inevitably, left lingering traces of erstwhile governmentalities. Yet, in composite, the changes have prized regulation away from specifically social priorities and produced several new governmental rationales and practices. These rather less than determined shifts in governmentalities should make us cautious of reifying complex and diverse regulatory processes through the closure of singular concepts (e.g., neo-liberal, post-social, and even advanced liberal—see Pat O'Malley, chapter 1 below). With this in mind, and reflecting this book's specific focus on the changing auspices of "social" governance, I propose that the shifting terrain be loosely referred to as a *co-social* ethos.

The idea here is to reference emerging governmentalities existing alongside, but not founded upon, images of the social. These governmentalities are not predicated *on*, or *after*, social governance, but emerge somewhat parasitically *with* social calculations of rule. Hence, one might point to a reason for using the prefix, "co". "Co-social" does not signal a nice, clear shift from previous disciplinary, social welfare governance. Nor do emerging "prudential" forms of risk management (O'Malley 1996a; 1998; see also Petersen and Lupton 1996), emphases on "security" calculations (Bauman 1997; see also Pavlich 2000), actuarial forms of justice (Feeley and Simon 1994), visions of community control (Cohen 1985; Pavlich 1996a and Pavlich 1996b), etc., necessarily overthrow all attemps to govern social orders. Rather, there are locally inflected, and heterogeneous, points of contact between different regulatory logics and practices. Our use of "co-social governmentalities" then signals these multiple, undetermined, dynamic and hybrid shifts in rationales and practices of rule away from regulatory arenas predicated on images of the social as a primordial being. These emerging contexts may well bear ancestral traces of social calculations but also bring with them different control rationales, agendas, practices and priorities.

With such definitional caveats in mind, one might say that as co-social governmentalities realign, so images of the social as an ontological fact of collective life are displaced; increasingly the social is viewed as a contingent political artefact of historically-situated welfare government rationales. Moreover, several emerging governmentalities oppose this artefact as too costly—in financial and other ways—to be sustained intact. This paves the way for images of the "family", or "community", to surface as primary (replacement?) forms of association, and to justify cutbacks on techniques of social governance (social security, social insurance, etc.). In the wake of such developments, the social may endure as a concept, but it does so without its past privilege.

If the above has significant ramifications for diagnosing the complex governmentalities that confront us nowadays, it also signals important changes for the identities of "law" (and "crime") no longer predicated upon clear-cut social foundations. That is, as the "social" basis of law weakens, erodes, or is fundamentally revamped, so modern law's associated identity is swept into torrents of re-identification—the previously intimate alliances between law and social order face redefinition. And as this happens, analysts are bound to reflect on how to speak critically within, and to, the tumults of a transforming governmental ethos. These broad concerns open themselves up to vast analytical possibilities, but the chapters of this collection address themselves to three specific themes: (i) calling for, and responding to, genealogical analyses directed to diagnosing the "emergence" and "lines of descent" of hybrid co-social governmentalities; (ii) naming how fracturing "social" governmentalities affect associated identities of law, order and crime; and (iii) exploring grammars of critique capable of confronting co-social governance.

No doubt, however, the chapters speak to these themes in diverse ways. There is little to gain from disguising the (sometimes profound) differences in their interpretations, insisting they fit snugly into a Procrustean bed of editorial making. If this requires some latitude when reading the whole, it also allows for voices to speak in unique ways to complex and emerging issues. Nonetheless, the essays are divided into three related parts, reflecting the above indicated themes. The first, entitled "Genealogical Entries: Governance, the Social and the Colonies", formulates several genealogies of particular sorts of governance centred on "society", its "laws" and emerging "co-social" images of rule. The second part, "Law, Crime and the Politics of Co-social Governance", focuses specifically on how transformations to social welfare governmentalities have affected on law, order and crime. Finally, "Reframing Ontology and Critique" offers future-orientated glances into possible ways to engage, methodologically and critically, the changing governmental terrains that have been discussed above

1 Genealogical entries: social governance and the colonies

This part begins with a plea to pursue genealogical analyses when charting the emergence of particular (e.g., co-social) governmentalities. Given the different locales of many contributors to this book, and following Foucault's genealogical emphasis on "local histories", the essays explore governmentalities in both colonial (Australian) and imperial contexts. Especially noteworthy here is the way colonial locales refract aspects of imperial social governmentalities in unusual ways, allowing the reader to discern novel contributions to wider governmentality debates.

The first chapter, Pat O'Malley's "Genealogy, Systematisation and Resistance in 'Advanced Liberalism' ", is an ideal starting point for the whole collection as it situates the three themes noted. O'Malley engages changes to governance through law and society by first discerning relevant Foucaultian "governmentality" arguments (especially as directed at neo-liberalism and the subtle shifts involved in the use of the near-synonym "advanced liberalism"). The discussion calls for vigilance to closures produced by singular categories, and the need to be aware of the pluralities that static concepts eclipse. Furthermore, O'Malley notes the concern of those who question whether governmentality work is capable of effective critical and political analysis. Whilst sympathetic to critics' calls for explicit political engagement, and clearer formulations of resistance, he nevertheless argues that governmentality frameworks can overcome their apparent weaknesses by according greater priority to Foucault's genealogical method. To illustrate the point, O'Malley looks to emerging punishment practices to show how governmentality analysts are too quick to interpret recent developments (e.g., attempts to foster self-governing, "enterprising" prisoners) as successful outcomes of neo-liberal attacks. Such thinking, however, overlooks complex and hybrid links between various neo-liberal and other mentalities of government (e.g., neo-conservative). This over-sight could be avoided by relying on sophisticated discussions of genealogical analyses that provide better strategic maps from which to engage (resist?) emerging governmental arenas.

Annette Pedersen's chapter implicitly accepts O'Malley's invitation to for-mulate rich genealogies in her unique analysis of the co-social governmentality theme. For her, the manner in which policing is understood and practised by a given locale reveals much about the governmentalities that license particular exercises of power. Looking at early Australian policing through pictorial rep-resentations of police functions in the nineteenth century state of Victoria, Pedersen develops vital links between Gramsci's images of civil society and Foucault's (as well as Donzelot's) images of disciplinary power relations. Forging these links allows her to chart the rise of social governmentalities in a colonial setting through a fascinating—and novel—discussion of William Strutt who, between 1850 and 1861, painted mounted police officers and troopers in Australia. Strutt's art provides a wonderfully rich canvass of images and ideas for extracting some key elements of the rationales and techniques of social gov-ernance developed by colonial policing. Pedersen uses the paintings as a window on the governmentalities through which state law and society were created in the mediating presence of the police trooper. This chapter also indicates the role of nineteenth century policing in helping to establish the basis of "the social" and disciplinary power as a constitutive "dark side" to formal expressions of colonial law.

Russell Hogg and Kerry Carrington's chapter 3 explores the genealogical theme of social governmentality in a somewhat different way. Noting the effects of the Australian High Court's *Wik* decision, permitting the co-existence of Aboriginal native title and pastoral leasehold land interests, Carrington and Hogg describe some complex, hybrid and diverse ways in which rural land title has been, and continues to be, governed in Australia. Like O'Malley, they are critical of the potential political apathy generated by governmentality analysis, but also see value in its ability to highlight the contingent rationales and techniques of specific "regimes of governance". Their focus is on the "rationalities of colonization and land settlement", indicating how, in Australia, this complexly involved the formation and development of social governance. They also reveal how singularly "illiberal" governmentalities directed the governance of Australia's Aboriginal peoples in rural land regulation, thereby pointing to an important, if overlooked, dimension to understanding the co-social governmentalities now present in colonial settings.

In the closing chapter of this part, "Governing Unemployment: Transforming the 'Social'?", William Walters outlines some distinctive features of government-ality literatures to show how these elucidate the complexities of "social governance". Walters distinguishes a "governmentality perspective" from other theories by emphasising its focus on such things as the "programmatic" and "practical" aspects of governing, the ways in which subjects are governed through images of autonomy, and especially its understanding of "the discursive character of government". After situating how this perspective might approach wider social welfare rationales, he charts several ways in which the social has been reconfigured by new ways of governing the unemployed in Britain. He focuses on how "political authorities" understand themselves, their tasks and the targets of their governance. The chapter also examines how unemployment is, "imagined within neo-liberal, neo-social democratic, communitarian strategies of government, as well as in terms of the strategy of criminalising the poor". In all, this chapter provides a complex genealogy of the "emergence" of present mutations in the "social", showing how its distinctive local lines of descent have produced a hybrid political ethos that bears traces of various political rationales and technologies used to govern the unemployed.

Law, crime and the politics of co-social governance

The second part of the book begins with a reflexive look at law's changing forms as it relates to new, co-social governmentalities. The chapters in this section pursue this broad theme quite differently. Jo Goodie's "The Invention of the Environment as a Subject of Legal Governance", insightfully alludes to the manner in which co-social governance has helped to etch new legal identities and subjects. She argues that law's previous reliance on the "autonomous, rational, legally capable individual" under conditions of social governance has effectively been supplanted by other "subjects"—the *environment* is a case in point examined here. Conceiving of the environment as a contingently negotiated subject of specific governmental politics allows Goodie to reflect on the ways in which legal subjects are created, showing how socio-legal politics bounces off social (public health), and increasingly co-social (new public health), governmentalities. Her account focuses on the law's emerging images of the environment, particularly in the budding area of toxic tort. She describes how legal identities are being reshaped by the priorities and popularity of rising co-social governmentalities. Goodie also tackles the specific ways in which co-social governmental techniques, such as the emphasis place on particular images of risk, require accommodation by new legal precepts and even institutions.

The changing identity of criminal law and institutions lies silhouetted behind Kevin Stenson's "Reconstructing the Government of Crime". His essay focuses on the changing forces involved with the "government of crime" in many co-social contexts, and explores important changes to some institutions of criminal law, policing and justice. Stenson sketches the complex background of this "reconstruction", focusing on how crime has been thrust into the centre of co-social governmental concerns with "safety" and "urban security" in Britain,

Europe and the United States. Part of this reconstruction involves the use of criminal law in the service of different governmental aims. Having contrasted two explanations of the change, Stenson offers "a cautious endorsement" of the governmentality literature, but wants to extend its alliances with some aspects of materialist thinking. He feels this would help to recognise the complex hybridism of governmental forms, and to appreciate better the "new sovereignty" that is in the processes of emerging. In many ways, this may be taken as an invitation to further analysis of co-social identities of criminal law. However, Stenson, like others in this collection, remains wary of the seeming lack of political engagement in many governmental analyses.

David Brown's "Governmentality and Law and Order" endorses Stenson's worry through a telling polemic against the tendency of much Foucaultian "governmentality" literature to "disdain politics", and to ignore or marginalise "any possibility that things might or should be different". He argues that whilst governmentality literatures reconceive politics in potentially insightful ways, they often spurn active political resistance strategies. Brown develops a possible response by drawing on fragments of the governmentality literature that echo his call for a greater emphasis on political engagement. This call serves as the basis for discussing how governmentality approaches might be used to help, rather than hinder, a critical understanding of co-social law-and-order politics. He exemplifies his plea by referring to recent developments around a dynamic law and order politics in Australia. Without the alleviating influence of commitments to social justice, co-social law and order debates embrace a hard retributive edge, as endorsed by developments in New South Wales. This chapter extends O'Malley's invitation for governmentality critics not to stand back from the politics of law and order and instead to use their insights to further active resistance strategies. It issues a challenge: to understand the auspices of political engagement and resistance in co-social governmental contexts—a task that leads us to the final section and its search for appropriate languages of critique.

③ Reframing ontology and critique

The final part of the collection seeks to develop apposite critical languages for addressing co-social governmental arenas. In many ways, this part entails a critique of co-social critique, and its two chapters tackle the theme in rather different ways. Malpas directs his "critique of metaphysics" to highlight the importance of ontology, not only in governmentality approaches, but also in attempts to think through methodologies appropriate to these. Pavlich, by contrast, speaks to the possibility of developing a grammar of critique, beyond discipline-based judgements, that is relevant to co-social contexts.

In his "Governmentality and the Critique of Metaphysics: Ontology, Methodology and Social Theory", Jeff Malpas closely argues for a message rarely heard in socio-legal studies, and even more rarely heard in Foucaultian socio-legal studies: our diagnoses of governmentalities always involve ontology, whether we think they do or not. His opening gambit makes clear that methodological questions are—for the most part—inseparable from ontological questions pertaining to the "entities and structures that are constitutive of that region". Those familiar with the general terrain at hand will recognise that this chapter implicitly takes issue with a strand of governmentality thinking that claims governmental diagnoses are not theoretical accounts of a particular being, only an "analytics of governance" directed to historical conditions for a given "emergence" (see Dean 1999: 20–1). Malpas rejects this, arguing that all forms of description and explanation, by definition, imply an ontology—it is crucial to realise this when approaching rationales and techniques of governance. But, he insists, all theoretical and practical ventures are limited, and so are failures; this should divest anyone of grand metaphysical pretensions. His intriguing analysis of this theme in social theory and Heideggerian philosophy provides an opportunity to signal the importance of sceptical thinking to the formation of critical selves involved with limited ontological analyses. All in all, this chapter raises several important considerations for imagining how to proceed with critical analyses of the change being brought by co-social governmentalities.

Concluding the collection, George Pavlich's essay "The Art of Critique or How Not to be Governed Thus" develops a co-social grammar of critique capable of naming, witnessing and politically engaging co-social governmentalities. He situates the dominant reign of "critic as expert judge" within disciplinary contexts that enable and sustain social governmentalities. In those contexts, the activity of critique as founded judgement holds considerable sway, and stands at the epicentre of its political critique. However, with the rising tides of co-social governance, he argues that critique as judgement is losing its centuries-old grip. Returning to etymological traces that link critique to images of separation, or discernment (rather than judgement), Pavlich tries to imagine an alternative "genre of critique". Drawing on Foucault, he traces the genealogy of an alternative critique that emerged with the art of government, and locates in this the possibility for a non-judgemental art of critique. He shows how critique might be recovered from discourses surrounding the art of governance since its early development. From Foucault, he notes the value of a critical language centred on this relentlessly evoked call: how not to be governed thus. . . In this call, he identifies a genre of critique that constantly searches for new life, beyond the limiting presence of given governmental regimes. From this, Pavlich extracts an alternative model of critique to confront the growing influence of dangers that surround co-social governmentalities.

PART ONE

Genealogical Entries: Governance, the Social and the Colonies

1

Genealogy, Systematisation and Resistance in "Advanced Liberalism"

PAT O'MALLEY

INTRODUCTION

IN "GOVERNMENTALITY" (1991), Foucault does not ask certain standard questions familiar in, even required of, conventional political analysis. He does not sociologically explain the emergence of governmentality, although he does attempt to understand what allowed it to emerge. He does not reduce governmentality to a reflex of some other phenomenon, but rather gives primacy to processes of imagination and problematisation. He does not ask after the complex sociological effects that it has generated, although he does outline a set of dimensions of rule in terms of which government subsequently is thought out. He does not, in short, concern himself with the approach to politics that can be thought of as relational, and which characterised certain other of his attempts to grapple with government, particularly those in which he discussed the place of "resistance". Rather, he examines politics as a mentality of rule, analysing it in terms of its own epistemologies and discoveries, its intended modes of investigation and operation, its internal moralities and evaluations. This approach to governmentality has fundamentally coloured the literature that has formed in the wake of "Governmentality". This literature:

> "draws attention to the fundamental role that knowledges play in rendering aspects of existence thinkable and calculable, and amenable to deliberated and planful initiatives: a complex intellectual labour involving not only the invention of new forms of thought, but also the invention of novel procedures of documentation, computation and evaluation. It suggests that we need to consider under what ethical conditions it became possible for different authorities to consider it legitimate, feasible and even necessary to conduct such interventions" (Miller and Rose 1990: 3).

Within this governmentality literature, it is possible to see that the development of mentalities of rule has come to be analysed in terms of two complementary processes. The first, concerned with the formation of mentalities, is that analytically valorised through genealogy. Genealogy here asks two questions: how did it become possible for a government mentality or particular government programme to form and, which elements were drawn together in this process of formation? It is virtually a fundamental principle of governmentality work that this process of formation involves a double moment of contingency. First:

> "there is no smooth path of development or evolution of policies . . . lasting inventions have often arisen in surprising and aleatory fashion and in relation to apparently marginal or obscure difficulties in social or economic existence which for particular reasons have come to assume political salience" (Miller and Rose 1990: 3).

Secondly, the formation of such policies and programmes is reliant on whatever intellectual, social or material resources are at hand. Consequently they do not start out with any coherence, but are pragmatic assemblages that somehow "do the job", being united only by the common characteristic of being thought of as appropriate to the task. The imagery of Heath Robinson's whimsical machines is often drawn upon in this respect (e.g., Rose 1996a).

The contingent and incoherent assemblages brought together by genealogy are then given a formal consistency and systematicity through the operation of the government mentalities. Over time, these assemblages are subjected to all manner of critical attention from within and without. "Inconsistencies" are explained away or reimagined; they are redescribed in "more appropriate terms" or renamed in language "more appropriate". Elements that contradict each other may be rearranged so that their clash is less visible and less problematic. Failing this, persistently jarring elements may be dropped altogether, sometimes to be substituted by other elements that are deemed more consistent (for an extended example, see O'Malley 1996a). It is this process of systematisation that generates government rationalities. For example:

> "It would be misleading to suggest that the neo-conservative political regimes that were elected in Britain and the United States in the late 1970s were underpinned by a coherent and elaborated political rationality that they sought to implement . . . Initially, no doubt, these regimes merely sought to engage with a multitude of different problems of welfare, to reduce cost, to undercut the power of professional lobbies, etc. But gradually these diverse skirmishes were rationalised within a relatively coherent mentality of government. Neo-liberalism managed to re-activate the sceptical vigilance over political government basic to classical liberalism by linking different elements to the rhetoric of reaction with a series of techniques . . . that could render these criticisms governmental" (Rose 1996a: 53).

These governmental rationalities are regarded as real, at least in the sense of actually occurring and being empirically grounded: formed and evidenced in texts of rule, in plans, programmes, formulae, manifestos, White Papers, ministerial statements. The process of systematisation produces "perfect knowledges" (Miller and Rose 1990: 11) in the sense that such knowledge is systematically rationalised, but precisely because they are formulated in empirically existing texts and practices of government, their status as ideal types is vigorously rejected by governmentality theorists from Foucault to Rose.

Despite this, and despite the fact that many studies in the genre are characterised by closely grounded analyses of government, it is questionable whether most of the governmentality-inspired analyses of (or in terms of) neo-liberalism—the form of liberal rationality most under scrutiny—make reference to the specific texts that express the mentality of neo-liberalism-at-large in any coherent and thorough-going fashion. Rather, reference is either to very specific programmes that are held to have neo-liberal characteristics (a process vulnerable to circularity), or to rather general typifications based on selected and highly abstract criteria of no particular provenance (e.g., Pratt 1996; Burchell 1993; O'Malley 1994). Most often, it is as though neo-liberalism is known unproblematically, directly from experience, and any examination of the texts of rule is largely the search for exemplars.

One reason for this feature, I suggest, is not that there are no neo-liberal texts, or even self-styled "neo-liberal" regimes, but rather that they are multitudinous and multifarious, with varying degrees of authorisation and regional or temporal identity and character. This point is obliquely alluded to by Rose (1990; 1996a) who uses it as one reason for developing a new term altogether: "advanced liberalism" (although it is vital to note that for most governmentality work in this domain, the terms neo-liberal and advanced liberal have become co-extensive). Consequently neo-liberalism as it is understood in most governmentality work is the outcome of a process of second order analysis. But in what sense are the neo-liberal or advanced liberal mentalities of rule that emerge from this process any longer empirically real, ideal knowledges? From whence comes their character as political rationalities: the texts of neo-liberalism(s) or the rationalising labours of the analyst? This sets up a rather characteristic tension peculiar to such governmentality work, between its claim to locate "empirically existing" rationalities, and its own formation of rational types.

ADVANCED LIBERALISM, NEO-LIBERALISM AND THE NEED FOR GENEALOGY

For Rose, whose work provides the most sophisticated and extensive analysis of current liberalisms within the governmentality literature, neo-liberalism is a set of historically specific formulae of liberal government—though never precisely identified in his work. Advanced liberalism on the other hand is understood to be "more modest yet more durable" and "much more significant than the brief flowering of neo-liberal political rhetorics" (Rose 1996a: 53). In some respects this is because advanced liberalism is a much broader and inclusive family of liberalism, equivalent to the "social liberalism" of the welfare state and the "classical" liberalism that predominated in the nineteenth century (Rose 1996a; 1996b). Like "social liberalism", this rationality is unambiguously a second order construct, a fact in itself indicated not only by the academic neologism "advanced liberalism", but also by the fact that there is almost no reference to definitive programmes or texts. Rather, it is constructed in terms of highly abstracted forms, techniques and relations.

As developed by Rose (1989; 1996a; 1996b), advanced liberalism is defined in terms of the following principal characteristics:

A relationship between expertise and politics that centres the calculative regimes of accounting and management

In social liberalism, governmental programmes related to "the social" were closely linked to the esoteric knowledges of the positive sciences of human conduct. Advanced liberalism has transferred its allegiance instead to an array of calculative and more abstract technologies, including budget disciplines, audit and accountancy. These require professionals and experts to translate their esoteric knowledges into a language of costs and benefits that can be given an accounting value, and made "transparent" to scrutiny. In the form of marketisation, the authority of experts is determined not by their own professional criteria, but by the play of the market. Consumers of expertise determine the authority and the reach of experts through the voluntary purchase (choice) of their services. In all such processes markets as "natural" phenomena, as understood by classical liberalism, are displaced by the conception of markets as purposively created as techniques of policy, in order to maximise choice, efficiency, accountability and competition.

A revised autonomy of the subject of government

Neo-liberal mentalities envisage the subjects of the state of welfare as over-governed: either restricted in their freedom by the constraints of the interventionist state; or rendered dependent by the clasp of the welfare state. Subjects constituted by the changed relations of expertise, however, emerge as sovereign customers and consumers, as making choices among advice and service providers—rather than citizens acted upon by various authorities. Subjects thus appear as "active" and innovative, as seeking to "enterprise themselves" as marketable entities maximising their personal value and achieving the means for self-fulfilment. As such, they are imagined as "empowered"— made free from debilitating state intervention—and encouraged to assemble their own lifestyles from among the array of commodified options available in the free market.

Through the same processes, subjects become more responsible for themselves and for the consequences of their choices. They are expected to form a calculative and prudent orientation toward life, to be aware of the opportunities and hazards in life, to acquire skills and knowledges that will place them to advantage in the face of a competitive and ever-changing world. They are expected to avail themselves of the skills, resources and knowledges made available in the market in order to maximise their security, health and well-being: to build self esteem, exercise care of their body, manage risks to their person and property, engage in life long learning, and so on. In this sense, Rose (1996b) suggests that there is a shift from governing through the social, to governing through the individual.

A pluralisation of "social" technologies

The prioritisation of the market, of choice makers and of individual responsibility is associated with the "death of the social" (Rose 1996b). In place of subjects united by common bonds of obligations and rights, through an organic unity of society, new norms and relations are established that are more fragmentary and variable. Communities, families and industries, imagined as a multiplicity of self-governing and/or voluntary associations displace the centralised vision of a single society. Gay communities develop and operate self-help health programmes for their members, neighbourhoods effect their own security and crime prevention through neighbourhood watch or private security, schools become the focus of communities of parents who govern the educational resources brought to bear on their children. Individuals bear responsibilities toward these entities, but they are imagined neither as morally or legally compulsory nor as naturally given, as under the state of "the social". Communities will rise and fall according to demand and satisfaction rather than bureaucratic or legal compulsion. At the same time, the social norms of dedication, obedience and service are displaced by other, more individualistic norms in keeping with the entrepreneurial ethos—such as competition, mutual benefit, and satisfaction. These parallel, and intermingle with, those of the changed "marketised" relations of expertise.

What emerges here, I would argue, is an analysis that outlines an abstracted set of characteristics, systematically and consistently arranged, and selectively isolated, accentuated and assembled through the lens of governmentality. They are presented in a systematically integrated form that, while analytically attractive (as is indicated by the plethora of studies that have deployed "advanced liberalism"), resemble an ideal type that does not appear empirically in this form. Nowhere does this constitute an account of an actually existing, unalloyed empirical arrangement, and yet it is understood as a "robust rationality", "that underpins mentalities of government from all parts of the political spectrum" (Rose 1996a: 60).

While it may at first appear as hair-splitting, I suggest that the deployment of either "advanced liberalism" or "neo-liberalism" readily slips into the mode of treating these second order constructs as real rationalities that are, in a sense, immanent in the present, either already established or—perhaps more frequently—unfolding. The form of advanced liberalism essentially is known already, even where it has yet fully to "emerge". It is this usage that has attracted the ire of critics such as Frankel, who see in it a new universal that replaces "late capitalism", "postmodernity" or the "risk society" as a totalising imagery—an "overbearing, excessive, portentous and singular concept" (Frankel 1997: 74). In key respects Frankel is certainly mistaken. Most importantly, he is mistaking "advanced liberalism" for a representation of an actually existing order, rather than as the representation of an actually existing mentality of rule. Taking direction from its origins in Foucault's (1991) "Governmentality", the literature has always been at pains to distinguish between its particular concern with governmental rationalities as empirical "ideal knowledges", and a sociological concern with whether, how and in what degree such government mentalities are translated into a social reality (e.g., Dean 1994; Miller and Rose 1990; Barry, Osborne and Rose 1993). Indeed, ironically, the literature's resolute resistance to such sociologising has been the subject of criticism from another direction (O'Malley, Weir and Shearing 1997).

Nevertheless, what Frankel's observation does point to is both the probable source of his own error and the locus of a difficulty with governmentality work on advanced liberalism. In travelling down this route of second order "idealisation" while at the same time refusing to recognise its accounts of political rationalities as ideal types, such governmentality analysis seemingly engages in and completes what at other points in the literature is considered as the governmental process of systematisation. The elimination of inconsistencies, the systematisation and axiomatic integration of constitutive elements, the silencing of dissenting voices, the clarification of ambiguity—are all processes that are understood to be activities internal to mentalities of rule. That is, such analysis, through its focus on the rationality of government, may involve a premature closure or termination of the other key element that characterises "Governmentality", namely genealogy.

As noted, this closure takes a characteristic form. Having identified advanced liberalism as a rationality and accorded it a reality, its deployment takes the form of instantiation. The process in much, if not most, governmentality work concerned with advanced liberalism/neo-liberalism (including my own) becomes one primarily of identifying new settings in which it appears, uncovering new forms in which it becomes manifest, locating new processes whereby it operates, and so on. In part as a consequence of this, the nature, pervasiveness and impact of other rationalities are virtually ignored, so that the representation of contemporary government becomes a process in which advanced liberalism ascends or unfolds unopposed, or has already advanced over previously existing mentalities of rule. The imagery of the death of social liberalism, for all that it was meant only as an image to be qualified in practice (Rose 1996b), is perhaps the most striking instance of this, and perhaps the most challenged (e.g., Dean 1998). But other rationalities have been even more completely eradicated from analysis, perhaps most significantly, I argue, neo-conservatism. At best such other rationalities become the raw materials out of which advanced liberalism is constituted, at worst they are merely more or less passive obstacles to be swept out of the way. What appears to be at work here is the combined effect of two features of the governmentality literature: the tendency to privilege systematisation over genealogy, and the vision of politics as a mentality of rule. When put together, these work virtually to exclude any notion of a politics as relational, allowing analysis readily to slip into a form which critics such as Frankel readily (if mistakenly) identify as totalisation.

Contrary to such critics' views, there is nothing theoretically necessary about this development, in the sense that a relational approach to politics is precluded from governmentality work by some internal axiom. Rather, overcoming or avoiding it is a matter of mobilising resources already in-built in governmentality's foundations, namely, to restore genealogy to a central place in analyses of the present in order to counter an over-emphasis on systematisation. Genealogical analysis brings to the fore attention to oppositions and inconsistencies, contingencies, diversity of voices—especially those voices silenced by political struggle and the subsequent rewriting of history (O'Malley, Weir and Shearing 1997). Precisely those other voices, in other words, that are either silenced, ignored or translated by the process of systematisation.

It is in the context of such genealogical analysis that Foucault's (1997a) well known, if rarely deployed, comments on resistance may take their place. His emphasis on the idea that "power comes from below", that "resistance is never in a position of exteriority in relation to power" that resistance is potentially positive, appearing "in the role of adversary, target, support or handle" for government, have rarely be taken up in Foucaultian work, perhaps because the term conjures up images of class, or of collective and heroic opposition (cf. Fitzpatrick 1988; O'Malley, Weir and Shearing 1997)

While these are readily avoided pitfalls, and provide no convincing reason to abandon "resistance", a more telling point would simply be to note that, in the sense of confrontation and opposition to rule, it is, at best, one particular form of political relation that should not be given any particular priority. If a concern with genealogy is foregrounded, then all manner of relations that destabilise, compromise, hybridise, translate or redirect, take on a place whose analytical importance is not provided by their oppositional nature as such (and hence even the currently favoured term "contestation" deserves no special status) but by their impact on the (re)shaping of government. To the extent that the analytic of governmentality achieves its effects by imagining its objects of study as governmental in nature, then this suggests that the relationships that do move into focus are relations between political or governmental mentalities. As suggested above, recent work on advanced liberalism has tended to eschew this. In the following section, I briefly examine one example of how such avoidance creates multiple problems: of silencing alternative rationalities and of attributing too much to neo- (or advanced) liberalism, and of prematurely closing off and rationalising the genealogy of advanced liberalism.

ASSESSING RECENT DEVELOPMENTS IN PUNISHMENT: ADVANCED LIBERAL OR NEO-CONSERVATIVE?

David Garland has recently pointed to the emergence, over the past two decades, of a "volatile and contradictory character of crime control policy" (Garland 1996: 445). Crime control policy is depicted by Garland as oscillating between two poles, punitive/authoritarian and inclusive/devolutionary. On the one hand is the punitive sovereign response, associated with law and order rhetorics that assert the state's right and power to govern by force of command and through its inherent authority to sustain order. On the other hand is a series of responses summed up in the formula: normalising crime, responsibilising others and defining deviance down. The latter provides a polar reaction in which the capacity of the state to govern crime effectively through sovereign remedies is downplayed: crime is presented as a pervasive feature of everyday life that cannot be managed by police, but requires the active involvement of the citizenry. The community in turn is rendered responsible for minimising exposure to crime, urged to form partnerships with police in order to render crime control feasible. For Garland (1996), this oscillation reflects a key dilemma. In the wake of the demonstrable emptiness of aggrandised sovereign state claims to provide security, governments now wish to deny primary responsibility for crime control. Yet they recognise that the political consequences of such a move are potentially disastrous. The result is a volatile and contradictory politics of punishment. However, there is another possible account, which can also make sense of other features of contemporary punishment. It is an account that brings to the fore the relationship between neo-conservatism and neo-liberalism in the unstable alliance of the "New Right".

We may begin by agreeing with Garland that the current state of penological inconsistency probably has few precedents in the history of modern criminal justice. This situation is all the more problematic because in some jurisdictions many contradictory sanctions are available (Lambert and Mason 1996). For the sake of brevity four examples will be examined (O'Malley 1999).

First, strict, hierarchical and authoritarian disciplinary programmes, based on the image of the military boot camp, have become quite widespread in many countries. All involve the inculcation of obedience and conformity. It is a model that echoes the nineteenth century penal regimens recognisable in Foucault's *Discipline and Punish* (1977). While superficially aligned with the discipline of the boot camp style, an array of retributive and just deserts regimes has also experienced renewed vigour and currency during the past twenty years. At one extreme, manifested in the death penalty and chain gangs, but also as a general rationale for incarceration, such punitive practices focus on the preservation of a moral order, the celebration and defence of sovereign legality, and the moral stigmatisation of wrongdoers.

Against this pair of "negative" sanctions, can be set another, and quite contradictory pair, also enjoying an ascendancy. The first of these is a family of programmes aimed at creating "enterprising prisoners" (Garland 1997). Such schemes, as Garland suggests, partake of a much more positive discipline in which prisoners are "trained for freedom"; they "enlist" as agents in their own rehabilitation, and as entrepreneurs of their own personal development. Prisoners "take part in the government of their own confinement" (Garland 1997: 191). More generally, such programmes display a positive vision for reform that has little use for the negative dynamic of punitive penalties, a feature they share with other developments that disconnect offending and the state, rendering the legal relation involved almost contractual. For example, recent developments in Australia and in the United Kingdom have moved to prevent courts imposing fines where it is possible to hand down a restitution order (Parliament of Victoria 1993). In place of collective morality driving retribution, and a process that centres the state as symbolic victim, individual victims and offenders privately negotiate restitution.

Reference to "neo-liberalism" (in the advanced liberal sense) has been held by theorists to explain all of these criminal justice developments (and many others; see O'Malley 1999). The arguments run as follows. Restitution reflects the ethic of individual responsibility, envisages the victim as the customer of justice, promotes quasi-contractual market-like relations and takes the state out of governance (e.g., White 1994). The schemes that "enterprise prisoners" reflect the neo-liberal affirmation of the autonomous, entrepreneurial spirit and the ethic of individual responsibility (Garland 1996; 1997). Punitive and just deserts penalties remove the welfare orientation of the previous penal regimes and bring to the fore the responsibilisation of individuals, while at the same time reducing correctional costs (Garland 1996). Strict discipline programmes likewise focus on individual responsibility, while at the same time promoting values of self-reliance and application consistent with neo-liberal images of the active citizen (Simon 1995).

Can all of these be "neo-liberal"? Retrospectively this appears possible through the argument that systematisation is in a sense laid on top of such Heath Robinson machines. But is this a genealogical assemblage being rationalised under one government mentality, or is this systematisation being achieved only in the work of these commentators? It is quite possible to chart an alternative neo-conservative rationality, in some ways seriously at odds with major features of the strategies of advanced liberalism, and plausibly underpinning elements of this volatile and contradictory penality.

To begin with, neo-conservatism is probably the source of much of the emphasis on order and discipline that is attributed to neo-liberalism in recent criminology. For neo-conservatives, discipline is essential for the social good— and the concept of the social here has very specific organic overtones that do not sit well with neo-liberals' radical individualism. Membership of and loyalty to traditional collectivities such as the nation, and indeed the social, are paramount. Obligations, whether to the family, the community or the nation, are in a sense given in the nature of social beings, rather than contractually, rationally or voluntarily chosen. Consequently the freedom and enhanced autonomy that is central to neo-liberalism "cannot occupy a central place in conservative thinking . . . Freedom is comprehensible as a social goal only when subordinate to something else, to an organisation or arrangement which defines the individual aim" (Scruton 1984: 24). For neo-conservatives, the state, particularly in its role as the preserver of order and the governor of the nation, is the privileged symbol of political rule, and allegiance to the state has little or nothing to do with a neo-liberal partnership. This strong assertion of state sovereignty in turn privileges both law and order as crucial, more important than the market and the individual. Thus, for neo-conservatives the law may "interfere" in all manner of "private" spheres, including contracts, family relationships, personal morality and so on, and if needs be must possess severe and ultimate penalties (Hayes 1994).

In all of this, it is not difficult to detect the source of those elements of penal policy that appear somewhat incongruous with the "switched on" capitalism of neo-liberalism and enterprise culture. Neo-conservatism would promote and find appeal in nineteenth century boot camp technologies of negative discipline and unthinking obedience, in retributive punishments, even in the death penalty. But equally, and for much the same reason, it rests uneasily with the model of the choice-maker/consumer that is at the heart of advanced liberalism. Neo-conservatism could not give such unfettered play to the market forces and consumer sovereignty crucial to neo-liberalism, and, as others have noted, this creates recurring tensions (Gamble 1988). Of course, this account is somewhat one-sided, it reveals little that binds neo-conservatism in a political alliance with neo-liberals. The free market, for example, is the site on which the neo-conservative virtues of a kind of Social Darwinism are held to be demonstrated and delivered. In the words of the British conservative Peregrine Worsthorne (1988: 14), "the battlefield and the economic jungle . . . [are] the proving place of character". Neo-conservatism also displays an hostility to welfarism that gives common cause with the neo-liberals, for welfare interventions tend toward the elimination of inequalities that for conservatism are the essential index and mechanism of Darwinian social selection (Levitas 1986). Alliances between neo-liberalism and neo-conservatism are thus likely to be marked by a degree of contradiction and instability.

As this suggests, the alliance of these two rationalities allows us to understand the rather bi-polar pattern of development that is extending the diversity or range of sanctions. On the one hand is the resurrection or revitalisation of formerly discredited penalties (retribution, strict discipline, death penalties and chain gangs). This neo-conservative "nostalgia" matches punishment and penal discipline with support for a unified and disciplinary moral order under the governance of state authority and paternalism. On the other hand is the addition to the penological repertory of quite radical and innovatory initiatives, which are largely associated with neo-liberalism—as suggested already, most notably the model of self-governing, enterprising and "active" prisoners, and victim-offender contractualism. Thus, within a penality generated by a loose alliance of neo-conservatives and neo-liberals (such as the New Right) the repertory or range of available sanctions is expanded in contradictory directions.

This bi-polar perspective on the penality of the new right can also explain, in terms of a rather more ordinary politics, the volatility in sanctioning policies that Garland has noted, between (neo-conservative) episodes of social authoritarianism, in which the state aggressively stamps down on crime, and episodes in which there appears to be a process of (neo-liberal) denial, in which state ministers and officials repudiate responsibility and devolve this to "the community". Thus, neo-conservatives have long called for a "remoralisation" of society as a means of fighting crime, and regard the role of the state and of law as crucial in this respect (e.g., Marsland 1991). At the other, neo-liberal, extreme, proponents such as the Chicago School economists, Milton Friedman (Friedman and Friedman 1984) and, in Australia, the Centre for Independent Studies (Buchanan and Hartley 1992) have proposed withdrawing state involvement in criminal justice from many areas of "victimless crimes", on the grounds that it is no business of the law to enforce a particular code of moral conduct. Likewise, it is neo-liberalism that can readily be understood as a mainspring of the moves toward responsibilising victims, and the empowering the community (O'Malley 1994). In such an alliance, oscillations between state bellicosity and devolution, of the sort observed by Garland, are a perfectly intelligible outcome.

My aim in this thumbnail sketch of volatility in crime control is not just to propose that neo-liberalism and advanced liberalism are tempered by other "isms" in practice. As well, it is to point to a lack of closure in politics, and to the need for an ongoing genealogy relevant to our understanding of "advanced liberalism". The appearance of volatile and contradictory punishment, I suggest, is not the effect of a remnant of an earlier conservative alliance that is being overtaken by advanced liberal governance, for, as Garland suggests, retribution and strict discipline seem to be gathering strength rather than diminishing. Raising our eyes only slightly to the horizon brings the "War on Drugs" into focus, with its militaristic nationalism and the coercive sovereignty, and array of neo-liberal opponents, most notably Milton Friedman (Friedman and Friedman 1984; Buchanan and Hartley 1992). More broadly, if neo-conservatism still appears a powerful force in the United States, with its strong links to religious fundamentalism, it is a rising rather than declining force in Europe, the former Soviet Union and even Australia. The importance of these observations, I suggest, is to re-establish the heterogeneous and multivocal nature of a politics (whether of penality or of broader issues) that has been reduced to expressions of one unified advanced liberal rationality.

CONCLUSION: GENEALOGY, RESISTANCE AND THE DIAGNOSIS
OF OUR TIMES

In his recent critique of governmentality scholars (whom he terms "Anglo-Foucauldians") Boris Frankel (1997: 85) suggests that they:

> "come close to appearing as new structural functionalists in their preoccupation with order and regulation . . . [O]n the whole they are happily immersed in the bleak patterns of 'system integration' and 'system adaptation'—even if they do not use these Parsonian terms. Thirty years ago, Parsonian functionalists also rejected criticisms that their theory was oriented toward system equilibrium and could not adequately accommodate social conflict. The Foucauldians would similarly argue that their work is cognisant of resistance and political contests . . . Yet their preoccupation with technologies of 'governmentality' leaves little room for emphasising alternative political processes".

If structural functionalism became homeostatic, it was because it had no theoretical space for social conflicts. However, as argued already, in the context of a Foucaultian project, the problem appears only through a tendency to prioritise the rationality of politics and consequently to render genealogy as appearing not in the present but in the past. Thus, in Rose's work (see esp. 1996a) we are provided with some notion of the variable forces, processes and conditions that brought advanced liberalism into being. These include: left critics' concerns with the fiscal crisis of the state and with the intrusiveness of welfarism; concerns from the right over welfare's impact on productive capital, and over the creation of welfare dependency; the erosion of confidence created by competition between professions and the resulting disputes over the authenticity of competing knowledges. The outcome, as we have seen in Rose's account, was not the establishment of a coherent rationality, but a cobbling together of various of these related themes and problems emerging from diverse sources, which only later came to be subjected to systematisation (Rose 1996a).

This process of systematisation is only in the most limited sense a genealogy, for its rationale is to minimise inconsistency and silence discordant voices. Of course, how it goes about this is in some degree open; any inventions that appear along the way cannot be known. But the development of systematisation turns the process inward upon itself. Programmes and rationalities begin to appear as if they are written by one hand, consistently ordered and accepted, rather than ambiguous, disputed and contradictory. They thus appear as static, or if in motion, appear as immanent ideal-real types unfolding.

Against this, it could be argued that the earlier discussion of criminal justice provides no more than an illustration of the heuristic use of an ideal type of advanced liberalism offered in order to understand the messy actualities of the empirical world. It does so in classically Weberian style, through observing and explaining the deviations of "reality" from the ideal model. By pitting one ideal type of advanced liberalism against another of neo-conservatism, we come up with an analysis of contemporary political configurations. In one sense I have no objection to this interpretation. It makes clear the status of advanced liberalism as a second order construct and it moves governmentality into active engagement of the "messy actualities" of political relations, although it has to be said that there is marked resistance to such an interpretation of governmentality work (for example, Barry, Osborne and Rose 1993). Such a usage would also militate against regarding the construct of advanced liberalism (or any other rationality) as immanent and unfolding. However, there are other dangers in this usage, for as seen with respect to the array of allegedly "neo-liberal" sanctions, it is all too easy for ideal types to be reified and over-extended, to be made compatible with whatever we see, and thus to become (as Frankel believes) totalising in their reach. As well, ideal types, in the last analysis, have an explanatory purpose, which in itself is generally not seen as a characteristic of governmentality work (e.g., O'Malley 1996a).

Making more explicit the idealised and second order character of such constructs is an important step, but ultimately this is no substitute for an emphasis on contingencies, instabilities and multivocalities. Restoring genealogy to its place alongside systematisation, in understanding the political rationalities of the present, is to question, for example, how far other mentalities or rationalities of rule stamp their form on what we take to be the symptoms of advanced liberalism. It is to interrogate rationalities for their hidden voices, ambiguities and contradictions. And it is, perhaps even more significantly, to move beyond rationalities and look for the disruptive and the different that may be inchoate, operating within or alongside—as well as in opposition to— the more visible rationalities. These are formed and sustained by minorities, the colonised and the outcast, and less visibly but equally importantly by all manner of people who carve out for themselves a space for self-government that is not programmatically articulated with more prominent and ascendant political rationalities (O'Malley 1996a).

It is in this sense that "resistance" can take its vital place within governmentality work, but reframed in a more heterogeneous form: as alternative and even allied formal governmentalities (such as neo-conservatism), or as marginalised or "indigenous" governances, such as those of minorities (O'Malley 1996a). Locating such sources of difference in governance: counters the tendency to subsume government under one ascendant rationality; creates spaces in which alternative governmental forms may be identified and contests facilitated; opens up the possibilities for recognising hybridisation, adaptation and change; in short, returns to political analysis the fluidity and contingency of relational politics without abandoning the characteristic analytics of governmentality. Politically and academically, such a recasting may also open up our examination of the present to questions that disrupt our own rationally formulated diagnoses.

2

Governing Images of the Australian Police Trooper

ANNETTE PEDERSEN

INTRODUCTION

"As we have seen, police in Australia were not some outgrowth of community innovation—they were a state-authorised imposition" (Finnane 1994: 17).

POLICE HISTORY, WHEN broadly conceived and investigated, is able to tell us much about the state and social history. The nature and duties of policemen, "the most conspicuous representatives of the political and social order", can speak volumes about a society's structure, dynamics and, importantly for this chapter, society's needs, both real and imagined (Palmer 1988: xix). William Strutt painted European and Aboriginal mounted police officers and troopers during his time in Australia between 1850 and 1861. It is a series of his paintings and sketches of police at various public functions and in the landscape that I examine and discuss here in relation to the history of the Australian state.

The theoretical basis of this chapter includes a limited engagement with the work of the Italian Marxist Antonio Gramsci. Gramsci's work is relevant to my research inasmuch as his treatment of hegemony can be seen to relate to Michel Foucault's arguments pertaining to disciplinary apparatuses and government. Gramsci discusses what he terms a "complex of superstructures", focusing on two main "levels", which he describes as:

> " 'civil society', that is the ensemble of organisms commonly called 'private', and that of 'political society' or 'the State'. These two levels correspond on the one hand to the function of 'hegemony' which the dominant group exercises throughout society and on the other hand to that of 'direct domination' or command exercised through the State and 'juridical' government" (Gramsci 1997: 12).

Civil society and political society are obviously connected and domination is achieved through consent and coercion via organisational means. This parallels Foucault's work. However, there is an important inflection to Gramsci's argument which enables me to make some interesting comments on possible meanings of Strutt's paintings and drawings of policing in relation to the Australian state. Furthermore, in my discussion of Strutt's paintings of European mounted police troopers in the Australian landscape, I am also keen to make a connection to notions of "civility" and political authority that stem from the work of Niccolo Machiavelli. According to Carl Boggs:

> "Gramsci often referred to Machiavelli as the 'first Jacobin' and praised him as a theorist who wanted to combine historical understanding with a strong commitment to creating a new human community through political action. But what Machiavelli does is to bring everything back to politics—i.e. to the art of governing men, of securing their permanent consent, and hence of founding 'great states' " (Boggs 1976: 106–7).

The link between the 'art of governing men', the meaning of politics and its role in establishing ideological and political hegemony in order to form a new colonial community, the basis for founding a "great state", that is what is important to my writing in relation to policing.

In seeing the Australian colony as a direct transplant from England there is a danger of misreading the cultural data or evidence. Nineteenth century Britain, as of course has been argued by countless historians and other scholars, was a highly industrialised urban society. Australia was not. While the First Fleet (the fleet which carried Australia's first British settlers) was the offshoot of a flourishing capitalist Britain, as a viable capitalist society in embryo it actually fell apart, rather than flourished, when the colonists arrived in 1788. The anxiety of the first few years of the colony, struggling to survive, did not necessarily inaugurate a zest for life that visibly improved on the ideas of modern society left behind in England. Rather, those first colonists witnessed a breakdown of all that was familiar to them by way of a highly industrialised modern urban European society. The colonists were isolated from their powerful mother country. Eventually the only way to assume control over the unfamiliar continent and establish a new social order was by force.

It is misleading to read institutions such as the early Australian police forces simply as direct relations of their English counterparts, with specific colonial or imperial inflections. The police troopers were integral to penetrating and controlling the Australian landscape. This was not an industrialised state with institutional control finally vested in the family, or consisting of "the proliferation of political technologies that invested the body, health modes of subsistence and lodging—the entire space of existence in European countries from the eighteenth century onward" (Donzelot 1979: 6). The Australian continent was a foreign province, conquest was difficult and in the nineteenth century the state had yet to be established along the lines of its imperial parent society. The aim of the police, states Jacques Donzelot, is "to make everything that composes the state serve to strengthen and increase its power, and likewise serve the public welfare" (Donzelot 1979: 7). The initial aim of the police in Australia was to facilitate the establishment of a capitalist state based on land ownership.

Although this discussion is focused on the work of the artist William Strutt, my concerns are with the history of the police, the law and the state in Australia.

I have selected some of Strutt's paintings and works for discussion on the basis of the insights they provide about colonial life generally and policing and law specifically. I am interested in attempting to discern what led Strutt to take such an intense interest in the police and I am interested in highlighting the fact that Strutt's Australian artworks owe much to European works he knew from his studies in the Louvre. I am seeking evidence of an iconography of the law in relation to policing in particular.

POLICING AS A GOVERNMENTAL PRACTICE

Policing of the public order and policing of the economy can adopt either civil or militaristic forms. Militaristic policing is usually described as the use of army tactics by the police to pacify a population. It involves the threat or use of physical force by police against internal and external challenges to the acceptance and survival of the colonial state and its authority. As is evidenced by the detailed and distinctive uniforms worn by both the Mounted and Native Troopers in Melbourne in the mid-nineteenth century, and other police troopers of that time in Australia, this style of policing (involving highly visible manoeuvres, often in conjunction with other organs of the state apparatus such as the army) was the main form of Australian colonial policing. Militaristic policing is by nature overtly political, not just in the sense of being part of the colonial state's agency, but in that it specifically focuses on challenges to the colonial state. In the case of Strutt's paintings and sketches of police from 1851 to 1861 in Victoria, the military "flavour" of these uniformed men raises some interesting issues related to European history and politics.

Although this chapter is concerned with Strutt's paintings of police officers in nineteenth century Victoria, I want to place my initial discussion of his work in the broader context of the Australian colony from its formal inception in 1788. Arthur Phillip was designated governor on 12 October 1786, his first commission specifying:

> "we do hereby strictly charge and command all our officers and soldiers who shall be employed within our said territory, and all others whom it may concern, to obey you as our Governor thereof; and you are to observe and follow such orders and directions from time to time as you shall receive from us or any other your superior officer according to the rules and disciplines of war" (quoted in Nagle 1996: 15).

The governor's powers were absolute, more appropriate to an autocracy than a colony with a civil government. Having said this, if the composition of the First Fleet is examined it is very easy to understand why the governor was given such clearly defined and wide-ranging powers. The original colonial settlement comprised:

> "approximately 750 convicts, of whom two thirds were male; a marine force of three companies, some 200 marines, approximately 20 of whom were of commissioned

rank; the governor and his staff of nine people. In addition, there was a small number of children of marines and convicts" (Nagle 1996: 19).

The convicts represented the largest part of the population of the original colony and from the outset the colony was governed as if by martial law. In his account of law and society in colonial New South Wales, Nagle notes that the first deputy judge-advocate of the colony was Captain David Collins, an officer in the marines. John Nagle describes this appointment as unique in that not only did Collins, who possessed no legal training, preside over the various courts set up in the colony, he was also responsible for their administration, and further, as a military officer, he was bound to obey the orders of superior officers even in matters related to law (Nagle 1996: 30).

The foundation of Victoria as a separate colony was formalised in 1851. A police force already existed, recruited in Sydney in September 1836 for service in Port Phillip (the original settlement for what became Victoria), it was initially administered from Sydney. This force arrived in Port Phillip on 5 October 1851 in a party which included thirty convicts. Kerry Milte describes the brief of these police: to "preserve the law and order, to protect the natives, to collect revenue and to survey land to be sold" (Milte 1977: 26). By 1852 the gold rush in Victoria had affected the police force to the extent that a Select Committee of the Legislative Council was appointed to investigate its operations. As a result of this initiative all policing was unified in the colony and the "Home Government" in Britain was asked to send some 200 experienced men to assist with policing (Milte 1977: 26). The rationale behind a centrally controlled police in Victoria was that remote regions dealing with problems related to bushrangers or Aboriginal communities were understood to be more likely to experience law-breaking: control therefore needed to be vested in the central government.

This instance underlines Gramsci's argument that the state, rather than being thought of as organised coercion, in a narrow sense, should be thought of in expanded terms such that it is both political and civil. Correspondingly he acknowledges two types of hegemony—political hegemony and ideological hegemony. Thus, the state rules not only by depending on the imposition of economic or physical power, but also by persuading the ruled to accept the system of beliefs of the ruling class and its moral, political and cultural values (Gramsci 1997: 257–63). The centralised police force enabled the authority of the colonial state to spread through the entire social fabric of the colony, in an attempt to create a civil society.

Both Foucault and Donzelot examine policing in terms of disciplinary power. Donzelot analyses the emergence of institutions such as brothels, hostels and so on as:

"a strategic base for a whole series of corrective interventions in family life. These assembly points for the society's misfortunes, miseries and failures facilitated the mobilization of philanthropic energies, providing it with a point of support, serving as a laboratory for observing working class behaviour, as a launching ramp for tactics designed to counter the socially negative effects of this behaviour, and to organize the working class family in terms of socio-economic urgencies" (Donzelot 1979: 26).

It is at this point that Foucault's and Donzelot's works become especially relevant to the Australian context. Why would a capitalist colony need to establish both political and ideological hegemony in a civil society? Foucaultian thinking suggests that the conditions for the social reproduction of capitalist relations are sustained in the so-called "unproductive" spaces of civil society and the state, particularly the family. To further enforce this "sustenance", a whole range of institutions emerged in nineteenth century industrialised Europe to regulate society and organise working class family life. However, in the Australian colonies, unlike industrialised Europe, initially the family was of very little importance, or, perhaps more accurately, there were few families: the small population was extremely fragmented with men greatly outnumbering women, and most of the women were convicts.

In colonial Australia, with a pre-industrial and embryonic capitalist society made up of indigenous peoples, convicts, ex-convicts, military and free settlers attempting to achieve self-sufficient statehood and expand exports, the need to establish hegemony over the entire social fabric became increasingly pressing. By the time of the gold rush in Victoria in the 1850s, this had been formalised in relation to policing by the 1853 Act for the Legislation of the Police Force (Milte 1977: 26). In relation to Aboriginal peoples, what was eventually established was coercive control, because the colonial state lacked the legitimate means of persuading the colonised to accept their domination. That is to say, the colonial state was unable to establish ideological hegemony over all its inhabitants.

From the inception of independent government in Victoria, policing and the political structure of the colony were linked. Strutt documents in drawings several events of governmental importance to the young Victorian colony: the swearing-in of the first governor of Victoria on 15 November 1851, the opening of the first Legislative Council of Victoria on 13 November 1851, and the opening of Parliament in 1856. In many of these drawings Strutt details both mounted police troopers and foot police. This link between police and government raises some interesting issues. In contrast to the police depicted in his works of Aboriginal police and mounted troopers in the rural landscape, these works are evidence of civil policing specifically in relation to government.

Civil policing refers to the regulation of public order and culture. It is a broad form of social intervention which involves police and other agencies, both within and outside the state, co-operating to establish order. The main means of control used in civil policing are legal-bureaucratic institutions. Hsi-Huey Liang sums up the basic principles of this type of policing in the following terms:

" 1. Police must operate on a legal basis only and prosecute suspects solely on objective (material) evidence.

2. Police should regulate the behaviour of individual persons rather than of collective groups and should not use terrorist methods, like hostage taking.

3. Police must apply no more physical coercion than is absolutely necessary in any given situation. Torture to exact confession is inadmissible.

4. Police serve the European state system by assuring the minimum of damage to civilian society during all the violent clashes—wars and revolutions—that inevitably accompany its perpetual movement towards improvement and reform." (Liang 1992: 4)

This view of policing sees police as, in a sense, agents of capitalism, instruments of progress and constitutional protection against arbitrary government. Strutt's paintings and sketches of police attending the ceremonies accompanying the swearing-in of the first governor of Victoria illustrate the importance of civil policing as a means employed by the state in its search for ideological hegemony—to generate consent for the established order. Yet, despite the apparently civil nature of these mounted police in Strutt's works, their elaborate military-style uniforms suggest the Australian context for civil policing had unusual nuances.

These works are evidence of the connection between political and ideological hegemony, and the relationship between population, government and security in terms of the colonial state. Strutt comments on the ceremony surrounding the foundation of the State of Victoria:

"On the arrival of the auspicious day, Mr Charles Joseph Latrobe, the actual superintendent, was appointed Lieutenant-Governor and sworn in by the Chief Justice, Sir William à Beckett and Judge Stawell, at Government House. This done, the National Anthem was played and a procession formed, when his Excellency, surrounded by the government officials and an escort of well trained and mounted black police, riding uncommonly well, wearing a picturesque dark green uniform, passed through the gaily decorated streets and proceeded to the official opening of the just-completed Prince's Bridge over the River Yarra; this having been effected a salute was fired by a detachment of the 11th Regiment of Infantry, stationed on the South Yarra Hill overlooking Melbourne" (Strutt 1979: 14–15).

In these artworks Strutt represents all the elements concerning government and the colonial state: the governor and "the officials and military, with the élite of the society of Melbourne and a great gathering of the people, the various Societies, their banners flying" (Strutt 1979: 15). The key word in this context is "people", which leads me to a consideration of Foucault's discussions regarding population.

In his famous lecture on governmentality, Foucault considers the shift which occurred from the sixteenth to the nineteenth century, from a focus on the role of the prince or sovereign, to the art of government itself. Much of the thinking involved here, Foucault points out, was not simply raised in terms of Machiavelli's key text on the role of the prince, but rather focused on the issue of the art of government itself (Foucault 1991, 89). By the eighteenth century the art of government was related to the problem of population and the family. A model of government—family—became an internal element of population and an integral instrument of government itself (Foucault 1991: 99). Foucault notes succinctly that, "in reality one has a triangle, sovereignty—discipline—government, which has as its primary target the population and as its essential mechanism the apparatuses of security" (Foucault 1991: 102).

This "triangle", its "primary target" and "essential mechanism" are clearly illustrated by Strutt's sketches. In these quick sketches Strutt depicts "foot police with muskets", "Black Troopers—Corporal", "a crowd hurraying (sic) and waving their hats", a "crowd scene in front of Government House" and "the swearing in of 'His Excellency Governor Latrobe' " (Strutt 1980: 34–35).

The depiction of the celebrations known as Separation Day demonstrates the profound historical link between sovereignty, colonial government and colonial population, on the one hand, and the essential role of the police in the establishment and maintenance of the colonial Australian state, on the other. These artworks also allude to the relationship between military and civil policing in the colony. The function in colonial Australia of the "essential mechanism the apparatuses of security", that is to say, the colonial police, as a model provides a contrast to its European equivalent. A detailed discussion of Strutt's work relating to police raises further questions.

In his painting on canvas, "Equestrian Portrait of Sergeant John Darby and Another Member of the Victorian Police Force", 1861, Strutt details two mounted European police officers dressed in "bush dress" and situated in a landscape. A L Haydon describes the uniform of the Victorian mounted trooper:

"The uniform of officers included a blue cloth single-breasted frock coat, with standing collar and service buttons; an overcoat of like fashion; blue cloth trousers with black lace stripe down the sides, white cloth being adopted for the summer; white cotton or buckskin gloves; high riding boots of the usual pattern; and a blue cloth cap with patent leather peak and black lace band. Police carbines, pistols and swords were the arms carried; swords, however, being only used for parade occasions" (Haydon 1911: 234–5).

In Strutt's painting, the two uniformed policemen are mounted on horses, and, although in full gallop, hold centre-stage of the canvas. The officers are upright, the foreground figure swivelled to face the viewer. In this painting there is a sense of urgency. That the horses are moving at some speed is indicated by the fact that none of their hooves touch the ground and there is a cloud of dust behind them. While the horses display some emotive behaviour—the foreground animal has flared nostrils and the white of his eye is prominent and the background beast is tossing his head vigorously—the police officers maintain an upright and disciplined posture.

Strutt considered his education in France of immense importance to his artistic practice (Strutt undated). In his autobiography he describes his education in Michael Drolling's *atelier* and his interest in the works of painting masters in the Louvre. He specifically mentions Peter Paul Rubens and his series of works known as the Marie d'Medici cycle of paintings. This series was of immense importance in post-revolutionary France, particularly for the way in which it leads the viewer to think about ideas of "kingship" and the state. As Lawrence Gowing points out in his book on the Louvre collection, this particular work embodies ideas of sovereignty that became a lasting motif in French romantic painting:

"The coronation of Marie d'Medici lent lasting solemnity to the French idea of kingship. Rubens' design was later borrowed by Jacques Louis David for his picture of the same rite in the career of Napoleon, marked with similar splendour and egoism" (Gowing 1987: 330).

Strutt mentions in his autobiography that one of his painting masters in Paris, Paul Delaroche, was a pupil of "the great David", and Strutt was obviously familiar with his work. The influence of Rubens's d'Medici cycle on David is well documented. It is not simply an influence on composition, in a painterly sense, it is an influence on the expression of the idea of the meaning of sovereignty in the new French state. As a new state, the French Empire, product of the Enlightenment, was not attempting to invent itself without precedents. The 1789 revolution deposed what was perceived as a decadent monarchy and replaced it with the new Empire founded on Enlightenment ideas of the imperial state of Rome. This move linked the eighteenth century French government to notions of the state and sovereignty that went back to Julius Caesar. Ideas of history and sovereignty were constant themes of classical and romantic Salon paintings in France throughout the eighteenth and nineteenth centuries. Painters such as David, Delaroche, Vernet, Delacroix and Géricault constantly explored significant historical themes in their art.

Thèodore Géricault, a close friend of Horace Vernet (one of Strutt's teachers) painted a large scale canvas "Mounted Officer of the Imperial Guard", which was featured in the Salon and was familiar to Strutt, who discusses Géricault in his journal. The precursors of Géricault's dramatic Napoleonic figure are the equestrian soldiers in Leonardo Da Vinci's "Battle of Anghiari". Géricault spent some time in Italy as a student and was very familiar with Da Vinci's work. Furthermore, Rubens's drawing, after Da Vinci's cartoon for this battle scene painted in 1605, is in the Louvre collection and was well known to artists in Paris during this period.

The intellectual inspiration for the Renaissance, especially for artists such as Da Vinci, was classical Greece and neo-Platonism. So it can be argued that Strutt had, through his intense interest in the Louvre collection and works by artists such as Titian, Michelangelo, Da Vinci, Gros, Rubens, David, Géricault, and Delaroche, a strong visual background in works celebrating the power of the state, sovereignty and Western civilisation. It is not Strutt's opinion of this that interests me here, I am interested in his artistic antecedents only in so far as they enable me to see a relationship, through artistic practice, which connects his work to classical Rome and Greece. In connecting Strutt and his art works to classical Greece, I am able to raise issues in regard to his paintings of mounted policemen in the Australian colony of Victoria and suggest a connection between colonial policing itself and ideas of Western civilisation.

During Strutt's student years in Paris the work of Géricault was legendary. Although not very many of Géricault's paintings were hung in public collections, hundreds of copies of his work and many lithographic reproductions were available. Strutt's work in Australia often reflects his intense interest in horses, which he dates back to his childhood—for example, his "Martyrs of the Road", and the famous canvas "Black Thursday". As Géricault's work was well known and reproduced both in Paris and in England, it appears very likely that Strutt both knew and studied his paintings depicting horses. That Géricault was a life-long friend of Strutt's teacher, Vernet, makes it even more likely that the young Strutt was familiar with his oeuvre (Grunchec 1982: 5–6).

Strutt's work, "Black Thursday", was completed in 1864. This work records the devastating bush fire which swept through large areas of Victoria on 6 February 1851. An early response to this event is Strutt's water-colour sketch in his text *Victoria The Golden* (Strutt 1980: 29). The sketch details a scene of a man in the bush on horseback driving a group of cattle before the fire. The small and vibrant scene is focused on the terror of the beasts and driven by a sense of urgency as flames lick over their heads. While man and beasts are described fully, the trees in the work are so huge that only a small part of their trunks are revealed—although the fleeing figures take up much of the scene, they are dwarfed by the enormity of nature and a fire out of control.

This sense of man and beast rendered insignificant by nature is played out with dramatic intensity in "Black Thursday", which Strutt completed some years after the fire and when he had returned to England. This work, oil on canvas, measuring 106.0 cm x 319.0 cm, has been discussed by other writers in relation to Rosa Bonheur's painting "The Horse Fair" and Vernet's "The Capture of the Smala" (Curnow 1980: 20). In his journal Strutt describes the morning of the fire in terms of horror:

> "The sun looked red all day, almost as blood, and the sky the colour of mahogany. We felt in town that something terrible (with the immense volumes of smoke) must be going on up country and sure enough messenger after messenger came flocking in with tales of distress and horror. One unfortunate man, severely burnt, tried in vain to rescue his wife and children, and just managed to escape with his own life" (Strutt 1979: 20).

Strutt's painting documents the terrified inhabitants of the land, people and animals, fleeing for their lives. Farmers, squatters, families, flocks and herds, and even a troupe of travelling players with a cart of costumes and props, mingle with native animals and birds in a panicked stampede. The foreground of the painting is littered with a debris of lost possessions and local fauna overcome by smoke, flames and fatigue.

Strutt further describes in his journal the angular dead trees sculpted into scorched memorials by the great fire:

"For years afterwards the traces of this storm were still visible in the Colony, and the charred skeletons of many venerable monarchs of the forest stood gaunt and black against the sky, testifying to the severity of their baptism of fire" (Strutt 1979: 21).

If, in the tradition of European painting, landscapes are culture before they are nature, this painting of Strutt's suggests that in Australia the reverse is true, the landscape is nature before it is culture (Schama 1995: Introduction). In fact, that very nature has the proven ability to threaten culture, as represented by the European settlers. "Thus the devouring element continued its course of destruction till, after burning through the Cape Otway forest, it was arrested by the sea" (Strutt 1979: 20). The raw uncontrollable force of the fire must have terrified the Victorian colonists, struggling to make some economic and social sense out of the alien landscape in order to organise a civil society after separation from New South Wales. Strutt illustrates the disastrous event in the manner of a European battle scene, in a manner similar to that employed in some works of his teacher, Vernet. Rather than recording the devastation that resulted from the fire, he concentrates on the effect of the fire on the people and animals caught up in its path, showing the heroism, terror and panic of flight. This approach is very different to that of Australian artist Eugene von Guérard who painted a bushfire scene in 1859, concentrating on the sublimely spectacular visual effects of the fire with the burning horizon silhouetted against a vivid sky.

Ten years after he observed the fire Strutt painted his "Equestrian Portrait". The colour in the Strutt painting is rich, the dark elements of police uniform and horse bridle are visually strung together and continue through the painting to be picked up in details of tails, manes, horses' ears and officers' hats and boots. White details highlighting a stirrup are echoed in a detail on the foreground officer's jacket sleeve and both their collars and then provides a luminous and cloudy backdrop to the work as a whole.

What can this painting tell the viewer about policing in 1861? Again, to quote Haydon,

"there is an appealing picturesque touch about the solitary, blue-coated, helmeted trooper at Wallaloo or Mudgeegonga, as the case may be, ruler of a good many square miles, doing several men's work in one and doing it remarkably well. In the country districts, in what may be termed generally 'the bush', the mounted constable is a highly important personage. 'Out back there', said an officer to the writer, 'the police are in absolute fact the Government. There's a good deal that they have to do off their own bat, so to speak, but they don't blow about it. It's just done, that's all' " (Haydon 1911: 244).

Both Géricault and Vernet are well-known for their battle scenes. Géricault in particular was interested in both officers and their favourite mounts and painted many representations of this subject matter set against the backdrop of the Napoleonic wars. This work of Strutt's owes much to works of Géricault's, particularly his artillery series. The point of departure for the two artists is that while Géricault was interested in the military and painted many scenes from the

Napoleonic wars, he did not paint police officers. The similarity between the works of Strutt and Géricault, despite Géricault's focus on military rather than police, raises some very interesting issues, particularly in relation to the positioning of Strutt's equestrian police officers in the landscape.

There is an acknowledged and recognisable relationship between early Australian police and the military. George Gordon McCrae, in his foreword to John Sadleir's book, first published in 1913, writes:

> "Our earlier police were, of necessity, semi-military in their organization and ideals; the mounted men especially, who numbered among them both troopers and officers who had previously served whether in the Imperial Army or the armies of the Continent. It is not one whit too much to add that in this bygone organization it is, that we trace the kernel whence sprang the ever-increasing army of the Commonwealth of today" (Sadleir 1973: 5).

Haydon, describing the formation of the first troop of mounted police in New South Wales by Governor Brisbane in 1825, writes:

> "As has already been noted, the members of this force were recruited mainly from the infantry regiments serving in the colony, so that it began with a distinctly military character. To further emphasise this the uniform worn was very much like that of the 14th Light Dragoons, consisting of a shell jacket with white facings, blue pants with a white stripe, and a cap without a peak This was for full dress order" (Haydon 1911: 33).

Finally, Robert Haldane in his comprehensive history of the Victorian police force quotes from a Government Commission of Inquiry criticising the "excessive military discipline in the police force" in 1854:

> "The attention of the officers had been too exclusively directed to imparting to the force the features of a military body, rather than those of a preventative force.
>
> It must be obvious that, although a preventative police may occasionally be called upon to act as a disciplined or quasi-military body, their useful action is much more frequently called in for their individual capacity as police constables.
>
> Their individual training and instruction as a preventative police is much more important than as a military force" (Haldane 1986: 40–1).

Haldane also refers to a unique aspect of the Victorian mounted police city patrol, formed in 1853, which he refers to as "the embryonic state of policing as a public service". Working as police to patrol the city of Melbourne day and night, the men of this unit were issued with a second uniform and "detailed to work as firemen should an alarm of fire be raised in the city" (Haldane 1986: 36). Although it may in fact be the case that this is the first sign of an idea of policing as a public service in the colony, I think it may equally be argued that the connection with fire-fighting came from different motives.

In the Introduction to his Victorian children's story, *Cooey* written in 1901 and finally published in 1989, Strutt makes the following observation:

"Most persons who have resided for some time in the great Metropolis have had their feelings of pity awakened by seeing a child of tender years lost. On such occasions a crowd soon gathers.

At length, a policeman breaks through the jostling crowd; stoops down; takes the little creature's tiny hand into his and then leads it to the nearest Station where every effort is made to comfort the lost one.

But with children lost in the backwoods of our Colonies, it is a different matter to stray. The result, not unfrequently, means death by starvation to the actual knowledge of the writer" (Strutt 1989: 2).

The British policeman had a clearly defined role. As John McQuilton reminds us:

"The London Metropolitan Police, however, was a civil policing force. Its members were unarmed, and it deliberately eschewed any military overtones in organisation and titles. In both training and spirit, its members were seen to be part of the community they served" (McQuilton 1987: 36–7).

The British policeman functioned in an urban environment familiar and understood by its population, a population used to operating within an institutionalised culture. Nigel Fielding observes in relation to British policing: "The historical inheritance of the nineteenth century was the local character of the office of the chief constable, the common law origin of police powers and the constables' subordination to justices of the peace" (Fielding 1991: 30–1).

The Australian bush, however, was a totally different situation. There was no "local character" to the office of the police constable and the tradition of common law enacted by police in Australia was an imported law, with no local knowledge or history before 1788 at the earliest. Commenting on the role of mounted police troopers in colonial Australia, Haydon observes:

"They are justly entitled to the major share of whatever romance and picturesqueness the period may possess. But the reputation of the trooper police does not rest solely on the criminal side of their duties, important though it be. It is as pioneers, as the advance guard of civilization in the wilderness, that they deserve our admiration. And this, be it remembered, is a work they are still performing, and will continue to perform so long as the expansion of Australia's settled area proceeds" (Haydon 1911: viii).

The "advance guard of civilization" implies a set of ideas that are the antithesis of the founding principles of the new British police founded in 1829. The "new police" was fundamentally about community policing, police being an integral part of the institutionalised state. Even the use of the term "advance guard" links the police in Australia to the military tradition of "avant-garde" with its specific meanings. While there may be a sense of this community policing in urban centres in the nineteenth century in Australia, there is evidence that other issues and concerns were at stake in the "bush". Haydon, for example, comments on the duties of the police trooper:

"If we read the Police Manual we find that 'the duties and powers of a mounted constable differ in no respect from those of an ordinary police constable', but the reality is far from the case. No doubt it was originally intended to be so, both in South Australia and other States. The development of the country, however, and the exigencies of the service under an economic government, have made this rule much 'honoured in the breach'. Today the mounted policeman has to perform duties of a multifarious character. As a policeman he is the sole representative, maybe, of the law in his district" (Haydon 1911: 263).

POLICE UNIFORMS, GOVERNMENT AND VISUAL EXPRESSION

To refer again to Strutt's works, in them we can see evidence of an anxiety about the landscape, anxiety about an uncontrollable nature and a colonial culture trying to make sense out of a dangerous environment. In that landscape, that environment, Strutt foregrounds the mounted trooper, "the sole representative, maybe, of the law in his district" and "advance guard of civilization". "Equestrian Portrait" foregrounds the police troopers so that they blot out the Australian landscape. They physically obliterate any features of the uniqueness of that landscape, the scene could be anywhere in the world, except for the officers' distinguishing uniforms. The identifying features of the work depend on the troopers' uniforms, the uniforms mark these men as the representatives of the law, colonial law, at a time when that law was being carried to the frontiers of the colony and Empire. Further, that law was utterly dependent on the troopers to uphold it and legitimise it such that: "Your trooper of the back-blocks, then, must needs be a man of resource and aptitude, of firm resolve and quick decision. Not only has he white settlers to look after, but those far more difficult children of nature, the blacks" (Haydon 1911: 264).

The distinctive uniform was an integral part of that law and tied to a long established tradition and history of law linked to the English monarchy and more contemporary notions of democracy. For example, writing about the establishment of police in the United States during the nineteenth century, Stanley Palmer notes:

"On the touchy subject of uniforms, the Americans were even more resistant than the English. Most of the new police wore only badges as a sign of their authority, and even this practice sometimes met with strong opposition. Uniforms were chided as 'undemocratic' and 'un-American', rejected as 'an imitation of royalty' or 'King's livery' " (Palmer 1988: 19–20).

However, with the establishment of the "new" English police in 1829:

"After 'discussion at great length', it was decided the police should be uniformed. The absence of a uniform could lead to charges about an army of spies. An initial suggestion that red and gold be the colours was rejected; perhaps the uniform of the Irish constabulary deterred Peel and the commissioners from outfitting the London police in anything remotely resembling military colors" (Palmer 1988: 297).

So, in having a highly distinctive uniform, military in character, the Australian trooper was decidedly unlike his British or American counterpart, and one can assume that the uniform was either of some importance or in response to needs not relevant in England or the United States.

The Australian landscape appears from Strutt's work to have been difficult to manage. The only thing between civilisation and chaos was the thin line of the law embodied in, and marked by, the police trooper. If there is any doubt of the trooper's importance in maintaining social and civil order, one simply has to examine their uniforms so lovingly detailed in anecdotal histories of policing such as A L Haydon's text, *The Trooper Police of Australia* (Haydon 1911) or in Strutt's artworks.

Why was the visual expression of policing so different in Australia to that of England? Mark Finnane discusses the instigation of the "new police" in Australia and its relation to settlement. He points out that the first "police" in the colony emerged as a result of convictism and indigenous resistance to the colonial settlement (Finnane 1994: 24–8). However, he also discusses the issue that the initial idea of policing in the early colony was based on existing structures in England where during the seventeenth and eighteenth centuries policing was not centralised, and the key figures of the system were the constable, the watchman and amateur justices (Reiner 1992: 14). This form of policing can be seen for example in Western Australia, where there was no convict population until well after settlement. James Stirling comments six months after Perth was settled in 1829:

> "Whilst amongst the heads of families there is a great majority of highly respected and independent persons, there is a working class of a greater variety, some having been carefully selected, but the greater part being the outcasts of parishes recommended to their employers by parish officers and possessing habits of the loosest description, the natural consequence being great inconvenience to their masters and endless trouble to the authorities. I have therefore been obliged to appoint a magistracy and a body of constables to maintain order, since which the drunkenness and similar evils have been less frequent" (quoted in Burton Jackson 1982: 78).

While the presence of convicts in, for example, New South Wales, would have been part of the impetus for some form of policing, in Western Australia community order was also an issue. By 1834 relations in Western Australia between the colonists and Aboriginal groups had deteriorated to the point that in October of that year Stirling led a party of twenty-five men, including five policemen, on an expedition which has become notorious as the "Pinjarra Massacre" (Burton Jackson 1982: 91–2). So policing in Western Australia had rapidly extended its perimeters from familiar community work to maintaining order at the frontier which, as Finnane argues, was also happening elsewhere in Australia (Finnane 1994: 23–8).

While it is clear that these contexts were powerful incentives for the development of policing in the early nineteenth century in Australia, the evidence of

PLATE 1: William Strutt, (Australia 1825–1915) "Equestrian Portrait of Sergeant John Darby and Another Member of the Victorian Police Force" (1861, Oil on canvas, Mrs Mary Overton Gift Fund) reproduced by permission of the Art Gallery of South Australia, Adelaide.

PLATE 3: Jacques-Louis David, (1748–1825) "The Consecration of the Emperor Napoleon and Coronation of the Empress Josephine in the Cathedral of Notre Dame de Paris" (detail from the central panel, 1804, Oil on canvas, The Louvre Collection) reproduced by permission of the Bridgeman Art Library, London.

PLATE 2: William Strutt, (Australia, 1825–1915) "Black Thursday" (1864, Oil on canvas, La Trobe Collection) reproduced by permission of the State Library of Victoria, Melbourne.

Strutt's paintings prompts the question: Is it that simple? Why do the early colonial troopers in his paintings have such distinctively uniformed appearances? What was there apart from the issues of convictism and Aborigines, that led to the distinctly visible nature of policing in colonial Australia?

In his discussion of what he terms the "science of policing" in his text *The Policing of Families*, Donzelot, in extending Foucault's identification of population as the focus for what he terms "the proliferation of political technologies", excises the family as the base social unit and essential component of population (Donzelot 1979: 6–7). These fundamental notions of population and family are grounded within a European industrialised urban society. Any discussion of the history of the "new" policing in England pays homage to the industrial revolution and rise of the middle class. Reiner, for example, states:

> "The basic causes of the need for police reform are seen as the twin pressures of urban and industrial revolution. As these spread through the country they brought with them new problems of order which were met by the institutions of the new police" (Reiner 1992: 10).

This industrialised urban context is the critical element in the formation of many European police forces.

In regard to European settlement in Australia, the tendency for population to concentrate in urban centres on the coast of the continent is well understood as a feature of local culture. The resultant urban order and disorder in Australia are therefore an integral part of the development of Australian colonial policing, as is evidenced by James Stirling's rapid appointment of constables in Perth in 1829. However, prior to the gold rushes in the eastern states during the mid- to late-nineteenth century, the population of Australia was relatively sparse. The composition of the First Fleet laid the foundation of a culture that was not based on notions of the family and society. The initial colonial population consisted instead of convicts, gaolers, military and a few free settlers focused on establishing a land-owning capitalist society. In that fledgling colonial population can be discerned the differing ingredients that give rise to the contradictions inherent in Australian policing.

As Finnane reminds us, it was convictism and Aboriginal resistance that prompted the initial demands for colonial police (Finnane 1994: 9–29). However, in this recognition he neglects another important element. The key to this less tangible ingredient is the presence of free settlers, the embryonic land-owning class of Australia. These colonists were coming from an industrialised, established, ordered community. They expected their property to be protected. As Finnane notes, the police were essential to this in relation to the Aboriginal presence in the landscape. The colonists had a sense of themselves as Englishmen, European; not at all how they saw not only the Aboriginal population, but also the landscape, which they viewed with some trepidation. Even by October 1849, when it was unanimously decided to establish a university in Sydney, the core of the curriculum was mathematics, Latin and Greek as it would be at the old universities in England, and the university motto was *Sidere mens eadem mutato* ("the same spirit under different skies") (Hirst 1988: 11).

CONCLUSION

In effect, this is what Strutt's "Equestrian Portrait" implies; the same spirit under different skies. The police trooper, immaculate in his uniform, stands as a marker of that spirit, linked to a centuries-old tradition of monarchy, law and order. The trooper reaffirms European control over the landscape—if there is chaos in the landscape, the police trooper can efface or control it. His uniform is "gorgeous" and "special" for specific reasons (Hill 1907: 39). It embodies law and order. An iconographical reading of the police trooper's uniform suggests that it actually symbolises the law in such a way that we can begin to understand the role of the nineteenth century policeman in the Australian colony from a slightly different perspective.

It is no accident or coincidence, then, that Strutt's "Equestrian Portrait" brings to mind Géricault's works such as "Epsom Derby" or "Trumpeter on Horseback", or that Strutt's "Black Thursday" echoes not only Vernet's works, but again Géricault's works such as "Retreat from Russia". The fledgling Australian colony was at war with the landscape and the trooper police were the avant-garde, the front line troops in that war. Their uniforms were as distinctive and ornate as military uniforms because the police actually symbolised and embodied the imperial state and all that it was striving to achieve in Australia. The uniform invoked and embodied a relationship with the imperial founding state, England. But more than that, the uniform linked the mounted police trooper to a long-standing tradition in the West of disciplined troops, law, order and good government going back to Rome and classical Greece; that is to say, the idea of Western civilisation. It is an iconography of law, war and legitimacy. It is no accident that mounted troops feature on the Arc de Triomph, or that mounted police troopers still have pride of place in public parades in Australia. W R O Hill recalls his experiences as a sub-inspector in the Queensland Native Mounted Police:

> "At this time, February 1868, the Duke of Edinburgh visited Brisbane and, probably as a salve for the unmerited annoyance I had caused, I was appointed second in command of an aboriginal escort formed in his honour. We did our best to outvie the white escort, and succeeded too, for the Duke himself told me he had never seen cavalry anywhere with such splendid seats in the saddle" (Hill 1907: 39).

Machiavelli says that: "The principal foundations of all states, whether new or old or mixed, are good laws and good arms, and where there are good arms it is appropriate that there be good laws" (Machiavelli 1996: 72). The foundation of the state of Australia was no exception. Whereas the law in England was naturalised to the point at which the policeman in the community was dressed like a civilian, in Australia this was not the case. The police trooper was an emblem of the state, the monarchy, the law and ultimately Western civilisation.

3

Governing Rural Australia: Land, Space and Race

RUSSELL HOGG AND KERRY CARRINGTON*

INTRODUCTION: DOING "GOVERNMENTALITY" WORK AND POLITICS

UNTIL THE CONTROVERSY surrounding the recent High Court of Australia decision in the case of *Wik*, many aspects of the legal and governmental regulation of the Australian interior had been a neglected aspect of governance and of socio-legal politics. That roughly 40 per cent of the Australian land mass was held under a peculiar form of statutory tenure, pastoral leasehold, involving a regime of government regulation of a most direct and interventionist kind, was hardly appreciated by the vast majority of urban dwelling, free-holding members of this "home owning democracy", including academics with a particular interest in law, government and politics. Until the High Court in *Wik* decided that Aboriginal native title could co-exist with pastoral leasehold interests in land, it was widely believed that virtually any Crown-dealing in land extinguished native title, with the consequence that effective Aboriginal title to actual tracts of land throughout most of the Australian mainland had been wiped out. When the *Wik* decision was delivered politicians, farmers' and pastoralists' organisations and newspaper leader writers went into a frenzy, gripped by the fear that suddenly its original owners were being positioned to reclaim rights to large tracts of the Australian land mass.

We write very much within this conjuncture of events, although the implications of the *Wik* decision are far from being the sole or primary focus of our concern. The debates about native title raise long neglected questions about the history and governance of land and race in rural Australia.

One of the attractions of the forms of intellectual work undertaken and fostered by Foucault is its resolute repudiation of essentialist, totalising forms of theoretical analysis. Attention has been directed to an understanding of power

* This chapter draws on an ongoing research project on communities, violence and government in rural NSW, funded by the Australian Research Council. This project includes localities in both the more closely settled agricultural parts of the state and the pastoral districts of the semi-arid far west. Other team members include Dr Peter Martin and Murray Lee, Critical Social Sciences, University of Western Sydney, Hawkesbury.

as diffuse and of government as comprised of practical, heterogeneous and contingent assemblages of rationalities, ideas, representations, techniques, and knowledges conforming to no general or necessary principles of social organisation. This in turn has suggested the importance of programmes of detailed empirical work conceived in a fairly open-minded and open-ended way.

That this body of work has also aimed for theoretical sophistication and innovation has, however, created its own attendant risks: of falling into a preoccupation with conceptual exposition, of excessive self-referentiality, of esoteric theoreticism, and of familiar forms of intellectual policing. The reception of Foucault's own work in some (especially Marxist) quarters is a reminder that this can lead to less than fruitful intellectual debate. It can also tend to confine researchers within tried and tested paths of theoretical and empirical inquiry and foreclose on the intellectually venturesome attitude fostered by Foucault's own work, which saw him direct attention to new, often mundane and ignoble, objects and materials of analysis. All of this can lead back into precisely the sort of totalising forms of analysis which, it was assumed, had been abandoned. There is a danger then that the otherwise laudably cosmopolitan and internationalist nature of the governmentality movement may engender a unity of, albeit somewhat Eurocentric, perspectives and concerns in which the much celebrated commitment to specificity produces a proliferation of analyses which essentially confirm, rather than add to, existing conceptualisations and understandings of power and governance. We turn to some of the instances in which this may be so below, after briefly considering their implications for the relationship of these forms of intellectual work to political activity.

A different, methodological pitfall has been recently identified by O'Malley, Weir and Shearing. They suggest the focus on official archives and political, administrative and policy discourses and programmes in governmentality work risks falling into a sophisticated "discourse determinism" (O'Malley, Weir and Shearing 1997).

Whilst there has been a refreshing absence of the sort of self-validating, self-congratulatory ideological posturing that characterises so much old style radical social theory, there is also a marked aversion in much of the governmentality work to political engagement. The analysis of power in its capillary and technical forms, the anti-reductionist approach to the state (Gordon 1991) and the scepticism shown towards grandiose political designs, all make Foucault's work attractive to many erstwhile Marxists and other radicals. Rather than drawing them more closely to practical questions and projects of reform, however, this seems to have led many "governmentality" scholars to disengage almost completely from conventional politics and policy debates, to become spectators rather than activists, as Richard Rorty has recently put it (1998).

For all their differences with their Marxist predecessors, many "governmentality" scholars seem to share with them a resigned acceptance—if you can't change the world at least you can theorise it. Rationalities, discourses, policies, programmes, government apparatuses, institutional practices and routines are analysed in ever more minute detail, but with an overwhelming sense of their refractoriness. This is reinforced by the air of clinical detachment with which such analyses are commonly undertaken and the adoption of an intellectual idiom seemingly calculated to engage only other governmentality scholars. Limited interest is shown even in the alignment and representation of govern- mental rationalities within particular party political programmes and strategies. Old political concerns and passions seem to have receded into the background of what has developed as a largely cosmopolitan academic project with few links to the processes and agents of political action and policy formulation in particular national settings. This is not to deny that there are many individuals who straddle these different domains. The question, however, is whether the analytical tools provided by work in the governmentality field are put to use or put aside in such engagements.

Although Richard Rorty is scathing about the influence of French social theory (involving all the usual suspects) on the formation of what he calls a "spectatorial cultural Left" in the United States, his complaint is not that this work is without powerful insights, but merely that its concerns are so limited and abstract and consequently of little political utility on pressing issues like economic inequality and redistribution. Post-Foucaultian work need not con- cern itself with socio-legal (or any other) politics of course, but if it is to do so, it needs to remind itself of the importance of these issues. It also needs to eschew the "discourse determinism" referred to by O'Malley and reflect more fully its avowed concern with specificity in its objects, methods and tools of analysis.

In the context of our own research this has required us to grapple with some residual tendencies towards essentialism in the agendas, objects and modes of analysis associated with much governmentality work.

The governmentality literature has defined the scope of its programme of research according to two recurrent themes:

(1)   the reference to "the West" as setting the implicit spatial-cultural para-
      meters of its analyses of government;
(2)   as part of an habitual tracing of the genealogy of "modern" government as
      a linear shift from sovereign to disciplinary and governmental forms of
      power in the transition from neo-feudal to modern European civilisation,
      a preoccupation with the elucidation of rationalities of government in their
      predominantly European liberal (and neo-liberal) variants.

We deal with each of these in turn before moving on.

"THE WEST"

It has perhaps been too readily assumed that analyses of power and government in "the West" apply not only to the European heartland but also to its "frag- ments" (Hartz 1964), colonial settler states like Canada, the United States, New

Zealand and Australia. To a considerable extent both tools and objects of analysis have been unproblematically transplanted from "centre" to "periphery". Barry, Osborne and Rose (1996), in the introduction to their collection *Foucault and Political Reason: Liberalism, Neo-liberalism and Rationalities of Government*, comment critically on what they see as "the comprehensive periodisation" implied by the concept "modernity" in the work of many contemporary social theorists, pointing to the problems of approaching it as an experience "without limits: geographical, social, temporal". However, the point applies with equal force to the idea of "the West" (often treated as the spatial counterpart of modernity), which has played such an important role in setting the limits to governmentality studies.

Barry, Osborne and Rose (1996) also acknowledge that their collection has little to say on the rationalities of race, nation, territory, and colonisation (Barry, Osborne and Rose 1996: 15) (it might be added that it also has nothing to say on the treatment and status of indigenous peoples). This point pertains to "governmentality" studies more generally, at least in the English-speaking world. And this is despite the central importance of such questions in the formation of Western societies and their urgent political significance at the present time. Much governmentality work does have a strangely placeless, even formalistic, quality about it.

The colonisation of other regions of the world by the European powers of course ensured to one degree or another that ideas, rationalities, techniques of government, systems of law and administration, and so on, were transplanted to these regions from Europe. But the metaphors that are common in much governmentality work—references to "migration", "travel", "regions" and "action-at-a-distance"—beg important empirical and theoretical questions as to what such a transplantation means within widely dispersed and differing locales where the boundaries of colonisation were themselves uncertain and shifting. What were its limits? What were the nature and effects of specific colonisation programmes? What unique problems were encountered? What of the resistance and subjugation of indigenous peoples? How were local conditions and resources (physical and cultural) variously understood and represented as problems for, and instruments of, government? How were the husbanding and augmentation (through immigration for example) of these resources to be managed in conditions profoundly unlike those of Europe? A "history of the present" of such societies would suggest the need to consider the relationship between imported and indigenous practices and their specific and contingent effects.

LIBERAL GOVERNANCE, "THE SOCIAL" AND THE STATUS OF THINGS

The efforts to elucidate the nature of practices of rule in "the West" have seen governmentality theorists devote considerable attention to liberal (and neo-liberal) rationalities of government. These rationalities could be said to entail a conception and practice of rule "at-a-distance" in two main ways.

First, it occurs in the broader and more literal sense that they posit as a core objective of government the maintenance of more or less continuous linkages as between the political authorities of a state and the needs, aspirations, attributes, pathologies, etc. of a population dispersed in space (usually that of a national territory). Secondly, it occurs in the more specific sense that liberal governance is to be primarily undertaken subject to, and through, the autonomous powers of free and equal persons (both individual and corporate), that is, involving formal legal and political authority which is limited in scope, and which in the private interest of safeguarding personal liberty and the public interest in creating a productive national economy respects the "natural liberty" of its citizens. A free society and a productive economy is to be fostered by refraining from, or restricting the scope of, government.

What might be identified as a tension between the broad conception of governance implied by the first of these ideas and the imposition of limits on the scope of formal political authority (of government) required by the second defines the terrain of "the social" in these analyses (Rose 1996c; Donzelot 1979). "The social" has been seen as at once providing the horizons, the domain and the resources for governing populations in liberal societies. The limited scope of political authority and action required that the domain of the social—the characteristics, problems, anxieties, aspirations, and resources of populations—be opened up to knowledge, calculation, activation and administration through non-political authorities and means. Chief amongst these in the twentieth century has been the power of expertise, notably medicine, the "psy" disciplines and other social sciences. These agencies and discourses link populations to political and social objectives, not through the coercive imposition of legal and political authority in a top-downwards movement, but by rendering them permeable: first, to forms of social inquiry which produce a "true" knowledge of the physical, mental, and moral condition of populations, their aptitudes, opinions, aspirations and so on; and secondly, to practical interventions variously taking the form of advice, assistance, education, supervision, treatment and promotion—in which individuals are led actively to align their conduct (their governance of themselves and others, such as children, families, etc.) with norms that are underscored by claims to truth. Such forms of rule involve not the erosion of personal autonomy and responsibility, but its intensification.

In the usual accounts, these liberal rationalities of government are depicted as the successor to those forms of mercantilist rule associated with European absolutism in which a well-ordered, happy and productive society was to be achieved by a total and continuous supervision of society conducted on the basis of a "science of police" (Chapman 1970; Raeff 1983). Attempts to transpose such forms of analysis into the Australian context (and that of other colonial settler states) run up against several difficulties. For one thing, it is only possible to talk of liberal rationalities of government in colonial settler states by overlooking the profoundly and overtly illiberal mechanisms of governance directed at indigenous peoples, at least until the quite recent past. These often seem to have had more in common with the "science of police" than with liberal governance. We consider this issue more thoroughly in a later section.

Further issues arise from the need to recognise how variable the conditions of "the social" can be in different spatial and political settings (national, regional, local, etc.). Major studies of the field of the social, such as those by Donzelot and by Rose, are (quite understandably) concerned with and premised upon the problematics of governance of the closely settled and predominantly urban populations that inhabit Western Europe. The studies, notably *Discipline and Punish*, in which Foucault first took up the question of power in an explicit way concern themselves with the conditions and questions of governance raised by demographic and other changes involving the increasing scale and concentration of population in settled (urban) spaces. Bentham's panopticon provided the spatial principle for a new technology of power in which the effects of a continuous, individualising, interiorising supervision could be achieved optimally with respect to large concentrations of people.

In many colonial settings, however, the first question was not one of how to govern the populations of settled places, but how to populate places which were (according to the perceptions and designs of their colonisers) uninhabited. The primary task of governments, both imperial and colonial, in such circumstances was of necessity not confined within the limits of a liberal rationality of government, even where the colony in question was not a penal colony, as was Australia in its early period of colonisation. This does not mean that the colonial authorities did not have aspirations to foster the creation of a liberal citizenry. They did and in each case land and space were regarded as central to its formation, although its precise role and the manner of its administration varied as between different projects of colonisation.

The points of significance here are twofold. First, the domain of "the social" in these colonial settings resembled a largely vacant and unsettled horizon whose occupation and cultivation necessitated action on the part of central government authorities on a scale and of a type which was quite novel to liberal rationalities in their European variants. Secondly, where governmentality studies have overwhelmingly concerned themselves with human populations and technical and normative means of their governance, knowledge and administration of non-humans was central to these colonising projects (cf. Latour 1993: 52–3). Rather than simply affording a sort of inert backdrop to the governance of human populations, things like land, natural resources, climate and its effects, feral animals and plants, were vital objects requiring representation, calculation and management in the field of government. This begins with the "discipline of exploration" (Carter 1987), but involves much else besides. In the semi-arid and arid interior of Australia the governance of things remains central to the problematics, calculations, tasks and practices of government. They in turn play an important role in the manner in which the role and scope of government at local, state and national levels is defined.

GOVERNMENTALITY AND THE AUSTRALIAN COLONIAL SETTLER STATE

A colonial settler state like Australia presents an interesting case study in governmentality. Australia, with a population of 18 million people, comprises a quite vast land mass (7,682,300 square kilometres), about the same size as China (population one billion) and three-quarters that of the United States (population 280 million). The continent is characterised by a very harsh physical geography throughout most of its interior and a highly uneven distribution of its small population, which is composed almost entirely from immigrant settlers or their descendants. Indigenous peoples constitute approximately 2 per cent of the population. The latitudinal position of the continent confines most of its land mass to "permanent aridity", exposing only its coastal fringes to regular rainfall (Macquarie Library 1984: 118).

These conditions presented particular problems for colonial and later governments, especially in respect of the manner in which the land and space of the interior was to be populated and "settled", the manner in which its inhospitable physical conditions and natural resources (poor soils, low rainfall, limited vegetation, limited natural means of inland navigation and sheer scale) were to be surmounted or managed in order to establish and foster productive industries, and the manner in which services like education, health, law, policing and communications were to be afforded a small and spatially dispersed population.

In the analysis which follows, our principal focus is upon the semi-arid interior of western New South Wales (New South Wales is one of Australia's six states, hereafter referred to as NSW). Known and administered under Crown lands legislation since the nineteenth century as the Western Division, this area comprises 336,600 square kilometres, 32.5 million hectares or 42 per cent of the land mass of NSW. That makes the Western Division about 38 per cent larger than the United Kingdom. It currently has a population of about 52,000 people (Western Lands Commission 1990: 8).

In the fragile and volatile physical environment of the Australian interior questions of optimality in terms of land management and population pose recurrent problems which continue to be central to Australian politics and government. In this fragile and volatile natural environment it is common for years of drought to be followed by the effects of floods or pest infestation. References to "invasion" refer here not usually to any human enemy but to the threat of rabbits or prickly pear. How are such environments to be managed so as to sustain productive enterprise and human population without depleting the resource base? How are these problems to be known and enumerated? What technical means can be used to manage them? What systems of land tenure and management might best facilitate the regulation of these lands?

The management of the natural environment has always been vital to its capacity to sustain human settlements. This of course was appreciated as much, or more, by its Aboriginal inhabitants as white settlers. By way of contrast to

Europe, the question in Australia was not one of governing an already settled population but of introducing population. Governance is not indifferent to spatial, physical and demographic conditions. Space, land and population are objects of, and resources for, government—for the calculated shaping and reshaping of the attributes of human subjects and environments.

If, for example, schooling and policing are regarded as integral to the formation and maintenance of a properly regulated population, it must be recognised that distance and limited population resources present major problems of governance. Questions thus arise as to how it is possible to create or foster human settlements in such country, to provide a population of the necessary size and composition to sustain the provision of services, if it is to be properly governed. That the available mechanisms of action and governance "at a distance" (market provision, bureaucratic delivery, local government, and so on) are necessarily limited and highly contingent is made palpable under these conditions.

Market provision at a local level, in areas like retailing, banking, and medical services, is intimately related to population size. Bureaucratic delivery of services may be less so, depending on factors like the division of powers and responsibilities between different levels of government, the fiscal powers of government and the organisation of political representation. In many of the more remote parts of rural Australia, bureaucratic government of education, health, courts, police, railways and communications (postal and telephone) has been absolutely central not only to the form in which such services were provided, but in its multiplier effect on these local communities and economies. In addition to providing the services required to support a local population and link it to principles, plans and programmes of rule formulated and undertaken by central political authorities (in this case of the Western Division, in Sydney or in Canberra), it has also generated the additional population and consequent demand for population-related services (retailing, banking, building and so on) which provide a foundation for a local market sector. This has nevertheless always constituted a very frail foundation for many local communities and a recurrent problem for political authorities at both state and Commonwealth government levels in Australia. This is apparent from the perennial debates about such matters as the under-provision of general practitioners and other health professionals in rural areas, the difficulty of getting trained personnel in education, the closure of banks and post offices, the costs and quality of telephone services, and access to new communications technologies.

These have been seen as pre-eminent political issues in Australia almost since European settlement, in the sense that the political authorities have been regarded as the key agents responsible for providing, subsidising or otherwise organising the delivery of basic services in remote communities. This has much to do with the historical formation of these human settlements and the role of government in this process.

SOVEREIGNTY, LAND AND GOVERNMENT

According to the principles of the English common law in 1788, when British sovereignty over Australia was declared, the territories it comprised were annexed to the British Crown in their entirety. Secure title to land could only be held (or so it was thought by many until the recent decision in the *Mabo* case, another landmark (literally) High Court case) by virtue of a grant or sale of an interest in land by the Crown. Such exercises of power by government, however, necessitate more than the abstract dominion of political authority over territory that is implied in the notion of sovereignty. In order to be treated as abstract interests—as divisible and alienable through paper transactions that may be wholly unrelated in space and time to the tracts of land to which they refer—they also have to be subject to a practical dominion. Territory must be partitioned if interests in it are to be ascertainable. This requires definite technical means and tasks, notably that of survey. A spatial history of Australian colonisation (Carter 1987) reveals the humble yet formidable burden of governance that this imposed, one not usually recognised as part of liberal philosophical depictions of property as the essential and highest expression of individual autonomy.

Other complex means used to demarcate and fix Aboriginal tribal relationships to particular tracts of land throughout Australia long pre-date European colonisation. On one (pre-*Mabo*) reading, the assertion of British sovereignty over Australia extinguished, in a single abstract moment, these relationships. Many settlers acted in accordance with this view—that the land was *terra nullius*, that for all intents and purposes it was uninhabited. Aboriginal presence, relationships and practices with respect to the territories of the continent did not need, in such a view, to be considered in the process of occupying and colonising them. This was not necessarily the view of the imperial authorities or their representatives in the colony, although Aboriginal resistance to the invasion of their lands inevitably led to a prolonged pattern of intermittent warfare, fought on highly unequal terms, down to the twentieth century. The actual dispossession of Aboriginal lands and suppression of indigenous culture and practices varied greatly in degree, chronology and the level of recourse to unauthorised and authorised violence from one region to the next (Goodall 1996; McGrath 1995).

The imperial and colonial authorities failed to arrive at anything vaguely resembling a political settlement with any of the indigenous peoples of Australia or to ensure compliance with their own principles relating to colonisation of other inhabited lands. Perhaps this is because they never adequately attempted to do so, or because they were completely lacking in the instruments (both normative and technical) for doing so in the conditions that prevailed on the Australian continent. This was simply the most profound of many related shortcomings of government in the colony of Australia. How was rule to be exercised in these circumstances?

The authorities sought to apply the principle of concentration in the early period of Australia's colonisation. This entailed restricting access to land and hence restricting the spatial limits of settlement within the boundaries and capacities of the civil administration (what by 1847 involved "the nineteen counties" or what was known as "the limits of location"). This, it was thought, would allow direct political supervision of the acquisition and use of land and, along with it, of the pattern of contact with its indigenous inhabitants. Not surprisingly, this was heavily influenced by the presence of large numbers of convicts, who were assumed not to be competent to own and work land in a responsible manner, or to acquire any of the other liberties and duties of citizenship.

By contrast, projects of "systematic colonisation" (notably that of Edward Wakefield) placed the sale of land, at a "sufficient price", at the centre of a programme of free settlement. Rather than imposing limits and controls on settlement by political fiat, land was to be sold at a price sufficient to discourage mere speculative land-holding and promote ownership for the purpose of cultivation. This in turn would foster a pattern of closely settled farming communities in which the population would be rendered amenable to the civilising effects of propinquity to land, parish and civil authority. The effects of concentration would be achieved not by political decree and direct control over the boundaries and conditions of settlement, but through the orderly sale of Crown lands. This, it was proposed, would produce the additional advantage that those lacking the immediate means to purchase land by virtue of being recently arrived or emancipated would form a much needed labouring class which would then be guided and disciplined by the expectation that they might in time and with hard work and sober habits ascend to the status of landholders.

Wakefield's scheme ensured that free settlement in the colony was integrally linked to the problems and exigencies of government in Britain, by providing that the proceeds of land sales in the colony were to constitute a land fund to finance the emigration of free settlers from Britain to the colony. This would afford the human resources needed progressively to build the new society whilst relieving the stresses on the old that were assuming a growing significance in the light of Malthusian population theory and anxieties.

We see here the relationship of a particular liberal rationality of home rule in Britain to rationalities of imperial rule through programmes of colonisation and emigration (not to mention penal transportation). It is worth remembering that at the birth of the penitentiary, that paradigmatic expression of disciplinary power, in the late eighteenth century, the British Crown lacked the institutional means to implement its own penitentiary legislation. Instead, it turned to the creation of a penal colony in NSW to which it might transport its criminals. The later schemes of the systematic colonisers, like Wakefield and his supporters, constitute a further example of the importance of colonial or imperial rationalities of government amongst the European powers, not only in the colonies but also in the forms and practices of "home" rule.

The above illustrates that there were different ways of conceiving the appropriate objectives and means of governance of the newly-founded colony of NSW. In each case, though, the rationalities of government all entailed the attempted exercise of quite direct forms of supervision and control of the population and its settlement (in the absence of anything like the dense fabric of social institutions to be found in the body of European societies) through which liberal rationalities of rule could operate. Our interest here is in the traces left by these schemes as they clash with the harsh realities they confronted. This can be seen most clearly in the policies, laws and administrative measures relating to the settlement of land and in particular in the failure of the programmes for an orderly colonisation of the interior, briefly outlined above.

Beginning in the early nineteenth century, pastoralists in search of lands upon which to depasture their sheep simply overran the official limits of the white settlement and occupied vast unsurveyed "runs" in the interior (hence, they became known as squatters). They were seen by many as a dangerous law unto themselves, as embodying a disorderly and rapacious mode of settlement which was antithetical to the extension of civilisation into the interior. On the one hand, the resources of government did not allow for their effective control, but, on the other, pastoralism quickly emerged as a major source of wealth for the colony, albeit one that threatened to choke off opportunities to "unlock the lands" to the private benefit of small landholders and to the public benefit of fostering a mode of closer settlement in which the arts of agriculture, the practice of religion and the presence of civic authority could form a dense disciplinary and civilising network around a sedentary population composed of virtuous citizens. An abiding question for the imperial and colonial political authorities throughout the nineteenth century was how to govern those people and activities beyond these rationalities, resources and practices of rule. Liberal rule on the European model was simply not feasible.

Squatting on unsurveyed Crown lands could not confer a legally enforceable proprietary interest but officialdom was powerless to stop it. Beyond the boundaries of location there was no system of legal administration. The squatters could not enjoy the protection of the law, but they could not be readily divested of the lands they occupied either; it seems most were content to be a law unto themselves. For much of the nineteenth century the colonial government accommodated what could not be adequately controlled. A system of administration was established over the lands beyond the boundaries of settlement which saw this area partitioned into administrative divisions each under the control of a Commissioner of Crown Lands. A paramilitary police force—the border police—was established to secure a semblance of law and order beyond the boundaries of settlement. And there were successive attempts to legally formalise, limit and demarcate squatter interests in the runs they occupied. These initially took the form of a licensing system, which conferred little in the way of formal security of tenure. Under later state land Acts, systems of statutory Crown leasehold were established as a vehicle for regulating the pastoral industry in the interior and over time security of tenure under such leases was increased, in exchange for higher rents and greater regulatory control. The mechanism of statutory leasehold was also adapted to the regulation of other forms of land use, such as mining.

As geographical knowledge of the interior increased, via the local experience of the pastoralists themselves and the systematic deployment of scientific expertise, so too did an appreciation of, and anxiety about, the limits to the natural environment itself and the need to manage carefully its use so as not to deplete its resource base. Drought was (and is) a recurrent problem; so too feral animals like rabbits, wild dogs, emus and kangaroos, which compete with livestock for feed, and noxious weeds such as lantana and prickly pear. Infestations of pests and weeds constantly threatened to render the land unproductive for grazing or for other agricultural uses. But so of course did its misuse by landholders, through, for example, overstocking. This initiated a quite complex and intense enterprise of governance centred on the population of non-humans that inhabited these environments—a sort of "census" of things designed to measure the presence and manage the impact of intrusions of all sorts on these fragile environments. The impact of different uses—cultivation of various sorts, grazing and so on—and the "carrying capacity" of different regions and tracts of land were carefully calculated, monitored and adjusted in the light of changing physical and climatic conditions.

These conditions, the sheer scale, volatility and physical and social marginality of these regions, have presented perennial problems of governance, of how effectively to police and supervise their occupation and use and how to reconcile their exploitation for short term productive purposes with the preservation of their long term viability. In such conditions the cultivation and maintenance of a particular pastoral "ethos"—of responsible self-management—was to be of critical importance to the governance of these regions.

Statutory leasehold (or pastoral leasehold as it is usually known) survives as a vital part of this system of governance, a core legal and administrative mechanism in the regulation of the pastoral industry in Australia. More land is held under leasehold than any other form of tenure in Australia. These tenures were made increasingly secure so as to give landholders the incentive to improve their holdings over the long term and allow them to attract finance for improvements.

In the Western Division of NSW most leaseholds are now held in perpetuity, but are subject to a quite extensive system of administrative control exercised by a public authority (the Western Lands Commission) under the Western Lands Act 1901. Regulatory controls are also exercised under other Crown lands Acts and environmental protection legislation. Under the legislation, leases are granted for a nominated purpose, usually grazing, although other purposes may be nominated instead of or in addition to grazing (such as agriculture, cultivation, recreation, etc.). Grazing leases are subject to conditions relating to the (sheep and livestock) "carrying capacity" of the land, which is the basis upon which rents are calculated. All important transactions relating to land, such as transfer, subleasing, subdivision, change of purpose and so on, are subject to ministerial control. Activities like clearing land can only be conducted under licence. The Western Lands Commission monitors the land use practices of leaseholders and may require (on pain of penalty) the destocking of holdings or particular tracts of land if they are judged to be overstocked, the regeneration or replanting of vegetation and the rehabilitation of degraded land.

From the late nineteenth century the policy was to divide the large station "runs" and supplant them with smaller holdings based on the concept of the "home maintenance" area: a holding that could sustain and in turn be supported by a man and his family with limited outside help for operations such as shearing, harvesting and fencing. This naturally produced more, smaller resident family holdings. The subdivision of the large holdings, by increasing the demand for local services, also attracted and supported a larger local population and rural economy.

On the other hand, there was always the risk that the smaller family holdings would prove unviable, especially in times of rural downturn. The play of market forces was thus highly circumscribed by a policy of managing the western lands within these polar constraints of promoting and safeguarding the model of the family farm, on the one hand, and applying the principle of a "minimal viable holding", on the other. In recent times greater flexibility has been introduced in land management policies in the Western Division and rigid adherence to these principles abandoned.

That leases are usually held in perpetuity encourages holders (some of whom are corporations, although most are families) to see themselves as de facto freeholders, as owners of the land. Pressure to formalise this relationship by converting the leasehold interests to freehold has been a constant feature of rural politics. This has been described to us as "the ethos of the Western Division". Yet it exists side by side with a high level of direct political and administrative control over land holdings and the private economic activities carried out on those lands. There has also been a very high level of dependence on government to afford relief in times of stress (such as drought, fire or flood), to provide directly or to cross-subsidise infrastructures (such as communications, transport, education, etc.) and to provide marketing boards and other agencies to regulate and stabilise commodity prices, something which has by no means been confined to the pastoral sector of Australian farming.

Out of this paternal governmental regime of land settlement has emerged a hybrid model of citizenship in which it might be said the classical agrarian independent freeholder at one pole wrestles with the figure of the supplicant petitioning government for public relief and assistance at the other. Public relief (especially in times of stress) is seen to be privately deserved because of the ethos of hard work, discipline, isolation and family responsibility according to which life is lived. Paternal regulation to secure the conditions in which these virtues might bring private material reward to producers has also (at least until recently) been conceived by political authorities as essential to the national interest, in particular to sustain and augment national wealth. This is a view that has been traditionally captured in the popular metaphor of Australia as a continent "riding on the sheep's back".

The political representation of this hybrid brand of governmental rationality has, for a good part of the twentieth century, been embodied in Australian party politics, in the shape of what was the Country Party, now known as the National Party. Both nationally and in several states the major conservative party, the Liberal Party (it is somewhat confusing that the main conservative party takes the name Liberal; the party and its beliefs and actions are sometimes referred to as big "L" liberal, to distinguish them from other forms of liberalism), is unable to form a government without a coalition with the Nationals. As such, the latter has exercised a powerful and enduring influence over conservative politics and government in Australia. This has introduced a powerful strain of support for protectionism and regulation within the conservative political bloc. Although looked upon as being on the right of the Coalition, the Nationals' commitment to economic regulation has often had greater affinities with the programme and philosophy of the left-leaning Australian Labor Party than with the traditions of Liberalism. National Party opposition to the privatisation of public agencies (notably, Australia's largest telecommunications instrumentality, Telstra) is a case in point. There is little doubt that in the Australian context this has blunted the influence of the so-called "New Right", and of economic liberalism more generally, on conservative party politics. It was primarily Labour federal governments that selectively deregulated the Australian economy in the 1980s and 1990s.

This regime of governance and the modes of life it sustains, its party political supports and forms of representation, are currently in crisis. The roots of this can be traced to what Barry Hindess refers to as the emergence of "a new problem of security" (Hindess 1998: 223). Following Hindess, it can be said (at some risk of oversimplification) that within twentieth century political and economic thought in Australia the national economy has been conceived as a more or less self-regulating entity whose output and productive potential are amenable to regulation and intensification by recourse to the tools of macro-economic management. Within this rationality of government, national economic prosperity is calculated to be integrally bound up with the protection of Australian industry and in particular the economic and social base of its pastoral and agricultural industries. As Hindess demonstrates, in the emergent problematisation of economic security the idea of a more or less autonomous national economic domain gives way to that of an international economy within which all economic conduct and calculation—from the level of the individual and small business up to the national economy itself—is to be governed by the need to compete efficiently within this international environment. The emphasis is thus placed on reform, to enhance efficiency across a multiplicity of sectors, on the assumption that the national economy and all the economic actors which compose it must outstrip or keep up with their international competitors if they are to be economically viable.

The effects of this are twofold. First, any attempt to protect actors and sectors that cannot compete (because for example they serve other important interests) threatens the efficiency and thus the security of the national economy, both as instances of inefficiency in themselves and as a drain on resources that might be more efficiently utilised elsewhere. Secondly, this model of the efficient economic actor is logically extended into manifold "non-economic" domains, such as health, education, labour market programmes and personal security, on the basis that efficient economic conduct depends upon efficiency in these other fields.

There is no doubt that this has intensified the direct economic pressures on farmers and pastoralists (as well as other sectors of the Australian economy). It has also meant that the increasingly competitive nature of sectors like banking and the extension of the market principle into the provision of "public" services (like postal, communications, transport, employment, education), through deregulation, corporatisation and privatisations are leading to the progressive rationalisation and closure of services in communities where they have in the past been heavily cross-subsidised. This is in turn producing a negative multiplier effect on local employment and population in many rural communities. It is also increasing the divide between those for whom distance is not an insurmountable obstacle to accessing services and those for whom it imposes a serious additional burden on economic and social well-being. This has also to be placed in the context of longer term shifts in the structure of production and employment, away from agriculture towards manufacturing and of course, more recently and dramatically, services and information industries.

This is currently placing enormous stress on the political bloc that has ensured, for much of the twentieth century, the representation of the "country interest" within a stable (effectively) "two party" national political system. At no time in the post-war period has this system been threatened by the advance of third parties or independents. A mid-1990s Queensland state election, however, saw this mould broken when the overtly xenophobic, racist, and protectionist One Nation party won eleven seats (13 per cent of the total number) with 23 per cent of the vote (as against around 30 per cent for the Liberal and National Parties together). This allowed the Labour Party to form a minority government with the support of an independent. In the 1998 Federal election, because of a preference deal between the major political parties, One Nation failed to win a seat in the (lower) House of Representatives and won only one (upper house) Senate seat. However, One Nation still polled strongly, with 8.4 per cent of the primary vote. Unlike the steady rise to electoral prominence of far right parties in Western Europe, the success of One Nation has been sudden and rapid, although signs of internal turmoil are straining its grip on popularity. With its principal base of support in rural, regional and urban fringe areas, this could herald the opening up of a political divide along spatial/geographical lines and the differing ways of life they are believed to embody (a new small party has even emerged called The Country Alliance). Although highly speculative and dependent upon the direction taken by these emergent political trends, this might even rekindle old, and widely overlooked, political traditions of secessionism and movements for the creation of new Australian states.

This would fracture the governmental linkages and forms of political representation that aligned communities, values, and ways of life in the interior with those of the principal, metropolitan centres and the policies and plans of central political authorities at both state and federal levels.

CONCLUSION: GOVERNING INDIGENOUS PEOPLES

The trends outlined in this chapter are also converging with, and connected to, another question: that of rights to land and the constitutional position and status of Australia's Aboriginal peoples. The rationalities of colonisation and land settlement are of course integrally bound up with the rationality of race. This relationship has taken a dramatic turn with the recent High Court decisions in the cases of *Mabo* and *Wik*. These have added another critical dimension to the current political divide.

We noted earlier that it is only possible to talk in unqualified terms of Australia as an "advanced liberal" state by ignoring the profoundly illiberal manner in which indigenous Australians have been governed. For evidence of this we need look no further than the policies of "protection" and (later) assimilation pursued from the nineteenth century through to the 1970s. These included such practices as: forced dispossession of traditional lands and removal to reserves, in which virtually all aspects of daily life (movement, education, finances, marriage, employment, etc.) were under the direction of government administrators; the forced removal of babies and young children from their families to special institutions from which they might be fostered out to white households (National Inquiry 1997); racial segregation in many institutions, notably schools, cinemas and municipal swimming pools; concerted attempts (successful up to the 1960s and 1970s) in many rural towns to prevent Aboriginal families from living within town boundaries; the failure until the 1967 referendum to include Aborigines in the national population census and to empower the Commonwealth to legislate with respect to Aboriginal affairs; and the effective denial and resistance by governments and courts until the late 1970s of Aboriginal claims to secure land tenure based on prior ownership and traditional rights (see Goodall 1996; McGrath 1995). Similar regimes and practices are to be found in other colonial settler states.

It is clear that the notion of autonomous citizenship played no part in the forms of rule to which Aboriginal Australians were subjected. However, it is important to note that the inauguration of policies of "protection" in the late nineteenth century were motivated in part by what was seen to be the inability of the authorities to otherwise safeguard Aboriginal people from white violence and to secure their access to schooling and other services in the face of white resistance.

It is not difficult to detect the source of a major tension emerging from the history of the interconnected regimes of governance recounted here. On the one hand we have examined a paternal regime of governance relating to white settlement of the interior. This was centred on providing the civic infrastructure for a particular way of life and protecting and rewarding the pastoral ethos of hard work, self discipline, and family responsibility that was assumed to embody it. Within it, Aboriginal people tended to be defined as a feature of the natural environment. In this respect they might be represented in a benign form as bearers of a unique and refined local know-how which derived from their unity with the physical environment, to which pastoralists were deeply indebted. There is often affection in such accounts, but there is rarely any sense of a people with rights or interests in the land with which they were so familiar. On the other hand, they might be reduced to the status of a dangerous pest, akin to other natural pests encountered in these harsh environments. It is this regime and its assumptions in particular that are now under substantial threat.

Paralleling the increasing fragility of pastoral paternalism, forms of "indigenous" governance have emerged under the rubric of "self determination" which have allowed Aboriginal people and organisations to purchase land, houses and businesses, establish services and constitute themselves as a visible civic and economic presence. From the point of view of the pastoral ethos, such policies are unfathomable except in terms of sheer government perversity or a conspiracy against the national interest. They are represented as a support for values and conducts that are the complete antithesis of the pastoral way of life, namely the idleness, dependency, drunkenness, neglect of family and disorderliness that they associate with Aboriginal town life. Of course, this discourse involves a conflation of the visible problems of poverty, crime and child neglect amongst some Aboriginal town residents with the new forms and strategies of Aboriginal politics and organisational life, so that the former are depicted as the product of these recent forms of government "welfare" and "handouts". This effaces any idea that they might have anything to do with the historical legacy of colonisation and dispossession (see Hogg and Carrington 1998).

This might prove to be a tolerable burden for whites in instances where it is confined within the perimeters of the towns and does not much affect their essentially instrumental orientation to town space. Ironically, after simultaneously dispossessing Aboriginal people of their lands and attempting to segregate them from town life, the town has itself become, for some whites at least, a space within which to confine and manage the disorders of Aboriginal life. The *Wik* decision, which held that native title to land could co-exist with the interests of pastoral leaseholders, threatens this as a *modus vivendi*. From the pastoralists' viewpoint *Wik* threatens to unleash the disorder they associate with Aboriginal presence in the towns into the surrounding hinterland. This is seen as a major threat on a material level because of the marginality of the land and the ethos of care, skill, and hard work required to work and maintain it in an economically productive manner. Aboriginal life is regarded as completely antithetical to the ethos required to govern these lands. It is of course also a major threat to their sense that they are, by virtue precisely of this ethos they bring to the management of the land, its rightful owners. This explains in large part the scale of the backlash against the *Wik* decision, the manner in which the theme of "uncertainty" circulated so freely in the wake of the decision and its wider and continuing repercussions in national politics.

Much of the national debate following *Wik* overlooks the depth of the difference between these modes of life, themselves the correlates of the rationalities of governance to which the interior was subject in the process of its colonisation. One short visit to the local sites of these differences is enough to dispel any optimism about the path to reconciliation. The widespread calls for total extinguishment of native title are based on the claim that in creating special rights only amenable to exercise by indigenous people, the principles of equality and neutrality in a liberal legal order are offended. But the attempt by these interests to "restore" an imagined past free from racial conflict appears doomed. On the other hand, many naive calls for co-existence ignore the difficulties of building local relationships and constituting spaces within which this might become possible. The more likely scenario at the moment may be further moves towards the forms of polarisation in rural Australia represented by the emergence of populist right-wing political forces like One Nation.

4

Governing Unemployment: Transforming "the Social"?

WILLIAM WALTERS

INTRODUCTION

GOVERNANCE HAS BECOME something of a "keyword" of late. Political economists have applied the term to the regulation of economic affairs (Jessop 1995). Political scientists are using notions of governance to analyse political systems which, in an age of "globalisation" and political fragmentation, seem to be increasingly polycentric and multilevelled (Marks *et al* 1996). Studies of public policy are also taking up the concept to make sense of new, sometimes looser, systems of regulation—brought into being by privatisation and new management techniques—where public objectives are often pursued through "partnerships" and other arrangements with private actors (Dale 1997). While these and many other literatures no doubt understand governance in diverse ways, one preoccupation they share is in understanding contemporary *transformations* in governance.

This chapter explores the kind of contribution which the governmentality literature can make to our understanding of mutations in (and in some cases away from) "social" government, a notion that is defined below, in the first section. There are several conceptual emphases which distinguish the governmentality perspective on governance from other theories of governance. These include a stress on the *programmatic* aspect of governing, the *liberal* character of dominant strategies of government (that is, their will to govern in terms of, and through the regulated autonomy of their subjects)for example, Foucault 1982)), and the *practical* dimension of rule (that is, the technical methods of inscription, calculation and influence on which this conduct of "distant" and relatively autonomous actors depends) (Barry, Osborne and Rose 1996; Rose and Miller 1992). But the one that is emphasised in this chapter is the *discursive* character of government. The governmentality literature is valuable for drawing our attention to some of the differing languages that political authorities have used historically to imagine their task, to picture the objects and the processes they have sought to govern. Governmentality does not employ as *a priori* categories of analysis the economic, the social, the psychological, the public and the private etc., as the social science disciplines tend to. Instead, it is interested in the manner in which governing mentalities and frameworks involve a characterisation of processes and variables *as* "economic", "social", etc.

This chapter examines some of the different conceptual "territories" in which the problem of unemployment has been posed and acted upon (Walters 2000). It begins with a discussion of the "social" government of unemployment which has been politically influential for much of this century. The second section then analyses a number of different strategies for governing unemployment today, each of which challenge the "social" approach. What is highlighted are the different ways in which unemployment is imagined within neo-liberal, neo-social democratic, communitarian strategies of government, as well as in terms of the strategy of criminalising the poor. In this way, the chapter seeks to suggest the possibility of a more nuanced and less reductionist account of shifts in governance.

UNEMPLOYMENT AND SOCIAL GOVERNMENT

As a concept, "the social" has a quite specific significance within the governmentality literature. It is not the eternal or necessary antithesis of "the economic". Neither is it a reference to the social world of human interactions and relationships that exists apart from, but in relation to, the natural world. Instead, "the social" refers to a particular style or ethos of governing societies and their problems, and it also refers to a "territory" of government (Rose 1996b), which is not transhistorical, but only came into being in Western countries some time in the nineteenth century, on a piecemeal and ad hoc basis. Today "the social" is undergoing profound mutations.

Pat O'Malley makes sense of the social by pointing out that under the regime of the social, at one time:

> "the principal objects of rule and the ways of engaging with them were constituted in terms of a collective entity with emergent properties that could not be reduced to the individual constituents, that could not be tackled adequately at the level of individuals, and that for these reasons required the intervention of the state. Social services, social insurances, social security, the social wage were constituted to deal with social problems, social forces, social injustices and social pathologies through various forms of social intervention, social work, social medicine and social engineering" (O'Malley 1996b).

Understood in this way, the social is particularly useful for the purposes of this chapter, namely analysing and historicising the government of unemployment in the twentieth century. The "social" nature of the regulation of unemployment can be appreciated on at least two levels.

First, we can inquire how it was that unemployment came to be constituted as a "social" object within governmental thought. In the nineteenth century and before, the condition of the unemployed was understood either as an issue of overpopulation (Malthus), or ascribed to factors exogenous to the market system (for example, a severe winter, sun spots (Jevons), Napoleonic wars). It was, of course, also ascribed to the moral failings of workers. Within political cultures dominated by liberal political economy it was not possible to conceptualise worklessness as a systemic and impersonal phenomenon.

But a number of developments towards the end of the century changed matters, so that by the 1890s, at least, "unemployment" was "discovered" (Harris 1972; Walters 1994). These developments include: the rise of social-survey based research which quantified the sheer scale of poverty and irregular employment in countries like Britain (Jones 1984); changes in political and social thought which repudiated the atomistic assumptions of liberal political economy in favour of a more holistic conception of society (Collini 1979); and the political activity of the labour movement and of poor people who began to make political demands in the name of the unemployed (Flanagan 1991). One result of this was that unemployment came to be officially recognised as an outcome of the functioning of a larger socio-economic system, or as William Beveridge (1909) put it, a "problem of industry". Henceforth, unemployment could be understood as a normal, albeit regrettable and deleterious, consequence of industrial life. Just like the various other dimensions of the social (suicide, crime, poverty, etc.) that were revealed through the statistical work of social experts and emerging social ministries, unemployment was seen to have its own regularity, its cycles, its social and geographical distribution.

Not only was unemployment now being conceptualised at a social level. The first six decades of this century also saw the development of a host of techniques for *acting* on it at this level of population and national economy. With the advent of unemployment insurance to socialise the wage, a labour exchange system to distribute the labour force more rationally, regional policy to distribute industrial activity geographically (Parsons 1988) and, by the end of the Second World War, a political technology of national economic management influenced by Keynes's formalisation of macro-economics (or, as Thompson (1992) has argued, by other economic rationalities in countries like France), more and more aspects of the problem of unemployment could be tackled at a national-aggregate, rather than an individual or local level.

Giddens (1994) provides a useful way of understanding the form in which social problems like unemployment, poverty and public health are constituted within regimes of social government. They become "external risks", phenomena which are not so much the property of eternal social groups (the poor, the residuum), but hazards which threaten whole populations. They are "external" in the sense that, understood as risks which traverse populations, these hazards become primarily the responsibility of systems of technocratic macro-management, of national health services, social security agencies, planning offices, etc.

However, to understand the place of unemployment within the strategy of social government solely in terms of "external risk" is itself risky. For it implies that the responsibility for the government of this, and other social problems, was somehow fully taken over by states and expert systems. It implies an overly linear and total shift from moralising and disciplinary techniques of governance to social-aggregative ones (O'Malley 1992). It also supports the argument made by neo-liberal critics of the welfare state, namely that the development of the latter demoralises and de-responsibilises the individual. With the understanding of modern power, which it takes from Foucault and Latour—as relational, as always working through the regulated and calculated autonomy of subjects and agents—the governmentality literature points to a different view. It is true that welfarist modes of government centre upon the aggregative, the collective pole, as it were. But by no means do they eclipse the role as self-governing entities which individuals, families, and autonomous groups like the professions, trade unions, employers and their representatives play in strategies of welfarist government. This much is nicely captured by Beveridge, writing in the early 1940s. In discussing the social obligations proper to social actors in societies of managed full employment, he clearly sees the connection between their self discipline and their enjoyment of liberties:

> "If the people of Britain generally under full employment become undisciplined in industry, that will show that they are not sufficiently civilized to be led by anything but fear of unemployment and are unworthy of freedom, or that control of industry must be changed" (Beveridge, quoted in Williams and Williams 1987: 34).

GOVERNING UNEMPLOYMENT TODAY: FOUR STRATEGIES

This brief overview of some of the ways in which the government of unemployment could be considered "social" this century is necessary to the main purpose of this chapter. For it allows us to now consider contemporary strategies for governing unemployment in terms of how they improvise, transform, or reject the presuppositions and techniques of social government.

It should be stressed that what follows does not aspire to offer any sort of structural or political explanation of the crisis of welfarism, nor the forces which contest it. There is a vast literature on this (for example, Scharpf 1991; Pierson 1994). Nor does this very schematic summary of different governmental strategies claim to be comprehensive. The objective is somewhat more restricted: to capture something of the diversity of languages which are being used by authorities to make sense of contemporary social problems, and the different ways in which social relations are now imagined.

Strategy one: neo-liberalism

Neo-liberalism is a widely and loosely employed term within the social sciences and in public debate. For the purposes of this chapter I am defining it somewhat heuristically, in terms of its differences from neo-social democracy (which is discussed in the following section). However, as strategies, both should be seen as positions along a continuum; both positions are loosely and pragmatically assembled.

Both neo-liberalism and neo-social democracy are typified at a most general level by the privileged role they accord to "markets" over "bureaucracies" within their programmes. "Markets" are held to be superior to "bureaucracies" not just as allocative and regulatory mechanisms, but also as devices for maximising the scope for individual freedoms and personal choice. Neo-liberalism and neo-social democracy both generally endorse certain core policies, most notably a limited role for the public sector, liberal trading regimes, price stability as a cardinal rule in monetary matters, and economic competitiveness as a key objective. However, they differ in terms of their hierarchy of political concerns and objectives. Neo-liberalism has little to say on questions of social justice, social inequality or discrimination. Its interest in social policy is largely connected with the contribution it is said to make to economic objectives. This is not the case for many neo-social democrats: while they recognise that economic competitiveness is key, they also seek to address the widening inequality associated with market liberalisation, social justice, and related issues. They are also more keen to build "partnerships" with a range of social actors. Quite how they attempt this is something I address in the next section. Here I am interested in neo-liberalism and the government of unemployment.

There are several levels at which we can consider the significance of neo-liberalism for a genealogy of the government of unemployment. But in order to take up this matter, we need to mention briefly the manner in which Keynes socialised economic theories of unemployment. For Keynes (1936), unemployment was the emergent property of the national economic system and could not be reduced to the economic behaviour or choices of workers. The most serious component of unemployment was involuntary: the outcome of inadequate aggregate demand in the system. This view of unemployment was challenged by the neo-classical and neo-liberal theories which had become powerful within policy-making circles, at least in the United States and the United Kingdom, by the early 1980s (for example, Minford 1991; Brittan 1975). These approaches turned Keynes on his head. There were strict limits to a strategy of reducing the jobless rate by manipulating aggregate demand in the economy, it was argued, since this did not improve the factors of supply, and risked aggravating inflation. The only way to effect a lasting solution to unemployment was to act on the factors which determine an economy's "natural rate of unemployment", factors located on the "supply side" of the economy—its institutional matrix of benefits, taxation, training etc. Consequently, while the left has seen deregulation of the labour market and the retrenchment of social security as an attack on the working class, and the reassertion of capital's power over the production process, the neo-liberal right has claimed it as a method of "job creation".

What is significant for our purposes is that these theories reinstate a view of unemployment as voluntary. It is no more than an aggregation of the countless preferences and choices individuals make, under a given set of circumstances, between work and "leisure" (Minford 1991: 22). This is one way in which unemployment ceases to be "external"—out there in the system—and moves closer to the choice-making individual of liberal discourse.

There is a correspondence between this reconstruction of theories of unemployment in terms of individual choices and the second level at which neo-liberalism is significant for a genealogy of governance. Neo-liberalism has made a lasting impression on public administration, introducing an ethos, and mechanisms, of "enterprise" into its workings (Hood 1991). The management of employment policy has not been exempt from this trend. For instance, in Britain the administration of training was devolved to a series of quasi-autonomous agencies, the Training and Enterprise Councils (King 1993). There is now a flourishing private sector providing job counselling and training services. But also the main task of regional and urban policy has been recast as one of stimulating local economies, and fostering the entrepreneurial capacities of disadvantaged communities, with economic development and enterprise agencies set up within and outside local government to this end (Deakin and Edwards 1993). The ethos of enterprise is also evident in the way in which employment programmes encourage the unemployed to become active and motivated "jobseekers" (Novak 1997), but also in all those programmes which encourage self-employment as an alternative to unemployment.

Strategy two: neo-social democracy

In an important sense, neo-social democracy wants to affirm the social. Where neo-liberalism is characterised by its neglect of, and in some cases contempt for, social questions, neo-social democracy seeks to keep problems of racism, sexism, unemployment, social inequality and deprivation in the foreground of the political agenda. Yet neo-social democrats evince little enthusiasm for the old technologies of the social—social insurance, social work, even trade unionism. Here they agree with the neo-liberals that these types of intervention are today counter-productive, fostering dependency amongst people, and doing little to "integrate" the "socially excluded" populations which the whirlwind of marketisation and globalisation has left in its wake. Jacques Donzelot (1991) has characterised the neo-liberal and neo-social democratic logics as being about "the mobilization of society". This seems an especially apt description of the neo-social democratic position. It works in terms of an "animator-state" that no longer positions itself as a manager who can solve society's problems. Instead, it deflects them back onto society, engaging it in a new form of social government in which the full gamut of societal actors and institutions—citizens, families, firms, communities, cities, schools, professions—are to be mobilised, resourced and steered towards the solution of social problems.

This logic is apparent in a series of high level policy documents that have emerged since the early 1990s concerning unemployment (EC 1994; ILO 1996). Here I focus on just one, the OECD's *Jobs Strategy* (OECD 1994). While the OECD's enthusiasm for market-oriented strategies has earnt it a neo-liberal reputation, the considerable attention it has paid in recent times to the positive reconstruction of social policy qualifies it here as neo-social democratic.

The *Jobs Strategy*, as with neo-liberalism, rejects the Keynesian conception of unemployment. Unemployment is first and foremost a "structural" problem, the symptom and expression of social and economic systems which are failing to adapt to the new global world.

There appears to be a growing gap between the need to adjust and the capacity of OECD economies to adjust. "This adjustment gap has arisen from practices that have made the economy rigid. Motivated to protect people from at least the worst vicissitudes of economic life, governments, unions and businesses have progressively introduced labour market and social policy measures which, in achieving their intended ends, also have had the unintended but more important side-effect of decreasing the economy's ability, and sometimes also society's will, to adapt" (OECD 1994: 29).

There are several points which need to be made on the strategy for governing unemployment proposed here. First, the mobilisation of society it calls for is permanent. Restructuring is no longer a once-off or periodic adjustment, as it was perhaps imagined to be in the 1970s when mass unemployment and inflation signalled the end of the post-war boom. Flexibility is a constant imperative: "structural reform should be seen as a continuous process responding to evolving constraints and opportunities, rather than being perceived as crisis management" (OECD 1990: 15).

The fact that the OECD, like so many organisations today, prefers the notion of "strategy" to "policy" is significant in this respect. It speaks to the changed conception of social and economic order, and to the task of political action, which is now associated with unemployment. In his historical overview of managerial thought, Charles Maier links this preference for "strategy" to a particular view of the economic world as somewhat "Hobbesian", a world marked by "the constant presence of uncertainty, and the existence of constraints". This is quite different from the "homeostatic vision" of their environments which managers of public, private and personal affairs took for much of this century, where the task of management was "to preserve or restore a high-level equilibrium" (Maier 1987: 69). The presupposition of the *Jobs Strategy qua* strategy is that economies and societies are no longer self-contained unities; the solution to unemployment is not the attainment of a managed "equilibrium" of full employment, as Keynes imagined it. Instead, it is about being adept at the game of "constant adaptation to a moving environment" (Carnoy and Castells 1997: 12).

The second point to note about the *Jobs Strategy* is that the causes of unemployment are no longer centred in one place, for example, in a deficiency of aggregate demand (Keynes) or friction within the labour market (Beveridge). Instead, the "jobs crisis" becomes the occasion for a sort of wide-ranging audit of social and economic institutions in terms of their flexibility. "Every part of the social and economic policy spectrum offers answers" (OECD 1994: 41). Accordingly, the *Jobs Strategy* contains more than sixty different recommendations for measures states can pursue to boost "job creation", including tax and benefit reform, the encouragement of entrepreneurship, the strengthening of the research and innovation base of the economy, and support for life-long learning. There is a clear sense that society is being implicated in this campaign. "The recommendations do not apply to governments alone. In many cases responsibility for action to improve employment performance lies most directly with employers, trade unions and individual workers" (OECD 1994: 43).

A third point can be made about the *Jobs Strategy* as part of a wider neo-social democratic strategy, one that requires us to consider the *Jobs Strategy* in the light of the historic commitment to full employment which most Western states made following the Second World War. It has been noted for some time that the rise of neo-liberalism signalled the demise of the full employment objective. The *Jobs Strategy* does not restore this objective, but it does indicate the existence of a new, positive objective which states can use to replace it. This is "job creation" which has emerged not just as a political objective, but a new empirical *object* of regulation: something to be counted, compared, theorised as to which methods best achieve this end.

But if job creation is replacing full employment as a policy goal and object, this is accompanied by a new relationship to the citizen around employment issues. In the past the guarantee of full employment suggested that the state would provide for the security of the individual in part by exercising a certain "external" control over her or his socio-economic environment. Neo-social democracy no longer conceives security in these terms. "A more realistic and positive approach is to accept the present world of employment instability, and to help citizens learn to deal with it as a permanent state of affairs" (OECD 1997: 5). A generalised state of insecurity is made the norm (Beck 1992). Hence, neo-social democracy looks to recast the social contract around "employability", a notion for which the "skills" of the individual becomes a key instrument and technology of government. The skills of the individual are to be governed and harnessed through a proliferation of new technologies, including various new systems of accreditation and assessment which are to make them visible; compacts with employers about training; the provision of financial and tax incentives for individuals to "invest" in their own "human capital"; and the recasting of education systems under the auspices of "lifelong learning". In these and other ways individuals are to be supported, encouraged, and steered towards a norm of constantly updating their marketable skills.

Finally, we should note that the neo-social democratic approach to unemployment, at least as exemplified by the OECD and its intellectuals, entails a novel kind of specification of the family as a site of human capital formation and economic partnership, and an attempt to redeploy it as a site of government. This is worth noting since, again, it illustrates the lines of continuity and rupture in relation to our earlier discussion of social government. For architects of the welfare state like Beveridge (1909), the family is seen as a *social* machine. The management of unemployment through political action and administrative means is crucial: only when the livelihood of the "breadwinner" is secured will the family be capable of meeting its "private" responsibilities and "social" obligations, especially towards the care and social development of children.

Within the neo-social democratic imagery, the family is still accorded certain "developmental" responsibilities. However, it is now also more akin to a small business, and a node within a larger training and retraining system. "When it is potentially 'strong' (with two highly educated adults at its core) it serves as a risk hedge against periods of unemployment, as a source of child development for its offspring, of investment capital for adult and child education and job training, and of personal security and growth. Networked into larger information and communication systems, it can also become a production unit" (Carnoy and Castells 1997: 41).

Strategy three: communitarianism

The third strategy we consider here is communitarianism. This is a well-established theoretical position within political philosophy, where it has served as a foil to liberalism. However, in recent years debate has flourished around this theme at the level of public policy and political rhetoric. This has been most pronounced in the United States where President Clinton, amongst others, has keenly adopted communitarian positions. However, communitarian arguments have also been espoused in the United Kingdom. Tony Blair's "new Labour" government has enthusiastically endorsed communitarian principles as part of its bid to chart a "third way" between the statism and technocracy of social democracy and the uncaring, anti-social and individualistic excesses of neo-liberalism (Driver and Martell 1997). It is in the name of community much more than class that Labour now governs.

A consideration of communitarian logics is relevant for this discussion of mutations in social government, since it seems that communitarians put forward a non-sociological account of social problems. This is a criticism that has been well made by Low (1999) of Amitai Etzioni, one of the most prominent voices of this new communitarianism.

Etzioni's communitarianism embodies a particular diagnosis of the present ills of the United States. In short, it is held to be suffering from a fraying of community. In a manner not dissimilar to neo-conservatism, the finger is pointed at the 1960s and 1970s, at the growth of "special interests", "individual rights" and moral narcissism. While the Reagan agenda of the 1980s defined itself against the moral drift of the 1960s, at the same time its pro-market emphasis only heightened a sense of individualism and contempt for communal values which in many ways made the situation worse. Hence, for Etzioni and other communitarians, a whole host of morbid symptoms stem from, and attest to, this weakening of community spirit, this dissolution of common core values. Among them are rising divorce rates, escalating crime and urban chaos, welfare dependency, economic insecurity, cultural conflict, a political system ridden with corruption and cynicism, and easily-available pornography. Any improvement will hinge upon a reawakening of a sense of individual and community responsibility.

Neo-liberalism and neo-social democracy might have reversed dominant understandings of unemployment. But they still situate it on a socio-economic plane. What is interesting about the communitarian strategy is that it displaces unemployment onto a space of community, of moral and ethical relations. Along with poor housing conditions, irregular work, family violence, it becomes one of a series of forms of "a-social malaise" (Low 1999: 95), a symptom of a deficit of civic activism and individual responsibility. Unemployment here becomes a tear in the social fabric, a site for a social and political campaign modelled along the lines of moral regeneration and repair. The unemployed must bear their responsibilities. According to the logic of community, society is no longer imagined as a space of interdependence or social determination (Rose 1996c). Instead, it is a delicate environment which we must nurture.

Etzioni doesn't write much directly about unemployment. He devotes more space to education, the need to "clean up" the polity, and to restore the socially-responsive family. But on the occasions where the issue does come up, it tends to confirm this argument. For instance, at one point Etzioni (1993: 127) observes that the closure of industrial plants which are the mainstay of communities cannot always be avoided. However, he goes on, the communities in question should be afforded the opportunity to help the corporation solve its economic problems, or to explore the opportunity of alternatives, like some sort of buyout. Employees should also be given time, and perhaps financial assistance, to help them and their communities adjust. There is no sense here of plant closure as an economic issue, structured by economic forces or dynamics. Instead, we have an essentially moral appeal to employers for better treatment of their employers.

Elsewhere, the subject of unemployment is broached in terms of subsidiarist principles: "We start with our responsibility to ourselves and to members of our community; we expand the reach of our moral claims and duties from there" (Etzioni 1993: 147). In the case of the unemployed, this could mean "continuing to look for a job following several rejections". The individual should only look to the nation—the "community of communities"—when other communities are incapable of helping. Hence, federal unemployment insurance only seems to be justified under *particular* circumstances, as a form of "intercommunity" assistance. Etzioni gives the example of an economic recession which strikes a particular town or community: "it is futile and unfair to expect that only members of those towns should bear the full brunt of resulting dislocations, which were caused by the federal government to benefit the nationwide economy" (Etzioni 1993: 146).

What is interesting here is that Etzioni's position reverses the assumptions of social government. For the social liberalism typified by Beveridge and by Churchill (1973), state action was to be the foundation, the substructure which guaranteed a basic and universal standard of living and security across society. "Voluntary action" (Beveridge) would then build on this. But universal provision had to come first so that poorer citizens had a stake in the social order, grounds for hope, a reason to strive to improve their situation. For the communitarian position set out by Etzioni, state provision is a measure of last resort, a back up when all else fails. This view of the welfare state is also implicit in contemporary political discussions whenever "social programmes" are referred to as "social safety nets"—as though the social existed solely to prevent the free-fall of the poorer sections of society who, unlike the majority, have no private means to secure themselves.

We noted that "new Labour" has assimilated certain communitarian themes into its programme for governing Britain. The New Deal (the name somewhat romantically recalling the leadership of another country in another era) is its flagship policy to deal with long-term and youth unemployment, as well as the integration of other categories (for example, single mothers) into the employment system (Finn 1997). For some commentators, the New Deal can be interpreted as "productivist" social policy, as a further step in the transition from the Fordist welfare state to a post-Fordist workfare state (Jessop 1994). However, the New Deal also seems to embody communitarian motifs. For one thing it eschews a sociological or economic understanding of unemployment. This much is demonstrated by the fact that the New Deal is funded by a one-off "windfall tax" on "greedy" former public enterprises. It does not assume that unemployment is a systemic or necessary feature of the social system mandating continuous supervision and a constant stream of public funds. Instead, it is more like an environmental disaster which can be redressed through a one-off public campaign.

But the New Deal is communitarian in other ways. It grasps the principle of "responsibility" in a bid to re-establish a social contract between the unemployed and the rest of society, to reverse the neglect for the disadvantaged and to counter the social disintegration spawned by the Thatcher years.

> Too many people in Britain have slipped through the labour market . . . We have a responsibility to offer people decent employment or training opportunities and these will be available under the New Deal. But it is a two way deal. In return people must take responsibility for their own development and their part of the bargain will be to make a positive contribution to society" (Blunkett 1997).

The responsibility of the unemployed, in this case, is to seize the "opportunities" which the New Deal offers them. These include subsidised work placements in the private and third sectors, involvement in the government's "environmental task force", and education or training. The Employment Service is to keep a watchful eye that such responsibilities are observed. But also, through its "Gateway" counselling process, it implicates the unemployed in a regime in which they exercise the responsibility of thinking strategically about their futures. "Gateway" does this by constituting the allocation of the unemployed between different retraining options in terms of a strategic "career choice". This choice is to be made by the subject in consultation with the "Gateway" job counsellors.

This emphasis on the responsibilities of the unemployed, rather than their social rights, is a feature of many social reforms which have been analysed as "workfare". It marks a direction in policy which has been advocated by conservative critics of welfare such as Lawrence Mead (1986). Less well noted in the literature is the discursive repositioning of the employer within these new types of welfare arrangements. A prominent feature of the New Deal has been its appeal to employers to form a new partnership with the government and young people, to attack the "waste" of unemployment. Through a high profile media campaign, and various government consultations, major businesses have been exhorted to recognise their "corporate social responsibility", to "pledge" themselves to the objectives of the New Deal by offering work placements and other forms of assistance to the unemployed. It is significant that their involvement is to be voluntary: this reflects the communitarian theme that social action should be first and foremost morally driven if it is to be sustainable.

My sense is that this appeal to the employer is more than just rhetorical. It reflects a broader reconstruction of the relationship of the firm to social issues according to the logic of community. For today we see a multitude of ways in which businesses are becoming involved in "their" communities. Whether it is supermarkets pledging a dollar towards computers for schools for every fifty dollars you spend on their merchandise, banks offering scholarships for disadvantaged young people, or local businesses offering managerial and marketing advice to help charities become more effective "social entrepreneurs", the forms by which the business world is becoming involved in social problems extends well beyond what used to be called business philanthropy.

This new governmental relationship of the employer stands in contrast to that which we observed under social-democratic and Keynesian forms of welfare government. Then the employer featured prominently as a partner, and a social actor alongside the union, in what was structured as a "corporatist" project of macro-managing of the economy. Now the idea that welfare can be managed in this way has passed. Today it is as a business "community", which partners other communities, that firms are to be enlisted in the promotion of the social good.

Strategy four: criminalisation

One of the positive features of governmentality research into social government is that it takes a broad and deeply historicist view. Unlike a great deal of work within political science and social policy, it does not take the social as self-evident or eternal, but as a particular way of governing. It is therefore sensitive to the existence of other ways of governing issues of security and population that have existed as competitors to social government, and that were, in some cases, subordinated by social insurance systems, social work, social justice, etc., as these became dominant elements of our present. Relevant to this discussion, as an illustration of such a competing strategy, is what Garland (1985) describes as a "penal solution" to the "social question" at the end of the nineteenth century. This "solution" accorded a much greater role for incarceral and repressive technologies than the social security strategy which, it transpires, successfully outflanked it (though not, perhaps, without drawing from it). Had the penal strategy been more successful, the space of unemployment would, presumably, have been constituted more as a law and order issue, and the proper target for such measures as labour colonies, anti-vagabondage measures, and a continuation of the logic of the Poor Law in assistance matters.

There are certain respects in which the present is marked by a revival of penal and criminological approaches to the government of population. As Stan Cohen, among many criminologists, has noted, "the crime problem has come to dominate the contemporary political rhetoric of Western democracies" (Cohen 1996: 7). At least within the English-speaking democracies, one can speak of a "new punitiveness" which seeks to engage certain "problem" sections of the population in a plethora of disciplinary measures, including boot camps, "tougher" sentencing, curfews, and "zero tolerance" policing. Society is mobilised around the theme of a "war on crime".

It seems this tendency cannot be explained in purely realist terms, that is, in terms of a public reaction to a secular rise in crime. For Garland (1996), these various wars on crime are a somewhat hysterical display of state sovereignty. By taking a "tough" stand on crime, politicians can reassert the symbolic power of the state at a time when its actual capacity to control the social and economic environment seems to be waning. (Something similar could be said about nationalist reactions to European integration.) For Wacquant (1999), the explanation is more political-instrumental: if a "moral panic" is now welling across Europe around themes of "urban violence", disorder and juvenile delinquency, this has much to do with the dominant flow of ideas from the United States. In this respect, he identifies what is now an international network that has come to link the interests of prestigious think-tanks, media commentators, academics, police departments and justice/home affairs ministries. Its core is in the United States, but its message and many of its instruments reach into Europe, with the United Kingdom serving as a relay station and a testing ground. This network has been instrumental in reconstituting social issues as questions of "order" and "security". It is tied in with "the withering away of the economic state, diminution of the social state, expansion of the penal state" (Wacquant 1999: 1). The emergent penal-industrial complex also has interests that converge with this network.

This network around the criminalisation strategy has also been instrumental in reviving the idea of "the underclass" (Lister 1996). This concept does import-ant bridging work in the sense that it links the question of the long-term un-employed to narratives of violent crime, single parenthood, drug abuse, racial alienation and welfare dependency. It shifts the place of unemployment within governmental imaginings so that it is no longer a systemic socio-economic con-dition which underpins a host of other ills, but rather part of a congeries of forms of immoral, irresponsible and anti-social behaviour. It associates unem-ployment with an alien "culture" that has formed on the margins, a culture in which the work ethic and social values of mainstream society are absent. As such, the underclass idea legitimates a more repressive approach to social prob-lems. It suggests that people without work can be conceptualised and governed in ways other than as "unemployed".

That intensive (public and private) policing, and ultimately incarcer-ation, presents an alternative, in terms of governing poor populations, to the unemployment/social security strategy is a conclusion implicit in one of the explanations given for the comparatively low rate of long-term unemployment in the United States. This comparatively low rate is partly explained by the tight-fistedness of the American social security system and partly by the higher rates of job creation achieved by the American economy. But it is also related, it seems, to the high numbers of men—and disproportionately young black men—in prison in the "land of the free".

CONCLUSION

The substantive core of this chapter has been the regulation of unemployment, understood here as a point of focus for a wider discussion of "the social" and its mutation. The chapter has sought to analyse this mutation mainly in terms of four schematic strategies. The presumption is that such an approach makes for a better appreciation of the complexity of governance. I do not claim for a moment to have offered a comprehensive overview of all the possible strategies for governing unemployment. For instance, I have said nothing about those who would revive a more Keynesian approach, perhaps through better systems of international policy co-ordination, and govern in terms of a kind of reregulation of the market (Eatwell 1995). Indeed the Group of Seven industrial nations observed in October 1998 that the present threat to the world economy was not inflation but lack of demand (Elliot and Milne 1999). Nevertheless, through a somewhat abbreviated overview, I have hinted at something of the hybridity and multiple logics of governance. This is in contrast to those who seek to interpret diverse phenomena in terms of a macro-logic—the transition to post-Fordism, the globalisation of the state, or late modernisation.

Many writers have observed that conservative, authoritarian approaches to law and social issues are frequently being twinned with the global resurgence of liberal economics and the retreat of the social state (Wacquant 1999). What Gamble (1994), among others, identifies as a trademark of "Thatcherism" seems to be a more general phenomenon. At some level it might seem logical to assert that the introduction of market logics into more and more sections of social life *necessitates* an intensification of policing and repression. By presenting matters in terms of different strategies, however, I hope to have left open the question of the connection between the neo-liberal and the conservative-authoritarian poles. Strategies compete with one another to gain hegemony over the social space. For instance, one cannot say deductively the extent to which a neo-social democratic strategy might be able to provide governmental solutions on an extensive basis, and relegate the criminalisation strategy to the margins. Much depends on political determinations.

PART TWO

Law, Crime and the Politics of Co-social Governance

5

The Invention of the Environment as a Subject of Legal Governance

JO GOODIE

INTRODUCTION

THE CONCEPT OF risk is employed readily in everyday discourse and mediates the relationships people have to certain activities. Douglas and Wildavsky argue that the environment is a pivotal focus of popular risk anxiety. People are afraid of "nothing much . . . except the food they eat, the water they drink, the air they breathe, the land they live on, and the energy they use" (Douglas and Wildavsky, quoted in Lupton 1993: 425).

Douglas and Wildavsky's project is to explore the use and construction of risk in everyday discourse. In this chapter I have a more particular focus, examining conceptions of risk in toxic tort litigation. Douglas argues that risk has a certain "forensic" quality, that the concept of risk has become vital to the adversarial nature of modern social and political discourse (Douglas 1992: 24). I want to take her observation a little further and consider three different ways in which the discourse of risk has become integral to the construction of public health environments in toxic tort cases, an emerging field of civil litigation. Toxic tort litigation provides a useful basis for considering the emergence of the environment as a legal subject because the law involved is an established arm of the common law, yet the harms for which toxic tort plaintiffs seek recognised legal remedies or compensation are novel, they have only become apparent in the last three decades (Christie 1992: 279).

The "governmentality" approach to socio-legal studies could afford to be more expansive. Foucaultian scholars interested in socio-legal studies have tended to focus on the practise of criminal law, rather than the uses and formation of civil laws, such as the law of tort, and administrative law. An examination of the manner in which the environment is legally managed and constructed is exemplary of the formation and practice of contemporary civil law, at least in the common law jurisdictions. As Malpas and Wickham observe: "[o]bjects are not merely defined by the governing practices under which they are taken up, but are themselves defining of those practices" (Malpas and Wickham 1997: 94).

The environment is a quite different legal subject from its precursor—the autonomous, rational, legally capable individual. While the latter could lay claim to the possession of substantive legal rights, the environment is a shifting subject which is the product of constant negotiation, attempting to resolve conflicting interests and exercise administrative discretion. This chapter considers some of the ways in which the environment has become a subject of legal governance. When thinking about the environment as a legal subject, it is necessary to move beyond the idea of the environment as a physical space. From the legal perspective, the environment is a contingent and instrumental object. As such, it is at the opposite end of the spectrum from the autonomous, rational individual, the darling of the common law. At the same time the environment only exists as a subject of legal concern inasmuch as it is the space in which the human legal subject lives, breathes or works.

MANY "ENVIRONMENTS" TO GOVERN

The environment is not a homogeneous entity. There are many different "environments", each the focus of social and legal interest. Since the middle of the nineteenth century the public health environment has emerged as a subject of increasing social and legal concern. One of the principal strategies of public health governance in the late twentieth century has been to manage the different environments in which people work, live and recreate. Armstrong delineates what he considers to be the four principal approaches to public health management since the late Middle Ages:

> "First, there was quarantine, which drew a line between places. Second, there was sanitary science which guarded the line between the body and its natural environment. Third, there was the regime of interpersonal hygiene which persuaded those bodies to maintain a line between each other. And finally there has been the new public health which deploys its lines of hygienic surveillance everywhere throughout the body politic" (Armstrong undated).

This process of environmental management is multi-dimensional, it relies upon a plethora of tactics and strategies (Petersen and Lupton 1996, ch 1). It is not limited to the control of physical space, it also involves attempts at directing the ways in which physical environments are used and inhabited. Some uses are deemed healthy and valorised, others deemed to pose a threat to the continued integrity of the environment:

> "The new public health encompasses such concepts and strategies as health promotion and health education, social marketing, epidemiology, biostatistics, diagnostic screening, immunisation, community participation, healthy public policy, intersectoral collaboration, ecology, health advocacy and health economics" (Petersen and Lupton 1996: 5).

Petersen and Lupton's list highlights strategies which involve a degree of co-operation between citizens, state agencies, health experts and community organisations. The coercive strategies which dominated public health governance until the late twentieth century have given away to a "contemporary focus on self-regulation, transformation and personal body 'maintenance' " (Petersen and Lupton 1996: 65). The tendency is to attempt to convince people and institutions to act in ways that are deemed good for them and others. Even the legislative regimes which accompany various schemes of public health management are not all directive or prescriptive. They allow administrators discretionary scope to negotiate the extent to which certain activity is tolerable.

Although the use of law is not central in the general scheme of public health management, neither has it been entirely displaced by other more co-operative or voluntarist strategies of governance.

> "While the overt rhetoric of the new public health is directed towards appeals to the notion of the 'civil citizen' in its emphasis on self-regulation and self-control . . . the state still takes a largely paternalistic approach to the task of monitoring and regulating its citizens' health, albeit cloaked in the discourse of individual and community 'voluntary participation' " (Petersen and Lupton 1996: 71).

Inasmuch as the central purpose of this chapter is to consider the construction of the public health environment as a subject of legal concern, one approach might be to conduct an audit of litigation and Acts of Parliament, to consider the conditions and factors which allow the identification of the public health environment as a proper subject of either legal action or regulation. However, it is possible and necessary to move beyond that approach, which typifies a somewhat restricted legal scholarship, to consider the confluence of legal consideration of the environment and broader non-legal discourses about the environment. Not all activities which play a significant part in the conditions of daily life are the subject of particular legal attention; for example if we recycle waste we do so voluntarily, not because of any legal edict. Attempts at the legal governance of the environment are a product of, and contemporaneous with, non-legal efforts to define and limit environmental space.

There is a range of non-legal discourses and activities which shape our environmental awareness and behaviour. Those discourses in turn have an impact upon our legal conception of the environment. If we think of the environment as being a particular field of legal attention and understanding then the object of this chapter is to investigate one of the key "practices which produce and organise" our legal conception of the public health environment (Hogg 1983: 12). I undertake this exploration by considering one way the courts engage with notions of risk in litigation, which has at its heart a consideration of the exposure of individuals to toxic substances in the course of their daily work, or as consumers.

TOXIC TORT AS LEGAL GOVERNANCE

Toxic tort claims are civil legal actions in which a person who has developed a chronic or terminal condition as a result of exposure to chemicals such as DDT, hazardous substances such as asbestos, radiation, or blood-borne viruses such as HIV, sues the person/corporation responsible for his/her toxic exposure. The defendant in these types of cases is usually an employer, a government body or a corporation.

I examine the process of toxic tort litigation because it has taken on an increasingly significant part in the governance of public health and environmental management. In a number of notable American toxic tort cases, damages awarded have been so large that they have undermined or destroyed the insurability of certain sorts of manufacture, such as the manufacture of asbestos building products. In expanding the categories of culpable behaviour, toxic tort litigation redefines the limits of corporate responsibility for public health. Because of the latent nature of quite significant injuries and disease which toxic tort plaintiffs suffer, the litigation exposes danger which was previously unnoticed, ignored or unregulated (Rabin 1993: 126). The litigation prompts better public health regulation, surveillance and renewed attempts at environmental management. It attracts media attention and inspires public indignation and anxiety. Rabin observes that "many of the great early successes in the public interest law movement were symbolic educational victories, in which there was no clear-cut courthouse victory" (Rabin 1993: 126). Litigation contributes to the formation of a certain ideal of healthy citizenship, in which the maintenance of a safe environment is both a right and an obligation (Petersen and Lupton 1996: 64–5).

Conceptions of risk play an integral role in shaping our non-legal and legal view of the public health environment and, I argue, there are at least three different ways in which calculations of risk determine liability in toxic tort litigation. In a toxic tort action the court has to assess whether or not the hazard or risk to which the plaintiff was exposed was the cause of the harm. It also has to determine whether or not the defendant was responsible for the plaintiff's exposure to the risk. There are two critical factors in determining the defendant's legal duties and responsibility to the plaintiff and consequently the defendant's liability. They are: the extent to which the defendant is expected to have known that certain activities or things to which the plaintiff was exposed would put the plaintiff at risk; and, the defendant's capacity to avoid exposing the plaintiff to that risk. Courts simultaneously consider the immediate harm and risk to which the particular plaintiff was exposed and take a global (actuarial) view of the knowable risk. Neither of these determinations is of course entirely objective.

USING THE NOTION OF RISK

There are three senses in which I use risk in this discussion. First, risk has a technical meaning: it is an insurantial calculation which indicates the likelihood of an event/catastrophe happening. Programmes aimed at the management of this definition of risk generally rely on these types of predictions. The manner in which other disciplines, such as epidemiology, conceive of and articulate risk has an impact upon legal conceptions of risk. Courts use such information to map a global picture of the potential hazards to which a plaintiff may have been exposed and it is from an appreciation of this global position that the conduct of both parties can be judged. Toxic tort litigation has very much followed the publication of scientific research which recognises the existence of harm peculiar to particular forms of toxic exposure (Christie 1992: 284; Rabin 1993: 112).

The second meaning of risk is what Ewald (1991) describes as its common everyday meaning. In its common everyday sense, risk is a term used to describe danger or hazard. Risks of this kind are not statistical calculations, they are social/cultural constructs. Such ideas of risk often have some genesis in a scientific prediction of risk, but they have developed to encompass an array of popular knowledge, beliefs and practices which are not limited to the confines of scientific discourse. Significantly, for the purposes of this chapter, this everyday sense of risk is a basis for ascribing moral culpability, whereas the technical risk calculations of my first definition are treated as predictive rather than moral assessments. In its commonly understood sense, risk has become inextricably linked with blame (Douglas 1992). This subjective appreciation of the plaintiff's dilemma and the defendant's conduct is a vital part of the evidence upon which the court ultimately makes a determination of legal liability. It is introduced through the accounts given by non-expert witnesses, of the risk and danger to which they perceive the plaintiff was exposed. In the courtroom, toxic tort litigation, despite its consideration of detailed scientific evidence, appears to turn ultimately upon moral evaluation rather than scientific argument and testimony, or even on points of law. Rabin describes American tobacco litigation as "a last vestige of a vision of nineteenth century tort law as an interpersonal morality play" (Rabin 1993: 122).

To these two understandings of risk we may add a third: a clinical appreciation of risk. This is an understanding of risk which is taken from health governance literature (see Weir 1996; O'Malley 1996a). Public health programmes use clinical risk techniques such as diagnoses and therapeutics as part of the process of managing public health. Clinical risk programmes aim to reduce the exposure of certain individuals, rather than whole populations, to risk. Toxic tort litigation is not therapeutic, beyond the fact that successful litigation and/or the threat of further litigation forces defendants who are found liable to reform their practices so that the hazard of exposure is limited or eradicated. However, the focus of clinical risk techniques on the individual's exposure to risk makes such an approach a useful way of thinking about the way toxic tort litigation constructs a certain type of legal subject. Despite the broader risk discourse within which any toxic tort litigation takes place, the individual litigating parties remain the primary focus of the court. It is the court's appreciation of the parties' personal and quite specific experience and exposure to risk, and their behaviour in the face of such exposure, which in large part determines the outcomes of the proceedings.

The shift from thinking about risk in non-legal terms—whether in a technical, clinical/individual, or everyday sense—to assessing its role in the litigation process is not a simple manoeuvre. As O'Malley observes:

> "Risk management or harm minimisation places an analytic and governmental grid across the social terrain it seeks to govern that does not necessarily correspond to the grid laid down by other governmental technologies, such as that of the law" (O'Malley 1996a: 6).

RISK MANAGEMENT AND LEGAL GOVERNANCE

At a certain level, the common law institutionalises certain norms of conduct. In practice it functions through the discipline and protection of the individual legal subject. This remains the case even though the privilege of the individual legal subject has been slowly eroded by the emergence of claims for collective rights from professional interest groups, indigenous peoples and by certain forms of class action. By comparison, the central rationale of risk management programmes is to move away from "the binary of free will and determinism" (O'Malley 1996a).

These types of programmes do not function through direct action on the individual. Programmes aimed at risk management and harm minimisation destabilise the use and role of law. What effect does this destabilisation have on the operation or value of legal regimes which have similar risk management strategies? The answer must obviously be predicated on the type of law at issue. The interaction of a risk management strategy with a system of criminal law, for example, which creates offences and has a power of punishment, must be quite different from its effects upon civil litigation or legislative regimes dedicated to environmental management.

Through the process of subjecting particular instances of risk and harm to close scrutiny and assessment, litigation insinuates itself into the public discourse about risk. Litigation can render hazards which had been ignored intolerable, risks which are latent or hidden can become visible and public (Rabin 1993: 126). Most tort texts include some discussion of the degree to which actions in tort actually have any deterrent effect. Deweews and Trebilcock argue that the deterrent effect is minimal, they base their conclusion on statistics which attempt to correlate incidents of injury and the number of relevant suits in tort (cited in Luntz and Hambly 1995: 42).

I argue, however, that litigation has a broader more subtle normative impact upon our conduct than such statistical correlation allows. Sometimes spectacularly, but usually slowly and incrementally, the liability of defendants sets the parameters for lawful insurable behaviour. It sets a standard which other individuals and corporate entities engaged in similar activities must adopt (Stapelton 1995).

The capacity to insure against legal liability has had a profound effect upon litigation in tort, although there is debate as to exactly what type of effect insurance and insurability has on the outcome of such litigation (Conaghan and Mansell 1993; Stapelton 1995). For example:

"Non-industrial, non-road accidents causing personal injury result in a negligible number of tort claims each year . . . The predominance of motor and industrial accident cases in courts and in settlement negotiations is due not so much to the law of torts, but to something that has been grafted on to that law: liability insurance" (Luntz and Hambly 1995: 6).

Actions in tort take place against/within the operation of various state-regulated and private schemes of insurance. There are a number of key effects insurance and insurability have upon the tort system in general and the conduct of litigation in particular. Perhaps the most profound effect is identified by Fleming, who argues that without liability insurance, "the tort system would have long ago collapsed under the weight of the demands placed upon it" (Fleming 1992: 11).

The proliferation of actions which followed industrialisation and the invention of new and more efficient ways of causing injury forced potential defendants to insure against liability (Derrington 1992: 165). Stapelton observes that the increasing "public policy reliance" on a prudential response to risk witnessed in the twentieth century has been paralleled by "a general broadening of the catchment of situations recognised by the courts as giving rise to tort entitlements" (Stapelton 1995: 820). As liability insurance became relatively common, the historical conservatism which mitigated against the emergence of new forms of action was displaced. While there are still numerous instances of judges refusing to be seen to be spreading the loss on the basis of the defendant's insurance status rather than fault, there is evidence of an expansion of the scope of negligence accompanying the spread of liability insurance (Luntz and Hambly 1995: 15–22). A fairly typical example of the oft-expressed attitude of courts to the question of insurance and culpability involves Lord Griffiths' 1990 observation:

"There was once a time when it was considered improper to mention the possible existence of insurance cover in a law suit . . . those days are long past. Everyone knows that all prudent professional men carry insurance and the availability of and cost of insurance must be a relevant factor when considering which of the two parties should be required to bear the risk of a loss" (*Smith* v. *Eric S. Bush* [1990] 1 AC 831, 858, HL).

That is, insurance made it possible for courts to shift the loss from:

"where it unjustly lay without imposing an injustice on a defendant and without harm
to the social and economic organisation of the community, the disturbance to which
had been the main impediment to full compensation" (Derrington 1992: 165).

Not only has the widespread reliance on insurance allowed the emergence of
new actions in tort, the insurer has become a dominant player in all litigation,
with considerable power to enforce and entrench its own calculation of risk.
Not every accident or incidence of negligence results in litigation. Insurers only
pursue and make defendants of those who can afford to pay damages—usually
those people and corporations who carry insurance (Luntz and Hambly 1995:
15). Insurers have also become quasi-regulators of certain industries
(Gunningham 1994: 277). The capacity to maintain insurance is a prerequisite
to doing business. Insurance is maintained solely on the insurer's terms. The
insurer will not insure in cases where it is not possible to reinsure or offset loss
(Luntz and Hambly 1995: 18). Writing about environmental insurance,
Gunningham observes that the insurance companies in the United States currently exclude pollution liability claims from policies and require corporations
to take out special "environmental impairment liability insurance". This form
of insurance is only available on proof that the corporation has the capacity to
manage environmental risk. In the United Kingdom pollution liability cover is
excluded unless the insured demonstrate that "cause was a sudden unexpected
and identifiable incident" (Gunningham 1994: 263). Gunningham expects this
trend will be followed in Australia. All Australian states have passed legislation
to protect suppliers of blood products against liability for transmission of the
HIV/AIDS virus, provided they meet certain procedures aimed at ensuring the
safety of the blood product. This legislation was a response to the inability of
blood product manufactures to obtain liability insurance following successful
litigation (Luntz and Hambly 1995: 18).

Even though litigation in tort is conducted within an insurantial framework,
it is generally still conducted as if the dispute were only between the two insured
parties, rather than their insurers. As Conaghan and Mansell observe:

"individual responsibility continues to be the perspective that informs most cases, collective responsibility and loss spreading through the mechanism of insurance tends to
be an incidental by product" (Conaghan and Mansell 1993: 11).

Horowitz argues, that this is despite the fact that:

"the problem of assigning liability has become simply a question of fairness of distribution of risks, 'a concealed half-conscious battle on the question of legislative policy'.
Liability for injury has become just another cost of doing business, which could be
'estimated, insured against, and ultimately included in the price paid by the public'.
The individualistic world of . . . 'moral causation' and 'free agency' had begun to be
transformed into a world of liability insurance in which the 'legislative' question of
who should pay would ultimately undermine the self contained, individualistic categories of private law" (Horowitz 1982: 211).

If one is talking about the standard personal injury claim then Horowitz's assessment of the current trajectory of tort litigation is accurate. Fleming observes that a defendant's insurance may very likely undermine any deterrent or punishment which might have followed a finding of legal liability (Fleming 1992: 10). However, in the case of toxic tort litigation, the notion of "moral causation" should not be discarded too readily. Such litigation is not resolved by a simple reference to an insurantial calculation of risk. Insurers may have the capacity to dominate the litigation process, but they do not litigate as if factors beyond their own actuarial calculations are irrelevant.

Stapelton argues that there is a tendency to conflate inappropriately "tort with the insurance model of response to misfortune" (Stapelton 1995: 820). She considers this conflation inappropriate because:

> "insurance is traditionally ignored by courts not because they want to pretend it does not exist, but because they reject its alleged relevance to the issue of whether liability should be imposed and find it an 'embarrassment' to be addressed on matters they intend to ignore" (Stapelton 1995: 824).

This is not to say that courts are explicit about the matters they take into account or find persuasive—the discursive framework of toxic tort litigation is rarely completely unpacked. A determination of legal liability in toxic tort cases inherently incorporates an assessment of the moral culpability of not only the defendant but also the plaintiff. In making such assessments the courts weigh up competing accounts of the type of risk to which the plaintiff was exposed. These accounts come from the parties themselves, from experts who provide technical assessments of the hazard or harm to which the plaintiff was exposed and also from other lay witnesses such as fellow workers, whose role is to provide the court with a real appreciation of the environment in which the plaintiff was exposed to risk.

As we saw above, Douglas argues that the concept of risk is vital to the adversarial nature of modern social and political discourse (Douglas 1992: 24). It is precisely because the probability of danger or harm can be predicted and calculated on the basis of objective criteria that modern forms of litigation are possible. A capacity to predict risk produces the possibility of apportioning responsibility for the probable outcomes of risky behaviour (Douglas 1992: 15–16). A simple example illustrates this point. In the middle of the nineteenth century actions in nuisance for air-borne pollution were rarely possible for want of proof. The possibility of such legal action depended upon the development of a scientific method which could predict how smoke was likely to disperse into the environment surrounding a factory. The court needed to have a capacity to separate and isolate the hazardous nature of the activities and things which are at the heart of the litigation from the subjective qualities and physical attributes of the litigating parties. The "objective" nature of risk assessment and the scientific method of the epidemiologist and the engineer allowed the courts to assume a role of "disinterested arbiter".

CONCLUSION: HAVING THEIR DAY IN COURT

Few commentators or participants in litigation would contend that legal judg-
ments pronounce upon the absolute truth of the matters they address. Yet the
courts operate with considerable authority. Their reputation as fair and final
arbiters is founded on the techniques they employ in resolving litigation.
Litigation involving allegations of harm caused by exposure to a toxic environment requires the parties to support their cases with expert testimony as to
the actual, rather than simply apprehended, nature of the risk to which the
plaintiff was exposed.

While the consideration of scientific, expert testimony is key to the technique
of legal adjudication, the allocation of blame and finding of liability is not
utterly divorced from subjective assessment of the moral character and reputation of the litigants. An attractive or successful plaintiff from the lawyer's point
of view is one whose sense of grievance and account of injury meets certain
requirements. Plaintiffs, by this ideal, must present with a particular attitude
towards the work which led to their toxic exposure; credibility is not only at
issue in criminal cases. Lawyers representing plaintiffs harmed by exposure to
toxic substances or hazardous activities reserve the tactic of the public trial for
the claims of those plaintiffs who have acted responsibly and, as far as possible,
protected themselves against harm. A test case plaintiff is, obviously, not an
individual who has voluntarily courted risk. The good citizen/plaintiff is one
who recognises and acts rationally to maintain good health. "Managing their
own relationship to risk has become an important means by which individuals
can express their ethical selves and fulfil their responsibilities and obligations as
'good citizens'" (Scott and Williams, quoted in Petersen and Lupton 1996: 65).

The knowability of risk—our scientific capacity to identify hazardous activities and substances—imposes responsibility not only on hazard creators but
also upon potential victims of such hazards. Risk, in modern society, has come
to replace the old-fashioned (and in modern secular society now largely discredited) notion of sin as a term that "runs across the gamut of social life to mor-
alize and politicise dangers" (Lupton 1993: 428). As Lupton, taking up
Douglas's thesis about the nexus between risk and blame, observes:

> "The modern concept of risk, like that of taboo, has a 'forensic' property, for it works
> backwards in explaining ill-fortune, as well as forwards in predicting future retribu-
> tion. Thus the experience of a heart attack, a positive HIV test result, or the discovery
> of a cancerous lesion are evidence that the ill person has failed to comply with direct-
> ives to reduce health risks and therefore is to be blamed for his or her predicament"
> (Lupton 1993: 430).

Nineteenth century tort doctrine was primarily concerned with questions of
moral culpability. Twentieth century tort is largely a vehicle for providing compensation; a means of shifting the economic burden of loss caused through some

types of accident and misfortune. For many plaintiffs, however, particularly those who have been exposed to a lethal toxic substance in circumstances where others had responsibility for their well-being, obtaining compensation is not the only goal of an action in tort. For them, there is an expectation that their "day in court" will be an opportunity for the righteousness of their claim to be recognised.

Unlike other routine or high volume tort litigation, toxic tort cases regularly go to trial. Such cases often involve difficult issues of causation, requiring lengthy inquiry into the circumstances of the toxic exposure. Galanter has observed that judicial pronouncements on a matter can have a particular value for either of the parties, or their insurers:

> "an insurance company functionary may want to avoid responsibility for a large pay-out . . . or there may be value to an actor in showing some external audience (a creditor or the public) that no stone has been left unturned . . . Or external decision may be sought where the case is so complex or the outcome so indeterminate that it is too unwieldy or too costly to arrange settlement" (quoted in Bottomley and Parker 1997: 126).

External, public, judicial pronouncements have equivalent worth for plaintiffs who want the litigation to acknowledge that a wrong was done. I am not suggesting that the court necessarily frames its decision in terms of moral culpability. However, blame and responsibility are central to the discourse within which the case is argued and considered.

In his account of the fate of tobacco litigation in the United States, Rabin (1993) has observed that there are two different types of plaintiffs in toxic tort litigation: those who are characterised as victims and those who are seen as irresponsible. Lung cancer sufferers exposed to asbestos in the workplace are clear victims and worthy plaintiffs. Cigarette smokers, on the other hand, are people who fail to overcome a habit known to have ill-effects, and as yet they have not won a suit against a tobacco manufacturer despite the scientific evidence that smoking is addictive.

We need to expand this profile of two potential toxic tort plaintiffs. It is much easier for an asbestos litigant to come to the court with clean hands for a number of reasons. For a start, most exposure to asbestos occurred before knowledge of the extremely toxic effects of asbestos was widely disseminated in the public domain (Christie 1992: 284). If the asbestos litigant is to be tainted, it can only be by the defence successfully pointing to some other feature of his/her lifestyle which might be responsible for the condition which he/she claims is caused by asbestos exposure alone.

In several asbestos cases which went to trial in Australia in the early 1990s, defendants challenged the aetiology of the plaintiffs' conditions and argued that the conditions were caused in part by the plaintiffs' smoking habits. In these cases tobacco manufacturers did not join readily as co-defendants. The defendants raised the issue of causation not so that they would be able to share the burden of any potential damages with other defendants, but in an attempt to undermine the plaintiffs' characters in the minds of the courts and juries. The spectre of tobacco as the cancerous agent also tended to make the plaintiffs' tasks of presenting expert medical and scientific evidence more onerous. It detracted from the appeal of the plaintiffs' cases by placing a greater burden on the juries in terms of the assimilation of complex expert testimony.

Plaintiffs exposed to asbestos were usually not in a position to limit voluntarily their exposure. Their exposure was an incidence of their work, whether as riggers, miners, laggers, builders, plumbers, process workers, teachers or office workers. Many children and spouses of people who worked in the asbestos injury were also exposed, as they washed overalls or played in a school yard covered in asbestos tailings. The exposure of workers and people living in asbestos towns was not only largely involuntary, it happened in ignorance of the hazard to which they were being exposed (Hogg 1983). The moral cleanliness of plaintiffs was illuminated in the trials being discussed by the fact that it was usually made known to courts early that the world's major asbestos producers knew of the dangers of asbestos exposure and conspired to keep it a secret. The responsibility of plaintiffs to act with regard for the recognised knowledge of the risk presented by toxic exposure is mediated by the type of relationship between plaintiffs and defendants. Children living in mining towns, the employees working in uncomfortable and intolerably dusty conditions are considered to be reliant on the defendants to protect them against known hazards. The defendants have a duty to be aware of relevant hazards, the extent of that duty depending upon the size of each defendant's operation. The smoker plaintiff by contrast has increasingly borne a duty to heed health warnings and protect him/her self against risk. Rabin shows that even scientific evidence of the health effects of smoking or the addictive nature of smoking has not shifted the burden of protecting against the risk to the defendant cigarette manufacturer (Rabin 1993: 122–4).

> "Moreover, in the courtroom, the addiction expert's translation of scientific data on reinforcement, withdrawal, reactive effects, and other esoteric phenomena into terms that make sense to the jury remains a rather abstract undertaking. The expert is in no position to say anything about the individual smoker . . . By contrast, the defence on the addiction issue is grounded in particulars: the claimant could have quit, knew the risks, evinced a life-long taste for dangerous activities, and so forth" (Rabin 1993: 124).

It is not only the courts' view of what is required by the law to establish causation which finds a plaintiff with lung cancer as a result of exposure to asbestos in a better position than a plaintiff with smoking-induced lung cancer. It is the focus of the litigation on "particulars"; on the individual's attitude to risk, the care and responsibility the individual has taken for him/herself. The scientific evidence does not counter the courts' attitude that smoking is almost entirely a habit of choice (Rabin 1993: 122–4). The capacity to exercise individual choice, to make a rational calculation about risk, sets such two potential plaintiffs apart.

Attitude to risk and the response of individuals to knowledge of the hazards of habits such as smoking is culturally mediated. It is perhaps not surprising that in the United States, where the ideal of individual freedom is socially and politically compelling, juries regularly find the free choice argument put to them by defence counsel persuasive.

The impact of broader cultural values upon risk-taking was acknowledged by the court in the case of *Christopher Harr* v. *Uneedus Scaffolding Pty Ltd* (Supreme Court of Victoria No. 4918 of 1989). In that case we find a hybrid of our two potential plaintiffs. Harr, a rigger who was exposed to asbestos on a building site in the 1970s, worked along side other workers employed by a different contractor to remove asbestos from the building. Harr's defendant employer did not provide any special clothing to protect Harr against asbestos, or require him to wear any, even though the asbestos removers wore special masks and suits. The defendant was in breach of a range of occupational health and safety regulations, the hazards of asbestos were deemed to be well known to employers of the defendant's size by that time. The principal legal issue was whether the exposure to asbestos was the sole cause of the plaintiff's cancer of the oesophagus. The defence argued that Harr's smoking was implicated in the development of his cancer and that because Harr was aware at that time of the hazards of smoking he was contributorily negligent. The jury reduced the damages award by 20 per cent for contributory negligence. However, the presiding judge, Justice O'Bryan, declined to accept the jury's finding of contributory negligence. Justice O'Bryan held that even though at the time of Harr's exposure health warnings were printed on all cigarette and tobacco packaging and, even though Harr had not denied that he had been aware that there was some scientific evidence that smoking could cause cancer, he had not acted negligently. The law of contributory negligence required the court to consider Harr's conduct in light of "the circumstances and conditions in which he had to do his work" (*Podreresek* v. *Australian Iron and Steel Pty Ltd* (1985) 59 ALR 529). Those conditions, it was held, included the fact that most manual workers smoked, such that site agreements allowed workers designated "smoko" breaks. Despite the increased public awareness of the hazards of tobacco consumption, smoking was a routine, normal and accepted practice of workers in Harr's circumstance at the time.

6

Reconstructing the Government of Crime

KEVIN STENSON*

INTRODUCTION

IN THIS CHAPTER I identify in descriptive terms some of the key features of the reconstruction of the government of crime that has taken place in most advanced liberal capitalist countries since the 1970s. This background description makes up the first main section. I then contrast, in sections two and three, two broad alternative theoretical narratives which attempt to explain the basis of this reconstruction. On the one hand is an explanatory framework influenced by the Marxist tradition; I refer to it as the neo-Marxist framework. This framework explains the changes at the heart of the reconstruction of the government of crime in terms of new modes of globally inter-dependent economic exploitation. This involves the shift from large-scale Fordist economic organisation to smaller-scale, high-tech organisations and the accompanying shifts towards new regulatory frameworks for this economy (Burrows and Loader 1994; Jessop 1995).

On the other hand is a narrative developed within a framework influenced by some of the later work of Michel Foucault, that which focuses on changing modes of government. This approach is sometimes called "governmentality studies" (Foucault 1991; Barry, Osborne and Rose 1996); I stick to this term, or close equivalents of it. In governmentality narratives, government is not a response to or support for material conditions, it is seen as essentially a set of discursive practices which create their own regimes of what counts as truth. These include the myriad ways in which populations and spaces are investigated, formulated as objects and concerns for government, differentiated and sorted into hierarchies. In this model the delineation of relatively autonomous orders, like the economy and the sphere of social policy and other institutions of civil society, is a product of government, of political rationalities, programmes, strategies and technologies of rule.

* I would like to thank Chris Crowther for help in the preparation of this chapter.

The chapter provides a cautious endorsement of the governmentality model of explanation, but it also explores and advocates, in the chapter's fourth main section, the need to build bridges to the neo-Marxist model in an effort to grasp the complexity and hybridity of forms of rule. I use the conclusion to the chapter to consolidate my arguments about the need to move analysis beyond general abstract narratives of change in an effort to understand the complexity of local practices of rule (Stenson and Watt 1999).

BACKGROUND TO THE RECONSTRUCTION OF THE GOVERNMENT OF CRIME

In the 1980s and 1990s, in the advanced liberal capitalist democracies, the control of crime and disorder has steadily ascended the political agenda, moving from a marginal position to centre stage in the struggle for votes. Long-term fiscal crises confronting all the varying models of welfare states, the growing influence since the late 1970s of neo-liberal parties and policy themes, the competitive pressures of increasingly interdependent, global markets and the diminishing political appeal, internationally, of parties with high tax-and-spend programmes have all undermined the political viability of universally available welfare services and rights of citizenship (Offe 1996). In this context, it has been argued, "social policies" are increasingly legitimated not in terms of the fostering of social solidarity, as in the high period of welfare states, but, principally, as subordinate supports to the goal of improving economic competitiveness, maintaining public order and reducing crime. In part, this retreat from universalism in favour of narrowly targeted policies could be seen as involving a criminalisation of social policy, directed towards perceivably poor and crime-prone populations and neighbourhoods, coded in the language of European Union (EU) social policy as the category of "social exclusion" (Crawford 1997; Stenson and Watt 1999).

In the United Kingdom, for example, there are continuities between the previous Conservative government's policies and those of the "New Labour' administration which has been in office since 1997. The youth service in the United Kingdom provides a salutary instance of this re-orientation of policy through crime control. While mainstream youth services provided by local authorities have been starved of resources and have progressively lost established career posts in the last twenty years, new youth jobs, on short-term, insecure contracts, have come on stream. These are defined under the heading of "urban/community regeneration" (with an accent on reducing crime) or "crime prevention" initiatives in poor neighbourhoods. As in other countries, these are often created as a governmental response to serious public order disturbances or burgeoning rates of burglaries, assaults and drug-related offences in poor neighbourhoods (Stenson and Factor 1994; 1995). Yet, curiously, as some commentators have noted, the disciplines of social policy and political science have shown only marginal interest in these issues, perhaps on the pragmatic assumption that they are the specialised concern of criminology and penology (Hill 1996; Crowther 1999).

The frequent reluctance within criminology and penology to confront the complexity of the wider social, economic and policy contexts within which crime policy emerges compounds the intellectual problem. Despite the selective and partial interests of the social science disciplines, new political rationalities in the United Kingdom, as articulated by politicians and their policy advisers, have tried to pull crime control from the ghettos of the criminal justice professions, the Home Office and a narrow, administrative criminology, at the same time emphasising the link between other mainstream policies and crime control. In 1998 an erstwhile Home Office minister in the Labour government, Alun Michael announced a crime-reduction investment programme of £250 million in these terms:

"our policies are not just to focus on crime itself but also on the underlying causes of crime. Social exclusion, under performance at school, peer group pressure, family background are all contributory factors which are being addressed by the Government. Through all these efforts and by working together we can succeed in cutting crime and making a radical difference to the quality of people's lives" (Michael 1998).

This crystallises the emphasis placed by the Labour government on the need for holistic, "joined up" approaches to such policy issues, under the orchestration of the Prime Minister's Social Exclusion Unit. In conjunction with its New Deal policies to get young people off the dole and into work and its more general welfare-to-work programmes, it also signals a shift away from the goal of egalitarian economic redistribution. Tackling social exclusion and criminality is be achieved, rather, through a redistribution of opportunities in the labour market and the education system (MacGregor 1998).

These developments must, in turn, be seen in the wider context of the rise of neo-liberal critiques of Keynesian social and economic policies. New institutions and practices, new political rationalities, visions, programmes, assemblages of persons and agencies and strategies and technologies of rule have emerged. These embody and pose classic liberal questions about the proper responsibilities and limits of state and municipal powers. Hence, the new paradigms of rationality are constructed by reference to the practices of commercial markets, and also draw on a variety of (left- and right-wing) libertarian critiques of bureaucratic and professional power, which stress the need to combat dependency, "empower" ordinary people from the "bottom up" and unleash their repressed creativity as players in the markets (Cruikshank 1994; Stenson 1996).

Therefore, it is argued, expensive, hierarchical state and municipal bureaucracies with their unionised labour forces, ossified and self-serving routines, should give way to smaller, leaner and more entrepreneurial agencies, devolving responsibilities to, and working in partnership with, agencies in the voluntary/ not-for-profit sector, commercial firms and organisations of active citizens at local levels, even though the new networks of governance operate remotely from lines of traditional democratic accountability (Rhodes 1990). This has created the space for a new class of social entrepreneurs, acting as brokers or relays between partners within and between agencies and equipped with new managerialist knowledge and skills, in which networking and problem-solving figure highly (Mulgan 1997; Clarke and Newman 1997). Increasingly, the message is that the task of the central and local state agencies is to "steer" rather than "row" the ship of governance (Burrows and Loader 1994; Shearing 1996).

In Britain, reflecting and reinforcing shifting debates conducted through talk and textual media, the dominant theme of partnership is crystallised in key texts across the terrain of social policy, but with a growing emphasis in political and media discourses on the seemingly intractable issues of crime and justice. "Partnership" solutions are seen as central within this field of policy (Stenson 1996; Hughes 1996). While in other policy fields these developments could be viewed as symptomatic of the fostering of new forms of freedom and creative entrepreneurship, in this sphere they are often seen by Keynesian social democratic critics of New Labour as parts of a larger pattern of control. This is seen as increasingly repressive, as targeting the poor and disadvantaged and as putting a sticking plaster over a surface lesion, rather than dealing with its deeper causes within the social body. It is argued that without a major investment of resources in social crime prevention and economically redistributive policies, prison populations will continue to grow apace under the Labour government (Downes 1998).

In many countries, a gloomy obsession with environmental and social risks has emerged as a driver of the reconstruction of government, with crime control, once a peripheral concern in most advanced countries, emerging as a key electoral issue. This increasing politicisation of crime control marks a significant shift in the status of the institutions of policing and justice in liberal capitalist polities. In most countries of continental Europe, police and justice agencies had suffered from a long association with the absolutism and oppression of the old police states, and absolutist and authoritarian regimes (Mawby 1990). This led to a premium, in the post-war period, on creating systems of policing and justice which at least maintained the appearance of being governed, not by politicians, but by the rule of law and codes of professional and administrative rationality (Lacey and Zedner 1995). In the United Kingdom, the long traditions, since 1829, of "policing by consent" and constabulary independence—to some degree transmitted to the old British Commonwealth countries—were seen as bulwarks of democratic freedom from state tyranny. These traditions, legally embodied in the Police Act 1964, became central to mythologies and legitimations of the British model of Peelite policing (Reiner 1992; Stenson 1993). Even in the United States, where police chiefs are elected or are political appointments and police agencies have always been more closely entwined with representative democracy, major struggles were conducted in the first half of the century to establish a recognition of the professional status and expertise of policing and a degree of operational independence from politicians. These were viewed as essential props to the democratic status of the law and the principle of the separation of governmental powers (Skolnick and Bayley 1988).

In a variety of ways, in different liberal democratic jurisdictions, policies and systems to control crime and provide justice were seen as spheres of policy and practice distinct from executive government and from the whims of (national or local) populist opinion or pressure—the spectre of mob justice or lynch law. The first significant post-war shift towards the politicisation of law and order in the United States by the Republican administration of Richard Nixon and Spiro Agnew in the early 1970s was maintained in successive Republican and Democrat administrations. A familiar criticism from the left is that the "New Democrats" in the 1990s have largely kept faith with the harsh populist punitivism characteristic of the Reagan and Bush Republican, neo-conservative and neo-liberal policies (Currie 1997; Simon 1996). The Clintonite emphasis on personal responsibility and human agency is consistent with right wing cynicism about the "excuse making industry" of traditional deterministic, positivist criminology (Tame 1991).

There is a reluctance to concede too much to the notion that crime may be symptomatic of poverty and social breakdown. Hence, there has been no effective challenge to inter alia: the use of harsh, zero tolerance, "quality of life" approaches to public order maintenance developed in Mayor Giuliani's New York in the 1990s, which involve displacing the homeless, petty criminals, the mentally disordered and other perceived nuisance groups; the erosion of public policing through the growth of private security; the use of the death penalty; escalating prison populations, increasingly contained in commercially run facilities; and, most profoundly, the erosion of support for a separate juvenile justice system oriented to salvaging and rehabilitating children. This is noted even in liberal Massachusetts, once an international beacon for progressive juvenile justice policies (Currie 1997; Singer 1996). Through the 1980s politicised law and order rhetorics were exported to the United Kingdom, other Anglophone countries and more recently to other Western European countries (Hall *et al* 1978; Taylor 1998; Stenson 1991; 1999).

It may seem ironic that the rhetoric of zero tolerance towards street crime and incivilities, associated with right-wing American criminology and New York's Republican Mayor Giuliani, should prove so attractive to British Labour politicians of the centre-left. This is particularly so given that they modelled their restructuring of New Labour so closely on Bill Clinton and Al Gore's refashioning of the Democratic Party in the 1980s (Johnston 1999). However, this becomes more intelligible when we take into account the broader formation of policy. The Democrats' suburban-friendly "Tough Love" approach to crime control and welfare reform (including welfare-to-work programmes), conceded much to the Reagan/Bush policy agenda and could be seen as close to Giuliani's ideology. Clinton's administration has coincided with a massive expansion in the prison population and spending on criminal justice, unwarrantable in relation to variations in the recorded crime rate (Currie 1997).

New Labour's promise of reform to reduce dependency upon welfare, promote welfare-to-work initiatives, and Blair's slogan as shadow Home Secretary, "Tough on crime and tough on the causes of crime", closely mirror the Clinton strategy and chime with key neo-liberal themes of the previous Conservative government. Labour's crime policies also provide a sharp challenge to Conservative policies, which, despite tough law and order rhetoric, failed to prevent a doubling of recorded crime between 1979 and 1992 (Blair 1998: 12). It is argued that the watershed came in 1993. In response to moral panics about youth crime, New Labour exposed the vulnerability of the Conservative government. In an interview on BBC Radio 4 on 10 January 1993, Blair distanced himself from deterministic explanations of crime which had underpinned much of the practice of old welfare-oriented penal strategies and practices during the high period of the welfare state. He emphasised the theme of personal responsibility and duty, key communitarian features of New Labour policy (Hughes 1998):

> "Anti-social behaviour should 'be punished, if necessary, severely'. Society has not merely a duty, it is in its interest, to try to create the conditions in which people get a chance in life. But the other side of that 'is: where people are given chances, they're expected to take them, and they're expected to take responsibility for their own individual actions' " (Blair quoted in Dunbar and Langdon 1998: 101).

Selective crackdowns and punitive rhetoric, stressing that "prison works", by Conservative politicians and the tabloid newspapers pressured judges into lengthening custodial sentences. Attacks by Blair and then later by Jack Straw, as shadow Home Secretary, on Conservative law and order policy led to a "bidding war" against the reactionary Conservative Home Secretary Michael Howard, over who could appear toughest (Dunbar and Langdon 1998). This continued until the election in 1997 and sharpened conflicts between New Labour and progressive opinion in the academy and the criminal justice professions. A powerful case was assembled, arguing that the punitive thrust of neo-conservative rhetoric under the Conservative regime, with its emphasis on restoring traditional authority, if necessary through the use of prison, was undermined by the neo-liberal, cost-cutting, budgetary and managerial disciplines that still drove government policy.

These conditions, it was argued, starved the Crown Prosecution Service and the police of the resources needed to develop consistent and coherent prosecution and crime prevention/reduction strategies in deprived areas. Existing research, particularly from the British Crime surveys, indicated the high concentration of criminal victimisation in these areas (Hope 1998). This undermined the morale of control agencies and of the populations most vulnerable to victimisation. It was claimed that, despite burgeoning prison populations, the police and criminal justice agencies had effectively abandoned large chunks of British territory to the hegemony of criminal gangs, the drugs economy and ill-disciplined children and young men (Rose 1996c; Davies 1997).

So, emulating the strategy of Clinton's New Democrats, in the 1997 British election campaign tackling crime came a close second to education as an election pledge for New Labour. The provisions of the Crime and Disorder Act 1998 include requirements for local authorities and police agencies to undertake local audits of crime and develop partnership-based community safety strategies, with an accent on crime prevention, which involve not just measures to "harden" crime targets, like the homes of multiple burglary victims, but also "early intervention" initiatives to improve parenting and school performance. These aim to reduce school exclusions and the associated risks of criminal careers. The new law also includes a radical expediting and institutional reform of the youth justice system, through inter-agency youth offender teams. Other initiatives entail controversial powers to require parents of young offenders to undertake parenting classes and new measures, using civil law rules of evidence, to deal with so-called "neighbours from hell". These measures are designed to harmonise with the welfare-to-work (workfare) project of the New Deal and other policies which aim to ameliorate social exclusion, policies orchestrated by the government's Social Exclusion Unit (Bright 1998).

Modelling himself to some extent on Blair, Gerhard Schröder, leader of the new-look German Social Democratic Party in Germany, in his successful bid for the Chancellorship in 1999, is another "leftist" who has recently talked tough on crime. And in his recent New Year's address, even France's Socialist prime minister Lionel Jospin, though further to the left than Schröder or Blair, declared crime to be his number one priority. France has 3.5 million unemployed, there has been a doubling in the rates of recorded juvenile crime between 1992 and 1998 and there have been regular, major public order disturbances in the bleak housing estates that house the poor and the minorities, many of which have become virtually no-go areas for the police and other agencies of government. This was graphically represented in the film "La Haine". It is not surprising therefore that faith in France's welfare-oriented youth justice system is beginning to weaken, with calls for a tougher approach (*Observer*, 17 January 1999). Yet, as in the United Kingdom and the United States, these tougher approaches in Germany and France co-exist with initiatives to stimulate community regeneration and crime prevention/reduction initiatives, operating from the "bottom up", involving local citizens and local government personnel.

Notwithstanding variations in history, culture and juridical traditions (Lacey and Zedner 1995), similar developments are visible in other European countries. Following a UN-sponsored international conference on urban insecurity and crime in Paris in 1991, the Paris-based European Forum for Urban Insecurity was set up. It has since held a series of workshops in cities across Europe. This is a fast-developing network of practitioners in the crime prevention/community safety field, academics and local city mayors and councillors. In a series of publications they have developed a new discourse which aims to bridge academic, professional and lay concerns to emphasise the experiences of victimisation and local professional practices. This new discourse is forged through a biting critique of the authoritarian remoteness and imperialism of the formal state bureaucracies of policing, welfare and criminal justice, challenging their monopoly over the right to define and manage social problems:

> "The bureaucrats designate targets: poverty, drugs, immigration, unemployment, housing, etc., or target groups: young people, immigrants, single parent families, secondary school pupils, drug addicts, etc. But these targets are only as coherent as the apparatus that designates them. This coherence is a way of looking at the world and establishing a series of statistics and a budgetary nomenclature and make everything else seem so futile, so fragile, so unimportant. Our old bureaucracies count and count again. But what picture do they present, who sees it, and what is done about it? All they do is frighten themselves, frighten us all" (European Forum for Urban Security 1994: 5).

The central concept of the European Forum is urban security, which has affinities with British conceptions of community safety (Hughes 1996). It is seen as intrinsically hybrid: a right, a commodity, and a public good. There is usually a breach between state agencies' conceptions of security and peoples' subjective needs. This breach is the problem space in which security must be rebuilt, through co-production and dialogue, diagnosis, proposals and assessment, but which simultaneously recognises the Europe-wide commonalities in the causes and nature of social problems and the challenges of managing them. State and EU conceptions of risk and threat have focused on organised crime, illegal immigration, money-laundering, drug-smuggling, or crimes which attack the profits of the major corporations. The new discourse, however, spotlights the routine, mass, petty crimes against the person and personal property, often invisible to the criminal justice systems, which corrode confidence in public spaces and also in the neglected domestic spaces: crimes against women, children, the elderly and ethnic minorities (European Forum for Urban Security 1994; 1996). Having provided this descriptive over-view of the reconstruction of the government of crime, I now turn to an examination of the two above-mentioned explanatory frameworks for making sense of these changes.

NEO-MARXIST EXPLANATIONS OF THE RECONSTRUCTION OF THE GOVERNMENT OF CRIME

I call the first of the two frameworks discussed "neo-Marxist" despite the fact that some of its adherents advocate reformist, social democratic, Keynesian policies for managing capitalism. Its "neo-Marxism" stems from the fact that it highlights the causal significance of political-economic processes: the drive for capital accumulation; the progressive subordination of particular local economies to the logic of an integrated and globalised capital market and the leading corporations; and the consequent growth of social and economic inequality and conflict. In the advanced societies, these factors have had greatest impact in the English-speaking democracies of Britain, the United States, Australia and New Zealand, where they have been doing battle with neo-liberal critiques of the role of the state, of "big government" and high tax-and-spend policies (Taylor 1990; 1998).

The neo-Marxist framework rejects neo-liberalism as an attack on the power of labour, one involving privatisation, downsizing of workforces, deregulation, promoting labour "flexibility" and part-time working. As such it is also seen by this framework to involve the creation of insecurity of employment, low wages and the growth of illegal economies. These are seen in turn as criminogenic conditions, requiring a reliance on the police and criminal justice, effectively to regulate the effects of neo-liberal market reforms (Brake and Hale 1991; Muncie, Coventry and Walters 1995). This is seen to require the rapid reconstruction of state powers and institutions at national, local and (nascent) international levels, effectively to secure unchallengeable arrangements for the production and circulation of commodities. The apparent redistribution of powers and responsibilities to locally based agencies and community groups, according to this account, masks a strengthening of centralised fiscal and administrative powers. In this endeavour, in the United Kingdom, the Audit Commission, in service to the House of Commons Public Finance Committee, has, we are told, played a central role in helping to import into the police, prisons and other public sector agencies the new disciplines of audit and the performance measures of the new managerialism (Power 1994; Clarke and Newman 1997; McLaughlin and Muncie 1994).

These developments have been initiated at national and local levels by secretive and often informal "partnership" groups of decision-makers and resource gatekeepers—scarcely accountable to democratic scrutiny—in the public, commercial and voluntary sectors, including social and professional networks of civil servants, corporate chiefs, senior police officers, urban managers, health, welfare and justice professionals and representatives of security firms. In some countries, it is argued within neo-Marxism, a steering role has been retained by government ministers and expert senior civil servants in the central ministries (Bowling 1993). These developments, it is said, are likely to be particularly visible in cities with large poor and/or unemployed populations, like Liverpool and Los Angeles (Coleman and Sim 1996; Davis 1993).

Central players in the new governing alliances are seen to include the major retailing chains, who are viewed as having a strong interest in promoting the values of consumerism and excluding perceivably impecunious and disruptive groups from high streets, and other owners and designers of shopping malls and city centres. For these players, urban regeneration, crime control and community safety mean the construction of safe spaces, under blanket surveillance, for capital investment and the spectacle of conspicuous consumption, rather than, for example, the protection of women from male violence, minorities from racial attack or the consumer from profiteering and the tainting of food and water supplies by producers contemptuous of regulatory safeguards (Coleman and Sim 1996).

It is argued that while the rationales and rhetoric for these alliances suggest a public good—the centrality of crime prevention and reduction within strategies of urban regeneration—the principal beneficiaries are the affluent classes, which have benefited from neo-liberal reforms and, more specifically, the tightly knit alliances of the new local governance. These groups are increasingly socially and spatially segregated from disparate collectivities of the threatening and disorderly poor. In an echo of Disraeli's England, the poor and the homeless are now censured and pathologised as residual, unproductive and burdensome for the elites and the majority, who are still able to retain a niche within the labour market (Sumner 1994; Levitas 1996). Their presence, and other perceived indicators of decline, like broken windows, homeless beggars, litter and graffiti, in major sites of consumption, upsets the aesthetic sensibilities of the agents of capital. They wish to see a tidy, decorative cityscape, as preconditions for attracting a talented urban service class, inward investment and the unleashing of market forces (Ferrel 1996). In this respect, for the neo-Marxists, the apparently contradictory commitment by both the last Conservative and the present New Labour administrations in the United Kingdom to both tough, street cleansing "zero-tolerance" policing strategies and urban regeneration strategies is intelligible. The two can be viewed as complementary technologies for controlling the poor underclass, which is the inevitable product of a globalised capitalist market and the pursuit of neo-liberal economic policies by all the major political parties (Crowther 1999).

It is important to note that while the dominant theme of this interpretive model hinges on the notion of class domination, other themes have emerged which recognise domination by gender and by race, albeit alongside domination by class: that the police and criminal justice agencies which support capitalism also support a dominant gender and racial order, helping to reproduce the subordination of women and sexual, racial and ethnic minorities. With respect to racial and ethnic minorities, this subordination, it is argued, is achieved through repressive policing and criminal justice and also by the discriminatory treatment of black people by immigration and customs officials, restricting mobility and involvement in the labour market (Hay 1996; Scraton and Chadwick 1991; Cook and Hudson 1993; European Commission 1996).

In this setting, criminal justice, particularly juvenile justice, shifts from the disciplining or rehabilitation of individuals towards the application of new managerial discourses and practices in the assessment of risks posed by those from perceivably high risk social categories and the cost effective modes of containing them (Pratt 1989). State agencies, it is thought, effectively manage the risks associated with the frustrations and resistance of the disaffected. Among the new weapons and resources acquired by the state are: new punitive legislation; new technologies of disciplinary surveillance, like the increasingly sophisticated techniques of CCTV (close circuit television surveillance) in urban centres and on national borders; the use of helicopters, armoured vehicles, and the development of new strategies and techniques of public order maintenance and riot control (Jefferson 1990; Scraton and Chadwick 1991; Coleman and Sim 1996; Davis 1993). It is argued that while these developments vary in their impact between nation states, they are elements in the international growth of policing, criminal justice and commercial security, with its attendant toughening of sentencing practices, expansion of prison populations and leech-like draining of tax-based funding from education and welfare budgets (Currie 1997). Seen most vividly in the destabilised former Soviet-bloc countries, this international growth has led to what Nils Christie (1994) calls the international "crime control industry".

While the principal focus of the neo-Marxist model remains the nation state, there is a growing recognition of the uncertain struggles to aggregate aspects of state sovereignty, in pursuit of security. With scant open democratic scrutiny, there has been a rapid development of international police co-ordination, the co-ordination of similar legislation (for example limiting rights to asylum) and cautious merging of jurisdictions, especially in the EU, for the purposes of controlling illegal immigration, cross-border drug-trading, fraud and other crimes (Sheptycki 1995). As with the Schengen Agreement on the policing of national borders, most of the developments are initiated within the Council of Ministers, the Trevi Group and the European Commission, remote from democratic scrutiny. In addition to fears about non-white immigration, a growing consciousness of the perceived threats to Western Europe of political instability and organised crime in the post-Soviet countries (Rawlinson 1997) provides the context and rationale for strengthening the apparatus of what may be the embryo of a "fortress Europe" superstate. Such a project, it is argued within neo-Marxism, requires the construction of populations outside and within as threateningly "other" to the mainstream, employed white populations. And within the apparatus of control, harsh treatment of the expanding prison populations demonstrates the tensions between the maintenance of sovereign control through the warehousing of marginalised populations and the liberal goals of rehabilitation, even in countries which have in other respects developed sophisticated welfare states (Ruggiero, Ryan and Sim 1995; Stern 1997).

GOVERNMENTALITY EXPLANATIONS OF THE RECONSTRUCTION OF THE GOVERNMENT OF CRIME

The governmentality school's narrative about the shift away from welfarist policies and practices challenges the neo-Marxist view that these shifts can be understood principally in terms of changes in the economy and the state (Rose and Miller 1992). Indeed, rather than viewing the market, commercial corporations, professional bodies, religious institutions and other institutions of civil society as lying outside the sphere of government, within this perspective these spheres are said to have gained a degree of separate existence only through governmental/legal action. Furthermore, they are seen as spheres of governance in their own right. Government is seen as operating in a range of sites beyond the confines of national and local state agencies and is rooted in political ratio-nalities whose provenance goes back to late-nineteenth century Europe (Gordon 1991).

Governmentality analysts talk of the "social" logic of government. The term refers to the range of ways (with censuses, studies of urban poverty and the social sciences playing a central role) in which the population is made thinkable and measurable for the purposes of government (Foucault 1991; Barry, Osborne and Rose 1996). Governing in the name of the social, which is not reducible to governing the economy, is holistic. It attempts to foster social solidarity, often at the level of the nation state, but also at more local, spatial sites, hence pro-viding an effective underpinning for the operation of markets (Stenson 1998; 1999).

The aims of the type of social government described by governmentality ana-lysts as dominant, at least from the late-nineteenth through to the mid-twentieth centuries, include the goals and technologies of redistributive social justice, tute-lage of the poor into the perceived norms of acceptable citizenship (Donzelot 1979) and the use of actuarial technologies of risk-sharing. The pool of risk-sharers is said ultimately to encapsulate the citizens of the state and protect against crime, unemployment, sickness, old age and other risks associated with the minimally regulated play of markets (Donzelot 1991). The agents at the heart of this logic are civil servants and local government officials, empowered by universalist statutory frameworks for service provision (Stenson and Watt 1999). To some extent, these mediate between the population and the everyday political fray; they reflect and reinforce a picture of the world that emphasises the shared rights and duties of citizenship.

To return to a theme raised at the beginning of the chapter, the social logic of government, according to governmentality thinking, fosters the differentia-tion of "social" policies and a "social" sphere from the "economic" sphere of economic/contractual relations. It is assisted in this, in part, by the academic dis-ciplines of social policy and other social sciences that conceptualise the "social" as a separate sphere.

Governmentality analysts argue that with the rise of neo-liberal modes of gov-ernment from the late 1970s, the social is now on the wane or even dying. Within this view, the fostering of social solidarity is no longer accorded priority as an end in itself (Rose 1996c). Broad, inclusive, national notions of the risk-sharing collectivity give way to smaller risk-sharing collectivities (O'Malley 1992; Stenson 1993). Local communities are encouraged to be more self-reliant, they are enrolled in crime prevention and other tasks of government, since there is decreasing confidence in the ability of the central state to provide effective secu-rity for its citizens. State agencies are encouraged to target their interventions more precisely towards particular "communities", groups and neighbourhoods.

These are seen as representing high levels of criminal and other modes of social risk for themselves and for the well-being of other groups and interests (O'Malley and Palmer 1996; Stenson 1996; 1998).

The apparent displacement of social government is seen to be allied to a utilitarian emphasis on economic rationality and "enterprise" within public discourse (Fairclough 1995: 112–29). For example, the enterprise-based urban policy of the 1980s was typified by the London Docklands Development Corporation and the credo of "trickle-down" (Deakin and Edwards 1993). There was a range of initiatives in the 1980s, some under the heading of crime prevention, such as "Safer Cities", emanating from central government. These initiatives attempted to provide short-term, pump-priming, targeted at specific neighbourhoods and groups (King 1991). However, they proved to be fragmentary, sometimes overlapped and lacked a clear rationale.

A MILD CRITIQUE OF THE GOVERNMENTALITY EXPLANATIONS OF THE RECONSTRUCTION OF THE GOVERNMENT OF CRIME

A number of criticisms can be made of the "decline of the social" narrative of the governmentality framework. First, while governing in the name of the social may have generic features recognisable internationally, governmental practices vary considerably in national, regional and local settings and operate in hybrid forms with other logics of government (Stenson and Factor 1995; Stenson 1998). It is important to recognise the complex interactions locally between state government strategies and those emanating from outside state agencies. Secondly, in the face of governmentality arguments about needing to focus on government through non-state agencies, many of the recent key initiatives—for example, those with respect to crime prevention—originate in central state ministries (Stenson 1996). Thirdly, it should also be recognised that the contested struggle for sovereign control over geographical territory remains a central thread within governing practices. The concern with bringing the writ of sovereign law, backed by the coercive apparatus of the state, to the rookeries of the poor at the time of the formation of the "social", has its late-twentieth century counterpart in attempting to regain control over perceived disorderly housing estates and the illegal economies which sustain them (Stenson 1996; Lea 1997). Fourthly, as I have argued elsewhere (Stenson 1996; 1999), there has been a relative neglect, by writers working in this framework, of issues of sovereignty. This is in contrast to the concerns of the neo-Marxist model, within which sovereign technologies are viewed through the prism of theories of the state. This matter warrants further discussion.

Within governmentality studies, sovereignty is conceived not as the functioning of a ready-made state, but rather as a set of technologies of rule, usually operating in hybrid interaction with other technologies, employed in the struggle to secure a legitimate (law- and state-sanctioned) monopoly over control of geographical territory (Foucault 1991; Stenson 1998; 1999). I see a need to go beyond a nominalist concern with unpacking the histories and discourses (narrowly conceived) of rule, towards more contemporary analyses of the operation and effects of complex assemblages of technologies of rule, particularly at local level. In other words, we need to go beyond the (initially helpful) governmentality narratives of change, like the death of the social, in order to see how "social" technologies operate with others in complex ways, in a variety of national, regional and local settings (Zedner 1995; Lacey and Zedner 1995). For, as I have argued elsewhere (Stenson 1996; Stenson and Factor 1995), the social sphere was not evenly developed. For instance, it was not as strongly developed in Britain as in some other European countries; there has been a richer tradition in Britain, ironically threatened by recent managerial innovations, of local independence, the use of discretionary powers and "community" based policing and crime prevention (Johnston 1992).

The "death/decline of the social" narrative also, perhaps, over-emphasises the role of welfare practices. As radical critics have stressed, in criminal justice agencies, particularly, there has long been a wide gulf between the lofty welfare rhetorics used to describe and legitimate practices and the reliance on harsh, body-centred sovereign technologies of control in prisons and elsewhere (Scraton and Chadwick 1991).

It is important to ground analyses by retaining the link between rule and geography. We should not lose sight of the struggle, particularly by police agencies, for sovereign control of geographical territory. This is particularly so where there are fierce contests locally for dominance over territory, for criminal and other purposes. Given that central state agendas of government must compete with multiple formal and informal agendas of governance in a liberal social order, this remains an enduring and central problem of governance. The concern with (state) sovereign technologies of control remains a strength of the neo-Marxist approach, albeit that their conception of the range of alternative modes of governance is somewhat selective and exaggerates the role of governance as "resistance" to central state authority. Sovereignty should be given greater prominence within governmentality research.

The key insights of the governmentality approach about the means whereby populations are made thinkable and measurable for the purposes of government are still relevant. We should not underestimate the power of the increasing international traffic of social science and policy ideas in helping to coalesce a new governmental discourse of the local and the communal. This discourse has the capacity to weave together new and traditional themes and transfer between nations similar ways of conceptualising social problems and appropriate solutions. In addition to a focus on local, problem-solving partnership-based crime prevention and policing initiatives, there is a growing emphasis on developing technologies that map patterns of crimes and crime opportunities, providing local policy-makers and residents with more finely grained data. These enable authorities to create, monitor and evaluate crime reduction and urban redevelopment measures and also signal a growing concern with the relation between crime and deprived, "excluded" populations and neighbourhoods, a concern now officially inscribed in EU social policy (Bottoms and Wiles 1996; Graham and Bennett 1995; Levitas 1996).

CONCLUSION: POLICING A NEW SOVEREIGNTY?

We are witnessing and contributing to nothing less than a fundamental rethinking of the nature of liberal government itself in an age of accelerating, profound social, economic and political changes. And it is not altogether fanciful to draw some parallels with police science theorists of the seventeenth and eighteenth centuries. The main difference is that liberalism then was a reaction against police states, even if it retained and incorporated some of their programmes and technologies. We should note that the central concern of earlier versions of "police science" as a governmental savoir was ultimately the securing of sovereign power—secured by sovereign law and the means of force over geographical territory against internal and external threats. The struggle to bring government to perceivably ungoverned areas and populations remains a central connecting thread within liberal government, particularly given the sharp growth in material inequalities since the 1970s at every spatial level. This is one of two central contradictions that lie at the heart of the reconstituted modes of liberal rule.

The first contradiction is that the apparent decline of the nation state and the redistribution of some sovereign powers to other authorities, for example at a European level, can create a crisis of jurisdiction and legitimation. In the EU context, the absence, as yet, of a stable transcendent European state fails to fill the vacuum left by the erosion of the sovereign powers and symbolic authority of nation states. Nevertheless, the struggles between communal groups at local levels over territorial dominance and by statutory agencies to maintain sovereign control over territory continue. We are witnessing a fracturing of levels of sovereignty from the local to the national and the international level, though that will probably proceed at different speeds in different areas. The second key contradiction of the shift towards local and communal modes of government is a tension over the transcendent nature of sovereign power. The mandate of statutory agencies to intervene locally is secured by notions of sovereign law, which must be legitimated in terms of supra-local, transcendent social collectivities.

Only thus can the police and urban managers (as required in the United Kingdom by the Crime and Disorder Act 1998) acquire the practical legitimacy to act as brokers between communal groups in conflict, whose norms may be at variance with each other and with wider legal norms. Yet, to the extent that the police and other statutory agencies become involved with local communal groups in partnership schemes, they risk compromising the illusion of transcendence and impartiality which underpins sovereignty (Stenson and Factor 1994). The attempt to enforce what may be seen as discriminatory powers in defence of sectional interests may create a proliferation of alternative strategies of governance by minorities, through criminal, political, religious and other modes of organisation and escalating spirals of resistance against sovereignty itself. In fact, the problem of sovereignty is likely to remain enduringly central for liberalism, rather than an archaic left-over. It seems that the price paid for the entrepreneurial and individualistic consumerist freedoms of the majority is a growing reliance on sovereign powers to contain the recalcitrant and disaffected minorities (Valverde 1996).

7

Governmentality and Law and Order

DAVID BROWN

INTRODUCTION

THIS CHAPTER EXPLORES a particular criticism of much of the Foucaultian "governmentality" literature: that it disdains politics. This is to say that in this body of work, with some notable exceptions (for example, Pat O'Malley, Lorna Weir and Clifford Shearing's recent "Governmentality, Criticism, Politics" (O'Malley, Weir and Shearing 1997)) politics has disappeared entirely from view. Any possibility that things might or should be different is being ignored; we are being served not just a disdain for politics, but also "a sense of it [politics] as being either wholly arbitrary in its effects (they are always the unintended ones) or as a secondary phenomenon of changing mentalities of government" (Hogg and Brown 1998: 229).

ELEMENTS OF THE DISDAIN FOR POLITICS

Some of the elements identified by O'Malley, Weir and Shearing (1997: 503–11) as contributing to the lack of politics in governmentality analyses include:

(a)   an avoidance of critique;
(b)   a tendency to ignore counter discourses such as feminism, queer theory and post-colonialism, leading to insularity;
(c)   a lack of reflexivity in what O'Malley, Weir and Shearing call the "diagnostic" metaphor of governmental inquiry—an "inattention to the building of a reflexive relation between diagnoser and diagnosed";
(d)   "[a] set against examining 'the messy actualities' of social relations";
(e)   an "attenuation of interest in the role of the public intellectual";
(f)   a limited regard for contests and resistances;
(g)   a tendency to focus on "official" or "serious" statements as against "everyday discourse".

In a major review of governmentality work, with particular reference to criminology, David Garland (1997) offers an overlapping set of what he calls "limits to governmentality analyses" (Garland 1997: 193–205). These include:

(a)   terminological confusion over key terms such as "liberal", "government-alised";

(b)   Foucault's incomplete genealogy of governmental reason;

(c)   A tendency to conflate agency and freedom via the motif of "governing through freedom";

(d)   a tendency to construct rationalities and technologies as ideal types, to the neglect of questions of how they function or are signified;

(e)   a neglect of "low politics" via an emphasis on programmes;

(f)   a neglect of non-instrumental rationalities of government;

(g)   a disdain (in some governmentality work) for more general sociologies.

To these lists I just add my own, again overlapping and no doubt baser, observations:

(a)   the extent to which governmentality analyses tend to become highly abstract and, hence, difficult to translate into popular and media discourses;

(b)   the "in-group" impression one gains when reading some of the governmentality work—there seems to be little effort to include readers who are not already within the networks and loops of reference;

(c)   the strange sense of "placelessness" paradoxically common to much governmentality work, paradoxical in that exhortations to specificity seem not to apply to geography. An example is the failure of some of this work to acknowledge certain legal conditions, such as the predominantly state-based jurisdiction of criminal law, and the differences between places to which they lead;

(d)   the "bloodless" quality of some governmentality work, presumably a response to the excessively florid and rhetorical tropes of leftist critique;

(e)   the feeling that despite the mantra of modesty and the useful move away from overarching origins and causes, from the univocal "state" and the hidden hand of capitalist or patriarchal interest, that the language of "logics", "programmes", "rationalities", "mentalities of rule" tends to set up a new sense of the onward march of unstoppable forces. These are no longer the logics of capital and the historic mission of the working classes but now the free floating technologies of the government of populations and government at a distance, logics and mentalities of rule, similarly driving all before them, underpinning every development. Paradoxically, genealogical analysis, which has as one of its key aims the history of the present, in the sense of showing how contingent the current state of affairs is and how it could have been/could be otherwise, often seems to suggest precisely the opposite, its inevitability.

Let me just try to test some of these issues a little further by reference to law and order debates.

STRATEGIES OF CRIME CONTROL

David Garland in a very influential article in the *British Journal of Criminology*, "The Limits of The Sovereign State: Strategies of Crime Control in Contemporary Society" (1996) provides a critique of what he calls the predicament of crime control in Western democracies. This predicament is characterised by high crime rates as a normal social fact (something I would not want to concede quite so readily, not without rehearsing the familiar "crime statistics as social constructions, measures of reporting behaviour and shifts in community tolerance and sensibilities" argument, at least in relation to violent crime), changes in official discourse and the myth of sovereign crime control. By the "myth of sovereign crime control" Garland means that the claims of the state to provide control over and protection against crime (always somewhat suspect) have become more obviously implausible.

Reactions to this predicament, according to Garland, are dichotomous and contradictory. One reaction is to *adapt* to the predicament, through developing "criminologies of everyday life" (for example, rational choice theory), the "responsibilisation" strategy, adapting to failure, defining deviance down, and redefining success and failure. The other (in what is essentially a politico-Freudian analysis) is "hysterical denial, and the emphatic reassertion of the old myth of the sovereign state" (Garland 1996: 449), manifest in elaborating "criminologies of the Other", and developing increasingly repressive penal and law and order regimes, a scenario fairly easily recognisable in the Australian context. Garland sees in both of these responses what he calls the "eclipse of the solidarity project" (Garland 1996: 463), that is, the end of the aspiration of the penal welfare complex that crime would be diminished and even eradicated through the correct application of social democratic welfare measures combined with the curative and rehabilitative effect of the corrections system.

The politics at work in Garland's analysis is one that can be readily understood and used by criminal justice activists. Ultimately it is still a form of modernist criminal justice politics, it seems to fit the local situation at a general level of tendency, it engenders a hostility to the neo-liberal measures involved in the adaptive strategy which many of us are familiar with (suspicion of crime prevention programmes) and it provides a Freudian basis for the pervasive populist politics of authoritarian and repressive law and order. It has the attraction of maintaining a sense of critique and opposition to current developments across the board. To this extent, it seems to offer precisely the elements that O'Malley, Weir and Shearing argue is missing from most of the governmentality analyses.

While I share the desire to maintain a politics and political engagement (not as necessary for everyone, but certainly as my preference), I think perhaps Garland's analysis is too dichotomous and too schematic. In relation to the "adaptation" strategy for example, Garland maintains:

(a)   a clear cut separation between neo-liberal, "responsibilising" (adaptation) strategies and traditional repressive law and order (denial) strategies;

(b)   an external "critical" stance in relation to both adaptation and "hysterical denial" strategies;

(c)   a sense of hostility to trucking with any of the wide variety of developments under the adaptation label.

ADAPTATION AND DENIAL

I am not so sure that "adaptation" and "hysterical denial" are dichotomous and contradictory, or are only so if one approaches them as part of some broad over-arching description at the level of tendency. To expect of politics and politicians, any more than of criminologists, a unified, complete and wholly consistent approach, is to deny the extent to which it is possible to speak in quite different registers and discourses in relation to different issues, in different fora and in different media. It is also to deny the extent to which quite different approaches and heterogenous voices co-exist within our own work and subjectivities. As Russell Hogg notes:

> "the model of the critical intellectual exists side by side in the same person with other models of the criminological intellectual, other understandings of the nature and meaning of criminology as a vocation, including the criminologist as scientific expert, as the Gramscian 'organic' intellectual whose knowledge is to serve the partisan interest of particular classes in struggle, or as the government bureaucrat" (Hogg 1996: 47).

Pat O'Malley, in his contribution to this volume, offers an alternative explanation of the volatility, contradiction and instability of contemporary crime control, namely in the loose alliance between neo-conservatism, promoting punishment, penal discipline and moral order, and neo-liberalism, promoting "self governing, enterprising and active" prisoners and "victim offender contractualism". In O'Malley's view then, "in such an alliance, oscillations between state bellicosity and devolution, of the sort observed by David Garland, are a perfectly intelligible outcome".

But O'Malley's more interesting arguments here, I think, concern the "lack of closure in politics", the importance of re-establishing "the heterogeneous and multivocal nature of politics . . . that has been reduced to expressions of one unified advanced liberal rationality". It may be that the desire to classify, hierarchise, differentiate, assign, which is common to both governmentality analyses and broader sociological conceptions such as Garland's, seem so often to have the effect of reawakening the structuralist remnants, the epistemes, of the earlier Foucault. Sometimes one is struck by the delights to be found in a piece of simple empiricism, a recitation of "facts" which have not already been inscribed within the big picture of liberal governance, neo-liberal rationality, modernity, pre-modernity, capitalism, patriarchy, corporatism, globalisation or whatever; delights of a simple mind perhaps.

One of the problems in both Garland's "adaptation" analysis and governmentality analyses which focus on the neo-liberal rationalities at work in insurantial and risk-based criminologies is precisely the tendency to homogenise the motivations and politics behind "programmes". The very notion of "programmes", with their components, formulation and implementation, itself imparts a sort of linear, rationalist, calculative feel. But in the law and order area "programmes" or policies often emerge in the most opportunist, random, "aleatory", single-instance way and are characterised by a profound disregard for research and for any calculation of the social and economic effects of the adoption and implementation of policies.

Examples are not hard to find, some in the realms of the absurd. In 1998 the New South Wales (NSW) state conference of the National Party of Australia (a rural conservative grouping) discussed law and order policy, including remits from some branches to "reintroduce the *Summary Offences Act*". It seemed to have escaped all concerned that the *Summary Offences Act* 1988 (NSW) had already been "reintroduced" ten years before, by a conservative government that included some of the same National Party figures presiding over the conference. At the same time as this conference was held, the NSW Liberal Party (another conservative force, the leading partner in a coalition with the Nationals) was announcing that it would move to introduce a "grid sentencing system", a system opposed by the NSW Law Reform Commission and slated in a considerable volume of research from the United States (as leading to inflexibility and burgeoning imprisonment rates with few benefits). Other examples might be the adoption of "one man" preventive detention legislation, such as that adopted by Victoria for Garry David and by NSW for Kable; and the adoption in Western Australia (WA) and the Northern Territory (NT) of various forms of mandatory sentencing policies. It is possible to dismiss such examples as illustrations of the "hysterical denial" response (Garland) or the punitive and "bellicose" desires of neo-conservatism (O'Malley) which have nothing to do with governmental programmes. But to do so is to miss the fact that such non-instrumental rationalities have a powerful hold in the field of law and order, they cannot be neatly confined to a bordered realm of "hysterical denial" or "neo-conservative" discipline.

Even if we go to a prime example of the formulation of a governmental "programme", *Creating a Safer Community* (1992), prepared by the Australian Commonwealth Federal Justice Office under the direction of a steering committee consisting of representatives of the Commonwealth and three state governments, there are clear limits to the extent to which it could be said that such a policy document or programme, many of the elements of which are in accord with but not reducible to neo-liberal strategies of government, commands the field of crime prevention in a unitary and coherent way.

The core elements of the *Creating a Safer Community* document include:

(1) a recognition of the limits and costs of the existing criminal justice system as the major institutional response to crime;

(2)   an emphasis on crime prevention rather than reactive law enforcement;
(3)   the devolution of a substantial responsibility for the prevention and regulation of crime to institutions and individuals within the community;
(4)   the engendering, in turn, of social responsibility and the development of a more active concept of citizenship;
(5)   a corresponding shift in the role of law enforcement agencies, especially the police, in accordance with the recognition of the necessary limits on their capacity to control crime and the responsibility of others for public safety and crime prevention (see Hogg and Brown 1998: 182–4).

Even if we take such as document as the epitome of a "governmental programme" in the crime prevention field, we should still recognise that its limits are many:

(a)   it was prepared by administrators and senior police, not politicians;
(b)   its release was barely noticed in the national news media;
(c)   its objectives and priorities are subject to the exigencies of electoral law and order politics;
(d)   its implementation would depend upon a diverse array of private, corporate and other non-government actors;
(e)   the budget allocation for the current conservative federal government's "Campaign Against Violence and Crime" (the successor to the Australian Labor Party's "Safer Australia") amounts to less than a quarter of one per cent (0.22%) of that government's Public Order and Safety budget (Hogg and Brown 1998: 200);
(f)   the difficulty in promoting the strategy in the light of the impact of growing socio-economic adversity and inequality on patterns of crime and the capacity of individuals, households and communities to manage it;
(g)   the question of how such a crime control strategy can significantly ameliorate crime problems if it is not combined with measures which seek to reorder "vertical" relations between communities and the "external" actors (government and non-government) which shape them, by redistributing power and resources as well as responsibility.

THE POLITICS OF CRITIQUE

The external critical stance in relation to Garland's adaptive strategies is, I find as someone who seeks to enter and influence public and media debate, a suspect one. In a context in which various sorts of crime prevention policies take up a fraction of one per cent of the total criminal justice/law and order budget, it is problematic to maintain a stance of uniform opposition to such developments. That does not mean that concerns and criticisms should be suspended, but that media comments in particular should be formulated in a way that does not have the effect of providing support for the strident conservative voices which oppose any shift of emphasis away from the reassuring "solutions" of policing and punishment. Beyond this tactical concern lies a "post-critical" stance which denies that the domain of politics and the academic discipline of criminology are or ever could be transparent to each other's objects, methods and knowledge. It is a stance which dismisses the claim of critique to occupy some privileged seat at the pinnacle of an ethical hierarchy of knowledge, in which it would make ethical and political sense to judge practical political outcomes and policies against the benchmarks supplied by critical theory.

Of course, particular crime prevention programmes can develop in extremely worrying ways. One of my students recently did some work on a crime prevention initiative in the Sydney suburb of Liverpool, around the mall and railway station area. Reporting back to the class he outlined various initiatives and was somewhat taken aback that they were met with widespread condemnation, even hilarity. Some of the suggestions did read like a Monty Python script. Problem: kids sitting on seats in the mall; solution—remove the seats. Problem: people gathering under an awning when it rained and disturbing local shops; solution—remove the awning. Problem: kids hanging around in the mall, especially outside shops which play youth-oriented music; solution—approach the shopkeepers and get them to play Mantovani and classical music which would drive the kids away. These are local versions of Mike Davis's "bum proof" bus seats and park benches in Los Angeles (Davis 1992); the Monty Python script given a real life in LA.

It seems to me that to engage constructively in law and order politics as an academic criminologist is to fashion a very specific and often somewhat schizoid stance, one which has its origins perhaps in Foucault's understanding that "if there was no resistance there would be no power relations" (seeing resistant political activity as "not simply a negation but a creative process") (Foucault 1997a: 168–9). That does not mean that it is not sometimes necessary to refuse to be involved. Such a refusal might be based on reluctance to be drafted in as an "expert" without having sufficient knowledge of, or involvement in, a particular community. Or it might be based on an assessment that a particular proposal or programme will impact adversely on already marginalised groups and has little prospect of being redirected or reformulated. Even here, such sentiments may have more effect if voiced from inside consultative processes. Here I would say, yes, I support the police being engaged in crime prevention initiatives in partnership with local councils and other organisations. But there should be youth and special interest group representation on such partnership enterprises. More than just commercial interests must be represented. There should be widespread discussion of any proposed actions. A reasonable period for comment should be provided. The police view should not automatically prevail. The local council should provide various fora for a more open, inclusive debate. There should be follow-up consultations and monitoring to see how things are working out from the viewpoints of different constituencies.

All this is fairly basic, even trite. But it is difficult to engage critically in such a process if one attempts to stand outside such developments and treat them as simply a response to the widely recognised myth of sovereign crime control and/or a distraction from the solidarity project of the penal welfare complex. We are all to some extent, whether in our professional competences or just as citizens, already caught up in making choices about the extent to which and how we personally engage in various forms of "adaptive" or risk-minimisation strategies in crime prevention; it is difficult to maintain a congruence between professional critique and personal involvement precisely because the choices are not dichotomous and we are already inside various networks of risk prevention and loss-spreading. To see insurance, for example, as merely a neo-liberal technology is to minimise its social-democratic and "solidarity project" origins and to downplay popular investment in such technologies. As private individuals, the management of our lives, health and security, the education of our children, and so on, are permeated with the themes of reflexive consumerism, efficiency, "responsibilisation" and privatism. That does not mean we have to lie back and let the neo-liberal rationalities of governance wash over us. But we do need to recognise the rising appeal of choice, diversity and active citizenship and the declining appeal of forms of collectivism, uniformity and bureaucratic management. The key question is how we might link the politics of community, identity, and local democracy to a reconstituted politics of redistribution appropriate to the times.

As a rule of thumb, it seems to me generally desirable to attempt to conduct a form of reflexive engagement with the practices and mentalities through which we live our lives, in an attempt to avoid the personally damaging cognitive dissonance which arises from exhorting a form of heroic "transgressive" conduct geared to exceptional circumstances which are difficult to act out in our more mundane daily lives (and indeed would be foolish). While George Pavlich's example of the Soweto youth throwing rocks at the troop carrier (see George Pavlich, chapter 9 below) is inspiring and instructive, for those of us who have the privilege of attending conferences such as the one from which this book ensued, our trials and tribulations are usually more prosaic and mundane; for example how to stimulate and challenge students in a context of significantly increased student numbers and significantly decreased resources. A focus on the fostering of co-operation, mutuality and trust in our daily lives may well be a more difficult and more constructive response to current educational conditions than a sometimes gestural, "transgressive" politics of opposition and critique.

ENGAGEMENT IN "LOW POLITICS"

It seems to me that the failure of governmentality analysis to "concern itself with struggles and conflicts and low politics" which Garland identifies in his detailed examination of governmentality analyses (1997), applies in part to his own earlier (1996) article. He says in the later version:

> "we must pay heed to the ways in which public fears and anxieties about crime are taken up in the political realm and represented there by populist discourses and 'expressive' measures of a punitive or incapacitative kind. The process of switching between rationalities, or moving from one discursive register (the economic-administrative) to another (the populist-political) is very much a political process, structured by conflicting interests *within* government departments and the offices of state, and motivated by all sorts of exigencies, political calculations and short term interests. The practices that make up the field of crime control may be structured by government rationalities, but in its detailed configuration, with all its incoherence and contradictions, the field is also the product of a rather aleatory history of political manoeuvres and calculations" (Garland 1997: 202, emphasis in original).

Aleatory (depending on chance), yes indeed, but also perhaps inflected by the "profoundly historical character" which Mark Finnane stresses against O'Malley when he notes that "the tide rises and falls on the shores of state action but in the democratic jurisdictions a great deal of a government's political fate rests on a commitment to programmes in which the state delivers identifiable resources to individuals and communities" (Finnane 1996: 40). Nor is the issue only one of "switching between rationalities" or different "discursive registers". For at the concrete level particular practices condense a complex array of potentially contradictory and non-unitary relations which cannot just be pressed into service in the interests of a particular "mentality of rule". It may be worth dusting off some earlier Garland here, his essay with Peter Young in *The Power to Punish* (1983) and his polemic against approaching penal practice by way of general moral philosophy (Garland 1983; see also Hirst 1986). In the *Power to Punish* Garland and Young convincingly argue the merits of the notion of penality rather than punishment, as signifying a "complex field of institutions, practices and relations rather than a singular type of social event" (Garland and Young 1983: 14). And earlier Garland stresses that "particular sanctions, such as incarceration, probation, residential care orders or simple fines, embody a whole series of objectives (and at this level 'retribution', 'deterrence' and 'reformation' are generally co-present and frequently indistinguishable) as well as definite techniques, knowledges, and ideological significance" (Garland 1983: 83).

Once we enter into a detailed empirical and historical, political analysis of any particular policy or "programme" then it often becomes difficult (if we are to try to be genuinely true to the phenomenon) to pass it off as merely a specific instance of some sweeping tendency, whether it be one of the "logics" or "rationalities" of governmentality, one of the dichotomous adaptive or denial responses of Garland, or one of the various species of nefarious extensions of social control common to so much "critique".

Almost any concrete example is invariably nuanced, contains a mixture of historical, aleatory, cultural, expressive, technological sensibilities; take for example the debate over the adversary system in the current Australian Law Reform Commission inquiry. While it is easy and relatively commonplace in legal circles for this debate to be read as a form of neo-liberal "technocratic justice", such a characterisation does not come so readily from activists with a history of agitation around miscarriages of justice. The demise of the pilot sentence indication scheme in New South Wales shows the real public limits to technocratic justice. And as soon as we start discussing forms of youth and family mediation, reparation and conferencing schemes, with a few predictable exceptions from the ranks of permanent revolution (whatever the context), the attributions of positions, tendencies, and characterisations are likely to run hither and thither.

David Garland is, in my view, correct in saying that governmentality analyses tend towards ideal types, are uneasy with non-instrumental rationalities, and might usefully be brought into clearer relation with more general sociologies. I also support O'Malley, Weir and Shearing's call for governmentality studies to be "deflected away from political irrelevance" (O'Malley, Weir and Shearing 1998: 514). However, I am not sure that a return to "critique" will ensure this "deflection". It seems to me that the relatively early critique of "critique" by Nik Rose, in his "Beyond the public/private division: law and the family" (1987), is very convincing.

Perhaps it depends, as George Pavlich argues in chapter 9 below, on exactly what we mean by critique. For me this term often conjures up earlier career incarnations of "dialectics" (a sort of simple physics that could be applied to explain, and in most cases explain away, everything); or the rather lazy way some add the word "critical" to every exam or essay question, as in "Critically evaluate the following statement by David Garland . . ."; or the increasingly tiresome stance of permanent opposition and refusal to take responsibility for any decisions, in the interests of resisting neo-liberal "responsibilisation" strategies, given that those decisions are always being forced on us by "the state", "the government", "the vice chancellor", "the dean", "the committee", "economic rationalism" and so on.

Pavlich is concerned to identify different legacies of critique and to differentiate judgemental critique from critique which seeks to "separate out, discern, differentiate", in the interests of exploring "how not to be governed thus" (see George Pavlich, chapter 9 below). Importantly this "how not to be governed thus" sits alongside the art of "how to govern", although, perhaps of necessity the concentration is on the former in Pavlich's account of the "critique of limits". One of my misgivings about this approach is that the emphasis on and valorisation of "transgression" may lead us back into the easy oppositionism of judgemental critique.

HAVING NO TRUCK WITH NEO-LIBERALISM

One of the points of contest here is the perceived necessity for critique to maintain a hostile attitude to neo-liberalism. But as Hogg and Brown argue in *Rethinking Law and Order*:

"while it would be easy to depict neo-liberalism as a right-wing individualist creed, it is important to recognise that it entails a more complex, flexible, composite and inventive approach to the management of a vast array of domains of life, such as the economy, paid work, health, education and personal life. It eschews simple ideological formulae and polarities such as state/civil society, market/state, individual/community and so on. We should not let ideological prejudices thwart our efforts to grasp the nature and novelty of these developments" (Hogg and Brown 1998: 139).

But then:

"On the other hand, neo-liberalism creates the prospect that for a significant minority, choice will be effectively curtailed by the conditions in which they are constrained to live by virtue of their lack of market power and the erosion of public systems of support and protection. Against the neo-liberal emphasis on choice, the political responses to current troubles by the Old left, the Old right, traditional social democrats and many of the new communitarians, commonly offer a return to 'communities of fate' defined by reference to class, neighbourhood, family, state collectivism and so on, and to the principles of collectivism, uniformity and compulsion. This is a source of their unpopularity. We doubt that any political strategy which fails to enlarge the domains and communities of choice is likely to meet with success in current conditions" (Hogg and Brown 1998: 213–14).

I suppose a response to this is that we should wait until conditions change. But we might be waiting a long time. In the meantime there are some fairly pressing issues to take on in the Australian context: mandatory sentencing regimes and high Indigenous imprisonment rates; law and order bidding auctions; the "zero tolerance" slogan is taken up with great gusto by politicians; elements of the right-wing One Nation party seek to exploit electorally race and immigration issues, opposition to gun control, law and order issues, and to promote referenda on the reintroduction of capital punishment; and the incidence of some of the most pervasive crime problems and violence remains relatively hidden in the strident law and order debate, as in various forms of intimate violence, child abuse, hate crimes, bullying in schools, sexual and physical abuse of vulnerable populations such as the elderly, children and prisoners.

PLURALISM AND ASSOCIATIVE DEMOCRACY

Another response to the current law and order climate is to try to fashion a pluralist approach which acknowledges the appeal of neo-liberal notions of choice, acknowledges the subtlety of governmentality analyses of mentalities of rule which are not yoked to overweening interests or functions and acknowledges the desire of critique for something other than we have, for being otherwise. Such an approach might at the same time recognise that existing relations of inequality of access to the repertoires and opportunities of choice necessitate a politics conducted at the level of reorganisation and regulation of markets to enlarge the domain of choice, but in a way which emphasises the importance of plural and decentralised forms of governance afforded by the associations of civil society and regional and local forms of government. In short, the choices are not only those of the "free market" or of new forms of state collectivism. It is perhaps worth considering the sorts of arguments put by writers like Paul Hirst (1994) under the banner of pluralism and associative democracy.

Hirst's associative democracy builds on the recognition that modern liberal democratic societies are characterised by a pluralism of beliefs, social purposes and forms of authority and association. The lives of individuals are lived out within many intermediate forms of association and authority other than the state: family, corporations, trade unions, professional associations, churches, schools, sporting clubs, cultural associations, and so on. As Bobbio observes, pluralism is not so much a theory as a reality (Bobbio 1987: 58). For Hirst, it is also normative. Many of these intermediate forms of association often constitute more direct sources of authority in the lives of individuals than the state. Furthermore, they are the main vehicles through which influence is exerted over governments on a day to day basis, as against the occasional and limited exercise of electoral choice.

Pluralist and associational approaches require that constitutional, political and legal structures recognise and protect the associational life of the society as well as individual rights and market freedoms. Effective economic, social and political institutions in a free and competitive market society depend upon strong forms of co-operation, mutuality and trust which are embedded in and enhanced by patterns of associative life. Unlike neo-liberalism, associative democracy aims not at the contraction of public provision and responsibility, but its extension and reconstitution through devolution and decentralisation of powers and functions of governance to associations within civil society and regional and local government. Or, in Hirst's terms, the associative approach "publicises civil society and pluralises the state" (Hirst 1994: 167; see also Hogg and Brown 1998: 210–17).

Hirst tends to assume that such arguments might have relevance to domains of life like work and welfare, but not to core responsibilities of state concerned with crime control and public safety. Hogg and Brown argue that this is not necessarily so, that there is abundant evidence that many of the functions of crime prevention and community safety are being increasingly carried out by individuals and associations within civil society alongside, and frequently in partnership with, various levels and agencies of government.

The wide variety of sanctioning agencies and practices do not provide a substitute for the traditional state criminal justice agencies, but a supplement to them. This more complex pattern of sanctioning not only cuts across the usual division between state and civil society and derogates from the traditional principles of equality and uniformity but is likely to have a more systematic influence on how different categories of offender are processed. It is primarily people integrated into the conventional institutions of paid employment, schooling, the family and professional life who enjoy a degree of immunity from the criminalising interventions of the state. But when people who are excluded from conventional social institutions offend, they are much more likely to feel the immediate punitive and stigmatising effects of the criminal justice system. Existing inequalities of access to the institutions of social citizenship are reproduced in patterns of sanctioning and then further compounded by the stigmatising and exclusionary effects of the criminal sanction on those who, by virtue of their marginality, are most vulnerable to its use.

CONCLUSION

It is for this reason that attempts to tackle the multitude of issues grouped under the label of crime or law and order require more than a new form of naturalistic description and more than an external critique. They require a form of governmental and government politics which seek to strengthen the basic fabric and institutions of civil society, to support and empower the growing minority of communities that currently risk being cast into a more or less permanent state of social marginality.

PART THREE

Reframing Ontology and Critique

8

Governing Theory: Ontology, Methodology and the Critique of Metaphysics

JEFF MALPAS

√ existence

INTRODUCTION

Q UESTIONS OF METHODOLOGY—questions concerning how inquiry into
a particular region should proceed—are rarely separable from questions
of ontology—questions concerning the entities and structures that are
constitutive of that region. There are, of course, certain general methodological
commitments, considerations of evidential adequacy, consistency, simplicity
and so forth that obtain, to some extent, irrespective of ontology, but, at a more
particular level, methodological recommendations typically reflect ontological
preferences. Thus, what count as the proper methods for identifying certain
phenomena within a region that require explanation or description, what sorts
of entities are admitted as relevant to the explanation or description of those
phenomena, and what counts as an adequate explanation or description, all
depend to a greater or lesser extent on what are taken to be the basic entities and
structures that make up the region in question.

Methodological commitments thus always bring ontological commitments in
their train one cannot avoid ontological entanglement by proclaiming one's
interests as "purely" methodological. And this is not just in the sense that certain ontological commitments are built in to our very language, but in the more
particular sense that methodological commitments typically derive from and
express certain theoretical preferences in relation to explanation and description. In this respect, to engage in any form of explanatory or descriptive enterprise is already to be involved in ontology. While there may be forms of
description or explanation that are neutral as between some limited set of alternative ontologies, there are no forms of description or explanation that are neutral with respect to all ontologies—every description or explanation brings
some ontological commitment with it. Social scientific theorists, and others,
who claim not to be involved in advancing any ontological theses, but to be

cant be purely methodological bring ontological elements in

involved merely in a descriptive enterprise, or to be involved only with establishing certain methodological principles, can be seen to have misunderstood the nature of their own activity. In this respect, the dichotomy between descriptive and explanatory modes of analysis that is sometimes invoked, and that is an important feature of some forms of Foucaultian analysis, can (though not always) be misleading. While there is a certain point to this dichotomy, as I note below, descriptive modes of analysis are typically embedded, if only implicitly, in modes of causal analysis (to describe is already, one might say, to embed the thing described in a certain causal-explanatory framework). The interconnection of description and explanation can, indeed, be seen as analogous with the interconnection of methodology and ontology. For this reason I often refer in this chapter to methodology and ontology, and to explanation and description, in combination.

[handwritten annotation: To explain + describe — when you describe — you're in your explaination]

THE SUSPICION OF METAPHYSICS

[handwritten annotation: being + knowing]

Social theory is invariably ontologically committed as is any form of inquiry, no matter what the domain. Social theorists have often, however, been suspicious of "ontology" and this suspicion is typically derivative of a more deep-seated and pervasive antagonism towards *metaphysics*. Such antagonism is not merely a function of the postmodern rejection of so-called "grand narratives", but is a characteristic and pervasive feature of social scientific inquiry as it has developed over the last two hundred years or so—it is, indeed, a suspicion rooted, paradoxical though it may sometimes seem, in the origins of social scientific inquiry in the Enlightenment. Part of this suspicion has undoubtedly arisen from an association of metaphysical with religious modes of thinking, together with a view of both the religious and the metaphysical as less than properly scientific and as insufficiently attentive either to the realities of life or the demands of concrete empirical analysis.

Jonathan H Turner, for example, begins his history of sociological theory by reporting Auguste Comte's division of the intellectual world into three stages— "the law of the three stages"—which he explains thus:

> "In the religious stage, interpretations of events are initially provided by religious beliefs or by reference to the activities of sacred and supernatural forces. Out of religion comes a metaphysical stage in which logic, mathematics, and other formal systems of reason come to dominate how events are interpreted. And out of these gains in formal reasoning in the metaphysical stage emerges the possibility for 'positivism' or a scientific stage, where formal statements are critically examined against carefully collected facts" (Turner 1991: 1–2).

Something of this Comtean spirit, which places a certain "positive" empiricism, directed towards the careful analysis of the particular and the concrete, above either religious or metaphysical systems of thought, remains an important

[handwritten annotation in left margin: suspicion of ontology ? connections with metaphysics]

and characteristic feature of much contemporary research, especially in disciplines such as sociology, anthropology and cultural studies. Something of this same spirit is also reflected in the writings of another of the "founding fathers" of sociology, Karl Marx. In *Die Deutsche Ideologie* Marx tells us that:

> "Morality, religion, metaphysics, and all the rest of ideology as well as the forms of consciousness corresponding to these . . . no longer retain the appearance of self-sufficiency. They have no history, they have no development; but in the development of their material production and their material intercourse, men thereby alter their material world, as well as their thinking and the products of their thinking . . . Where speculation gives out, where real life starts, there begins real, positive science, the expounding of the practical activity, of the practical process of development of men" (Marx 1971: 23–4, my translation).

The "suspicion" of metaphysics that can be found in Marx is closely tied to a conception of metaphysics that associates it with religion and that treats both as separated from the concrete empirical reality that is the primary concern of science. It is a suspicion that can also be seen in Marx's famous pronouncement that, "The philosophers have only given different interpretations of the world, what comes now is to change it" (Marx 1971: 4).

To some extent, more recent expressions of a similar suspicion of metaphysics, or, more precisely, of metaphysics understood as "idealism", and arising from within Marxist and "post-Marxist" perspectives (see, for instance, Coward and Ellis 1977: 9) stand within much the same framework: metaphysics, like religion, is representative of a view *on* the world, rather than a view *from* the world; it attempts to impose meaning onto the world from outside, rather than understand meaning as generated from the concrete materiality within.

One of the oddities of social-theoretic suspicion of metaphysics, however, is that it has often failed to recognise the way in which it itself stems from a particular metaphysical perspective. Both the Comtean prioritisation of "positive" science and the Marxist emphasis on the material and the empirical over the ideal and the rational exemplify thoroughly metaphysical positions in that they take a certain "ontology"—typically a certain "scientific" or materialist ontology—as fundamental to all forms of inquiry. And even when the Marxist and Comtean narratives are explicitly abandoned, the general metaphysical standpoints on which they are based often remain. Of the various forms of postmodernist social theory, most remain essentially committed, in spite of the fact that they often employ a rhetoric that is typically anti-metaphysical, to a certain empiricist materialism. Postmodernism, in this sense, remains within a thoroughly modernist frame.

Moreover, the original emphasis on an empiricist and materialist metaphysics within social theory was also paralleled by a view of social theory as essentially directed towards the achievement of certain socially beneficial outcomes. The tendency for social theory to see itself as associated both with a "realistic" and practically oriented empiricism and with an ameliorative and progressive politics has survived even the challenge of postmodernist thinking. Indeed, as it is manifest within social theory, postmodernist thought can be viewed as simply the latest manifestation of the long-standing social-theoretic suspicion of metaphysics that not only takes metaphysics to be identical with an essentially religious, and so anti-empiricist, mode of thought, but that also rejects metaphysics in favour of a more "practically" (and politically) oriented form of concrete social analysis and critique.

[handwritten margin note: Postmodernist – just a new manifestation – inc reject metaphysics]

METAPHYSICS AND ONTOLOGY

[handwritten margin note (left): metaphysics can include ontology]

Of course, this social scientific suspicion or antagonism towards metaphysics need not always entail a suspicion of ontology in general. Although philosophers have often viewed "ontology" and "metaphysics" as almost coextensive terms—both being understood as constituted by the inquiry into, or the theory of, "what is"—metaphysics can also be viewed as designating that particular form of ontology that looks to provide an account of "what is" in the most basic and all-encompassing sense. In this respect, while any and every inquiry or theory brings a certain ontology with it that is, any and every inquiry or theory presupposes a certain structure or set of entities that are constitutive of the particular region inquired into or theorised about metaphysics is the attempt to inquire into that which underlies and also unifies any and every such region; it is the attempt to formulate an ontology that precedes all other ontologies and that provides an account of the unique structure or set of entities that are presupposed by all forms of inquiry or theorisation. In this sense, social scientific suspicion of metaphysics can be seen as consisting in a suspicion of the attempt to ground everything that is—the reality of both the natural and the social or cultural world—in some single, underlying entity or structure. What is often in question is whether the anti-metaphysical spirit evident within social theory does itself escape this same metaphysical tendency—whether it does not in fact merely substitute one form of metaphysics for another.

[handwritten margin note (left): When you create a social theory without metaphysics – actual have a form of metaphysics.]

A suspicion of metaphysics, in the particular sense of the term just outlined, is not, however, only to be found in social theory. An anti-metaphysical tendency is also to be found within philosophy, and not merely as a recently emerged phenomenon, since it can be traced back at least as far as the scepticism of Sextus Empiricus (who is thought to have flourished in the second century AD), and of his predecessor Pyrrho of Elis (c. 365–270 BC). David Hume and Immanuel Kant are perhaps the two most notable representatives of the anti-metaphysical tendency within philosophy as it developed after Descartes and prior to the twentieth century. More recently, the philosophical suspicion of metaphysics has arisen in at least two other main forms: the first springs from empiricist and scientistic modes of thought (often inspired as much by John Locke and Isaac Newton as by Hume) that are exemplified in the work of

Rudolf Carnap and W V Quine; the second derives from the critical tradition inaugurated by Kant (a tradition that took on a historical turn in the nineteenth century), and that develops in a particular form in the work of Heidegger. A number of contemporary philosophers set out anti-metaphysical positions that draw on elements from both these streams, a notable example here being Richard Rorty, whose "postmodernist" stance combines elements from both Quine and Heidegger, amongst others.

Clearly there is a good deal of overlap between the anti-metaphysical positions that have developed within philosophy and those that are present within social theory. But there are also some important differences that obtain between those positions, particularly, in my view, between the sort of anti-metaphysical stance to be found in Heidegger and that to be found in Quine, Carnap or in much social theory. At times, particularly in his earlier work (prior to about 1933), Heidegger's own project is clearly, in important senses, a metaphysical one, albeit a metaphysical project that also attempts a rethinking and refounding of metaphysics at the same time as it engages in a critique of the previous metaphysical tradition. In this respect Heidegger's project bears comparison with Kant's in the *Kritik der Reinen Vernunft* (Kant 1781/1787): both attempt to rescue a certain sort of metaphysics, and certainly the possibility of ontological inquiry, from dogmatic metaphysics and scepticism. In his *Kantbuch* of 1929 Heidegger presents the Kantian project as a "laying of the ground of metaphysics" ("*eine Grundlegung der Metaphysik auszulegen*" (see Heidegger 1991: 1 *et seq*).

In his later work, while Heidegger can still be viewed as engaged in a form of "ontology" (though we have to be careful how we use the term), "metaphysics" designates a way of thinking about the world, to which we are inevitably prone, that continually tries to reduce the world and "what is" to some underlying rational principle or ground that is properly only a part or aspect of the world—to understand being, as Heidegger puts it, always and only in terms of some particular being among beings. From this Heideggerian perspective, the anti-metaphysics that is associated with empiricist and scientistic thinking, as well as with much social scientific theorising, remains metaphysical in spite of itself. Such thinking, while rejecting certain forms of metaphysics, nevertheless prioritises a certain particular way of understanding the world over all others, and insists on understanding the world in terms only of some particular aspect of the world.

THE ONTOLOGY OF GOVERNANCE

The Heideggerian attack on metaphysics seems to be given a particularly social scientific turn in the work of Michel Foucault. Foucault has acknowledged the central influence of Heidegger, along with Nietzsche, on his own thinking. Although Foucault is not explicit about the exact nature of this influence, one respect in which Heideggerian thinking is apparent in his work is in his similar rejection of the "metaphysical". Here the reference to "metaphysics" has to be understood in the Heideggerian sense of a reference to a mode of understanding that privileges a particular feature or aspect of the world over all others—that attempts to explain all entities or structures in terms of a single entity or structure. This is how, I suggest, we should understand, for instance, Foucault's critique of the idea of "man" in *Les Mots et les Choses* (Foucault 1966: 314 *et seq*). Indeed, Foucault's anti-humanist position in this work, in particular, can usefully be compared with Heidegger's own critique of humanism in the influential "Brief über Humanismus" (Heidegger 1976). Such anti-humanism (though it is not an opposition to or neglect of the human) is a reiterated feature of the work of both thinkers throughout their respective intellectual careers.

Yet the comparison, and the line of influence, between Heidegger and Foucault does not end with the critique of metaphysics notwithstanding their anti-metaphysical positions, both Heidegger and Foucault can be viewed as offering a certain model of ontological analysis that stands as a counter to the analysis proposed by the traditional metaphysician or social theorist. The style and nature of this analysis is perhaps sometimes clearer in Heidegger than in Foucault—indeed, Foucault provides us less with an analysis as with a series of suggestions and exemplars indicating how such an analysis might proceed—but it is an analysis that can, nevertheless, be given a reasonably clear exposition and that also connects up with a number of other themes in contemporary social theory as well as philosophy. The analysis that I have in mind here is one that I have already tried to spell out in work I have undertaken with Gary Wickham that centres on the notion of governance (see Malpas and Wickham 1995; 1997). It is a mode of analysis that is developed in Foucault's work by means of the work on power and discipline, for instance, as well as through the late work on governmentality and self-governance. In Heidegger, the approach at issue can be seen to be evident in a number of different ways: in *Sein und Zeit* (Heidegger 1993), in the idea of the structure of *Dasein* as constituted through a number of equiprimordial ("*gleichursprunglich*") elements that are worked out in terms of *Dasein*'s concrete "being-in-the-world", and, in later Heidegger, through the idea of disclosure as something that always takes place within a complex structure of interlocking elements that "clear" a space—a world—within which things can appear.

The features of this approach that interest me here are not only to be found in Foucault and Heidegger, but can also be discerned, to a greater or lesser extent, in the work of a number of other theorists. I treat Weber as another figure who can be seen as making an important contribution to the ideas at issue here, as they develop within a social scientific context in particular. For my present purposes, however, it is on Foucault and Heidegger that I want to concentrate.

In its general outline, the analysis at issue here combines two fundamental ontological, but also, of course, methodological, ideas. The first idea involves a

[margin note: Foucault offers a different ontological analysis]

focus on a certain *structural* mode of analysis. Immediately, I have to say that this should not be taken to imply that the analysis is therefore to be categorised as a variety of *structuralism*: there is no particular level of structure that can be deemed to be primary on this account; while the focus on structure itself has to be understood as allied with other concepts; the appeal to structure thus lacks the specificity of "structuralist" approaches. In Heidegger's *Sein und Zeit*, the emphasis on structure is evident in two ways: in the commitment to a structural analysis of *Dasein* as "being-in-the-world" that takes *Dasein* to be a unitary phenomenon that is nevertheless constituted only through the integration of a complex set of differentiated elements or aspects; and, in the commitment to the equiprimordial character of these different elements or aspects, such that they have to be seen as together originating in the unitary structure of *Dasein*, even though that structure is itself only constituted by means of those elements.

The second idea involves a focus on a certain "dynamic" mode of analysis that brings with it a certain reciprocity of effect. In Foucault, this is most clearly evident in the turn towards the notion of power as a central focus for inquiry. It is not just the focus on power alone that is important—power is only understood in relation to the resistance which is generated along with it. If we think in terms of a structure, then the sort of structural model we should have in mind is not the structure of a static system of inter-defined elements. Rather, it is the dynamic functional system that is exemplified in an engine, in which every stroke has its counter-stoke, in which power produces resistance, in which resistance produces power.

In Heidegger, this dynamic mode of analysis arises not through any direct focus on power as such, but rather through giving central stage to concepts of projective activity. *Dasein*'s projecting of itself into the world through its concrete involvement with things both determines the ordering of things in the world and the ordering of *Dasein*. Moreover, such projecting is generative of both possibility and constraint. In this respect, the emphasis on the structure, and the elements within it, as defined by, but also constrained by, reciprocating activity, can be seen to bring with it an emphasis on the necessarily limited and partial character of every form of activity or exercise of power—what is acted upon is constituted by activity and yet always extends beyond any particular instance of such activity, while every exercise of power, seeking to exercise control over that which is subject to it, is itself constrained and limited by just that which it attempts to control. With partiality and limitation is also conjoined a thesis concerning multiplicity the necessarily limited character of projective activity, of the exercise of power, of governmental practice, brings with it a commitment to the multiplicity of such projects, the multiple forms of power and the multiple practices of governance (see Malpas and Wickham 1995; 1997).

If we think of both power/resistance and the reflexive projection of *Dasein* as productive of both ordering and constraint, then we can see how both might be assimilated to an account that takes a general notion of governance as the overarching concept. The idea of governance can be seen as neatly combining a certain structural mode of analysis and an emphasis on activity as both productive and constraining. Governance, on this sort of account, is not be understood as some activity in which pre-existing entities are brought under control by the directing influence of an agent (whether individual or collective), but rather as a dynamic structure in which agents define themselves through their attempts to exercise control over objects that, while constituted in terms of the activities of governance to which they are subject, nevertheless always extend beyond the confines of any particular governing activity. Moreover, there can be no single level of analysis that completely captures the governmental structure at issue: both objects and agents stand at the intersection of multiple governing practices, and no single agent or any single object is completely encompassed by any single such practice. An analysis that is geared towards the notion of governance, as deployed here, is thus an analysis that is always incomplete, that always looks towards governance as operating on various levels and in multiple forms. In the account that Wickham and I have developed, the necessary binding together of productivity with constraint, of power with resistance, of activity generation with a limit generation, is expressed through the idea of the inevitable failure of all governing practices. Such failure is, on our account, a mark of the dynamic and reciprocal character of the structure of governance as such and can be seen to be operative at every level of analysis, description or explanation. Indeed, such a tendency towards partiality, towards limitation, towards "failure", can be seen as characteristic of the theoretical activity of the social scientist or philosopher as much as of the "practical" activity of the citizen, the householder, the business person, the politician, the corporation, or the state.

Now it might be supposed that in looking to the sort of account that I have been outlining here—the sort of account that I have been presenting as a feature of both Heidegger and Foucault, as well as of the work of Wickham and myself—what is really being advanced is an account that looks only to some very general level of collective structure as the basic level for explanation or description. I recently read a brief newspaper characterisation of Foucault according to which a Foucaultian account of the game of football (this was during the World Cup in France in 1998) views the game as consisting of a set of rules but no players. Only the rules—the structure—matters. This characterisation is seriously mistaken about the ontology that is actually being proposed.

On the reading of Foucault and Heidegger that I am presenting, and on the account of governance that I have set out, it is not that the real level of analysis is to be identified with the level of structural interrelation between elements, but rather that elements cannot be removed from the dynamic, relational structures in which they are embedded without loss of both the structural whole itself and the elements that make it up. The reciprocity—the mutual constitution—that obtains between elements within the structure is reflected in a mutual reciprocity between the elements and the overall structure. The structure is itself constituted through the interplay of the elements within it, even as those elements are

Nobody is above the law because the law is not a thing - it is something that we are a part of

constituted through their interrelation within the whole structure. It is not that the "rules" are simply what constitute the game, since the rules themselves depend upon the elements—players, officials, field, ball—to which those rules make reference, even as those elements are given definition through the rules. Rather than look to some reified notion of "structure", we have to think of both structure and elements as forming part of a single field—a field, moreover, that is capable of multiple forms of analysis depending on our own projection of that field, on the relations of power in which our own theoretical activities are enmeshed, on the practices of "governance" on the basis of which our theorising proceeds. On this model, it is not a matter of finding certain entities or structures, or even a level of structuration, that gives the primary ontology, but rather of understanding ontology as itself a matter of grasping the generation of a domain through the dynamic, structured, reciprocal interplay of elements within it. Similarly, if we take seriously the interconnection of ontology with methodology, then a proper understanding of method ought to involve an understanding of the way in which any domain is indeed generated through this sort of interplay, and cannot be understood through appeal to any "methodology" that insists on a single level of explanation or description or on a single structure or entity as the basis for all else. Here the necessary interconnection of ontology and methodology is reinforced once again.

THE GENERALITY OF UNDERSTANDING

The concern with the "generality" of any ontological account can, however, be put in slightly different terms to those which I have just considered. Indeed, it can be put in terms of an objection to the account I have advanced: that in looking to such a general "ontological" account, one is thereby looking to identify a general explanatory factor *in addition* to those more specific and concrete factors that are operative in any particular instance. This objection can be seen as an instance of the "suspicion of metaphysics" that I discussed earlier as a feature of much social scientific theorising a suspicion that is manifest in an emphasis on concrete, empirical circumstances, particular to each case, over any more general account. In the case of my emphasis on failure within the account of governance, one might say that the objection at issue is that we do not need an "ontological" account to explain or describe failure (or incompleteness or partiality)—we already have all we need in the particular circumstances that obtain in each case. To look for more than this is to look for an unnecessary additional level of explanation or description.

It seems to me, however, that this sort of objection essentially misunderstands the nature of explanation or description. It is like claiming that to explain or to describe the operation of a particular car engine on the basis of an abstract understanding of the processes involved in the internal combustion engine in general, is to postulate another cause of that engine's capacity to do work in addition to the *explain x -because when you explain x -take on a view of x - x-can't be completely objectively explained*

particular instances of those processes—the igniting of gas in this chamber producing an expansion of this gas moving this piston—involved in the operation of that particular engine. In fact, the general level of analysis is not additional to the more particular level. There is no primary level of explanation or description, to assume otherwise is precisely what is entailed in the tendency towards metaphysicality. Moreover, particular levels of explanation or description typically call upon or entail more general levels. Thus, certain explanations and descriptions of the operation of *this* engine—the very one that is installed in the car I drive—are not independent of, but do indeed call upon other, more general explanatory and descriptive frameworks.

Of course, the type of account that I have been sketching here is not merely characterised by its generality; it is also a type of account that is intended to apply at a level of generality that encompasses almost all and every domain. In this respect, it might be thought that, whatever else might be said, such an account is merely a disguised form of metaphysics after all. Yet the account that I claim can be found in Heidegger and in Foucault, and that I have elaborated in terms of the notion of governance, is an account that, unlike traditional metaphysical accounts, does not propose any single entity or substantive principle as the basis of any and every domain. In this respect, if the approach is viewed in any way as "metaphysical", then it is a sort of "empty" metaphysics, a metaphysics, if it is that, that can be seen to consist in a rethinking of the metaphysical demand for explanation or reason itself. This is evident, I think, in Foucault, in the turn towards description rather than explanation. The idea that a strict dichotomy between these two can actually be sustained is, as I noted earlier, problematic, but if we take this emphasis on description as having a fundamentally rhetorical point, then we can understand Foucault's concern with description over explanation as a matter of directing our attention away from the typically metaphysical attempt to discover some deeper rationale for things that is to be found in some ultimate level of causes or explanatory principles (Foucault's emphasis on description can be seen to have some affinities with a similar emphasis in Wittgenstein, in whose work there is a strong anti-metaphysical tendency also).

In Heidegger, the possibility of rethinking the metaphysical is evident in his attempts to rethink the very concept of "ground", or "*Grund*" (see especially Heidegger 1957). This emphasis on rethinking fundamental concepts and modes of procedure may lead one to view the approach at issue here as really more methodological than ontological, but on this point I reiterate my earlier argument that ontology and methodology are always bound together. The approach advanced here, and that I suggest can be found in Heidegger and Foucault, is both ontological and methodological, it may or may not be construed as "metaphysical" depending on exactly how the metaphysical is understood.

The fact that this approach does indeed retain a commitment to providing a certain general level of analysis that obtains across domains should not, then, be seen as compromising the analysis generated, as retaining some problematically

Empty metaphysics

more descriptive than explanatory

Easier to describe phenomena generally –

"metaphysical" orientation. To argue that the very attempt at generalisation across domains is problematic is to misunderstand the project of understanding itself. It is only by looking to integrate phenomena within broader frames of analysis and to connect different phenomena together within more general schemas that phenomena are made intelligible, amenable to description, and accessible to even limited forms of explanation. Indeed, it is precisely through such a generalising and unifying approach to phenomena that governance itself operates in defining the objects to which its attention is directed. And, in this respect, all governing projects are the same, inasmuch as they establish—or, if one prefers, "subjugate"—certain phenomena as objects within specific governmental frames. Consequently, one need not view the tendency towards generality that is an element in "metaphysicality" as problematic in itself. It merely exemplifies, in a particular form, a tendency that is an inevitable feature of any project of understanding and of any project of governance. There is no escape from the need to attend to questions of ontology to think that we can, as a way of somehow escaping metaphysics, only throws us back into it once more.

The critique of metaphysics cannot be accomplished by simply rejecting any form of general ontological analysis. In this respect, while the account I have offered here does indeed oppose itself to metaphysics, it does not do so simply by the outright rejection of metaphysics (a rejection that typically abjures metaphysics on the one hand while nevertheless reasserting it on the other). Thus, the account I have advanced is one that takes a stand against traditional metaphysics on the basis of a certain definite ontological, and therefore also methodological, position. Indeed, the account offered here actually makes possible an answer to the question of why traditional metaphysics is problematic and to the question of why the tendency towards metaphysicality is nevertheless a recurrent feature of inquiry.

For Heidegger, of course, the tendency towards metaphysics is a function of what he called, in *Sein und Zeit*, "falling" ("*Verfallenheit*") and that is exemplified, in one form, in the tendency on the part of agents to become immersed in their activities such that they are blinded to anything that lies outside, in a way that also leads agents to identify activities with their results. Thus, agents are typically forgetful of the larger frameworks in which particular activities are embedded, typically viewing things only in terms of the extent to which they can be acted upon so as to achieve certain results. Agents come to view activity itself in ways that often fail to reflect its dynamic character. Modern empiricism and scientism, and modern technology, are, for Heidegger, one manifestation of this tendency towards understanding the world in terms of what is achievable and manipulable. In general terms, metaphysics can be seen as rising out of a tendency to view the world in terms of only those aspects or features that are presented within particular forms of activity within the world. In terms of my account of governance, the metaphysical tendency towards understanding things in terms of a single structure, entity or set of entities arises as a natural consequence of viewing the world from within the framework of particular governing projects such a narrowing of vision arising as a natural consequence of the need to focus on objects in just those respects in which they are subject to governing control. The generalising and "reductive" character of metaphysics thus arises as a consequence of the way in which governance involves the combination of a certain narrowness of focus, onto just those aspects relevant to governmental control, and the breadth of governmental ambition that is implicit in the very attempt at control. Metaphysics is governance writ large, but with its narrowness of vision and breadth of ambition writ larger still.

SCEPTICISM AND HISTORICISATION

The sort of ontological account I have sketched here is one that gives special emphasis to the partial and limited character of every project, whether "theoretical" or "practical", and to the inevitable tendency for those projects to fall short of their goals. But understanding the limited and partial character of any and every project is only possible on the basis of an ontological account of what makes possible any such project at all. In this respect, the critique of metaphysics is only possible on the basis, not of some set of supposedly "neutral" methodological observations or precepts, but of an account of the ontological and methodological basis for all forms of inquiry and for all domains of inquiry. This is a point that is already clearly evident in Kant's *Kritik der Reinen Verkunft* and it is a point that marks out the Kantian critique of metaphysics from almost any previous attempt at such a critique. Indeed, one can view the anti-metaphysical positions formulated prior to Kant as largely consisting in forms of scepticism that were unable to stop their own sceptical weapons being used against them (this was certainly Kant's view of Hume's position for instance). Kant is not hostile to scepticism and its anti-metaphysical tendencies, but explicitly views it as an advance over the dogmatism that is typical of the metaphysician (see Kant 1781/1787: A761/B789). The Kantian criticism of scepticism, and so of earlier forms of anti-metaphysics, consists simply in the fact that, while scepticism sets limits to understanding, and so shows the pretensions of metaphysics to be false, it provides no account of how those limits obtain (see Kant 1781/1787: A767–8/B795–6). Consequently, it cannot provide any ground for those limits without itself lapsing into dogmatism.

It is this deficiency in previous "sceptical" critiques that Kant aims, in part, to remedy (though he also, of course, has certain practical-ethical objectives to advance). I would characterise my account of governance, along with the "ontological" projects I have attempted to discern in Foucault and Heidegger, as operating along rather similar lines to those found in Kant as establishing the limits and parameters of social scientific or philosophical inquiry through the articulation of the ontological and methodological structure that underlies it. In this respect, such approaches can be viewed as attempts to formulate a position that retains the anti-metaphysicality of scepticism, while resisting the dogmatism to which scepticism is prone, by providing an account of that which both constitutes and limits all forms of inquiry.

Of course, the thinking of both Foucault and Heidegger is often associated with a tendency towards historicisation and this might be thought a common feature of many such "sceptical" and "anti-metaphysical" approaches. One escapes metaphysics, it seems, through an assertion of absolute socio-historical particularity and determination. This has been especially true of the way in which Foucault's thought has often been taken up within the social sciences. Foucault, by this reading, is seen as promoting a mode of analysis that looks only to the particular socio-historical circumstances in which phenomena are embedded. Sometimes a similar tendency is discerned in Heidegger, particularly in the emphasis, in the later Heidegger, on the idea of there being successive stages in the "History of Being" (direct parallels are sometimes drawn with Foucault on this point).

This might be seen as presenting certain problems for the analysis I have advanced here, in the sense that such an historicised approach must be inconsistent with my emphasis on a general ontological analysis. Alternatively it might be thought to imply that the general ontological account I have sketched must be instantiated differently in different socio-historical circumstances in such a way that the ontology could be viewed as determined by those circumstances and unique to them (thereby effectively making spurious any claims to real generality).

In fact, while it is, of course, the case that how any ontological structure is instantiated will depend very much on concrete socio-historical circumstances, this need not imply that one cannot generalise in such cases. Moreover, it is important to recognise the way in which, once again, the tendency to historicisation can be viewed as another manifestation of a tendency towards metaphysicality. This is so whether we treat such historicisation in terms of the idea of a "History of Being" or in terms of the more mundane idea that all phenomena are socio-historical products to be explained only socio-historically. The thrust of my reading of Foucault and Heidegger as engaged in an anti-metaphysical critique (albeit a constructive critique), is that there is no level of analysis, no single structure or entity that is ontologically—and this means explanatorily or descriptively—primary. Historical circumstance is no more a privileged level of analysis than is any other. Moreover the necessary partiality and multiplicity that accompanies all activity, every exercise of power, every governmental practice, implies a corresponding multiplicity in the ways in which particular phenomena can be addressed.

CONCLUSION: TRUTH AND SELF-FORMATION

Recognising the ways in which objects and practices arise as elements within complex, differentiated and interconnected fields ought to lead to a recognition of the need to attend carefully to the complexity and differentiated character of those interconnections. But it ought also to lead to a recognition of the impossibility of any specification of the interconnections in their entirety. Inquiry, whether social scientific or philosophical, is always characterised by a partiality of vision and a multiplicity of approaches. Understanding phenomena in their socio-historical specificity need not entail any form of ontological relativisation, nor need it imply the priority of the historical over other forms of analysis.

This point is especially important when it comes to the attempt to understand, describe or explain intellectual practices or productions. The project of careful, historically situated description of particular practices, objects, ways of life, or modes of thought does not rule out other projects that may take up those practices, objects and so forth under different, if sometimes related, frames. Thus, a particular philosophical position, or a specific political movement, may be understood both as it arises within a quite specific and localised set of historical circumstances, on the one hand, and, on the other, in terms of those elements within it that have, or purport to have, a broader and more universal application. To suppose otherwise, and to think that the necessary situatedness of intellectual production implies the necessary restriction of the ideas produced to just the original situation in which they appeared, is to confuse the conditions of intellectual production with the conditions of intellectual concern. Moreover, that a position is elaborated under quite specific historical or cultural circumstances, while it may shed useful light on the question of how that position is to be understood, has little relevance for the question of whether that position is logically consistent, supported by the available evidence, or, most fundamentally perhaps, whether the claims in which that position consists are true (for more on truth see Malpas 1996).

It may well be said, of course, that truth itself is constituted only within particular governing practices and so within quite specific historical, cultural or even political locations. In that case, truth would itself be an "effect" of the complex ontology of "governance" or "power". Yet, while the terms in which any particular claim may be couched are certainly dependent for their meaning on the particular context in which that claim is situated, the truth of the claim is not, for the most part, determined by context in just that way. A particular governing practice, a particular field of power-relations, can be seen as establishing, in Foucault's phrase, a particular "regime of truth". But to say that it does this is to say no more than that it establishes a certain "semantics"—it establishes the meanings of the terms employed within it—and a certain framework for verifying the truth or falsity of particular claims. Such a regime of truth does not establish any system of *truths* as such, but only a method for deciding on what is to be *held true*.

For example, the governing or ordering practice associated with the maintenance of a motor vehicle provides us with a framework within which we can assign a certain meaning to particular terms and utterances. It also provides us at the same time with a framework within which we can decide whether or not certain utterances should be held true, but it does not determine the actual truth

Truth/failure — manner of interpretation

or falsity of those utterances. Indeed, that it cannot do so is a corollary of the necessary incompleteness and partiality of all practices, projects and power. Truth extends beyond any particular governmental practice or system of power relations, just as things themselves do. Indeed, in Heidegger, truth is itself tied to the very possibility of the appearance—the disclosure—of things (see the discussion of this in Malpas 1992: 260 *et seq*).

The emphasis on the limited and partial character of all theoretical and practical activity is something that ought to lead us to be sceptical of the pretensions of metaphysics, wherever they arise. But it ought also lead us to be sceptical of the metaphysical pretensions that are expressed, quite frequently in social scientific circles, in the idea that social theory is committed to a certain set of socially ameliorative or politically progressive goals. Often the commitment to such ideals springs both from an exaggerated view of the capacities of governmental control and from a tendency towards metaphysical modes of thought— from a view that governance is geared towards success rather than failure, and from a tendency to understand the world as ordered around single structures or entities, rather than in terms of a field constituted by the reciprocal interplay or contestation among mutually defining and mutually limiting elements. The ontologically constructive "anti-metaphysics" outlined here suggests, however, that practical social and political intervention can only ever be partial and localised, and must always be prepared to adjust itself in the face of the resisting and recalcitrant character of its objects. In this respect, a theoretically sophisticated social theory ought to be a constant reminder, to those who would offer narratives of social improvement and political progress, of the necessary limitation, and inevitable tendency to failure, of all such narratives, rather than being itself caught up in the formulation of such stories.

— Always be failure

* —

The critique of metaphysics need not imply a rejection of ontological modes of analysis, but does indeed depend on such analysis. Moreover, the connection of ontology with methodology suggests that not only is ontological analysis a necessary component in the formulation of social, and philosophical, theorising, but it also indicates the way in which the articulation of a social-theoretical or philosophical self-conception must be bound up, not only with methodological, but also with ontological considerations. To reflect on the nature and practice of social theory, of philosophy, and of socio-legal study, is also to reflect on the ontology that governs these and all such domains. Moreover, the self-reflexivity that is implied here does not function only at the theoretical or even disciplinary level.

Pierre Hadot's *Exercices Spirituels et Philosophie Antique* (Hadot 1987), translated into English as *Philosophy as a Way of Life,* emphasises the way in which Classical and Hellenistic conceptions of philosophy were tied to the idea of philosophy as an activity essentially directed, not so much at the achievement of knowledge, as at a certain kind of self-formation. Philosophical practice was thus directed primarily at the self rather than the world. This idea is, of course, an important element in the late Foucault's interest in practices of

- Nobody is above the law - interpretation includes the self "

self-government (it can also be discerned in some of Nietzsche's writing). Such an emphasis on self-formation is, in fact, a characteristic feature of philosophy, and, perhaps, of intellectual disciplines in general. Such disciplines are typically directed at the formation of a certain kind of self, as much as they are directed at the achievement of certain forms of knowledge.

One might take this as exemplary of the "metaphysical" or even "religious" background in which intellectual life has often been embedded. It certainly is partly indicative of this. Of greater significance, however, is the way in which the characterisation of intellectual work as always a work of self-formation can be seen to derive from the ontological constitution of selves and practices within the same "governmental" field. Every form of activity or practice involves self-formation and self-constitution, inasmuch as the self is a structure defined and established only through its involvement in projective activity, in systems of power and resistance, in practices of governance. Of course, such processes of self-formation, precisely because they are self-formative, can never be completely controlled or directed. The project of self-formation is as limited and constrained, and just as unpredictable, as is any other project whether at the governmental, corporative, or individual level. In this respect, the task of the social theorist, and perhaps of the philosopher also, is not so much one of attempting, in any large-scale fashion, to change or to redirect the field of governmental activity, as of mapping its dynamic, complex and differentiated character.

9

The Art of Critique or How Not to be Governed Thus

GEORGE PAVLICH

INTRODUCTION

R EVIEWING WHAT PASSES for current knowledge on how to govern people, one is likely to apprehend the privilege granted to technocratic political rationalities. Claims to improve the efficiency and cost effectiveness of almost any regulatory technique abound. The discourses of critics who question the founding logic and aspirations of dominant governmental patterns are much less prominent. I doubt any social analyst would now confidently declare, as did Kant when reflecting on his times, anything like this: "our age is, in especial degree, the age of criticism, and to criticism everything must submit" (Kant 1958: 7). Ours is more an age of the technocrat, and to achieving the maximum efficiency of any system all must submit. We might well ponder the plight of critique, or how to resist a rolling neo-conservative juggernaut that declares the "end of ideology" and eschews criticism as irrelevant. The entrepreneurial technocrat as line manager, spouting neo-liberal languages of cost efficiency and accountable outcomes, has muscled in as the mainstay of a political climate in which critical (revolutionary?) punditry lies in ruins.

The fading image of the critic as expert judge, prescriptive guru, or revolutionary, leaves ashen traces of a spirit which once leaned out towards universal justice and perpetual peace (Ransom 1997: 1–3). Noble and laudable aspirations indeed, but such critics confined themselves to independently founded judgement aimed at guiding us towards social advancement. Critique and the founded judgement of the expert became virtually synonymous. Yet, our knowledge-producing arenas have altered markedly, and the language of critical judgement has lost the epistemological cachet it once commanded (Lyotard 1984; Bauman 1997). In the current ethos of uncertainty, enunciating one universally valid social order through expert judgement is met with indifference, if not incredulity (Pavlich 1995). Prescribing, ordering, preaching, admonishing, and condemning are activities whose legitimacy is tied to the fate of the experts and authorities ordained by erstwhile regulatory modes. In an ethos that recognises value in masking naked coercion, and heralds the technical efficiency of governing from invisible shadows, the judgements of previously demarcated experts are increasingly irrelevant (Bauman 1987; Rose 1996b).

With the abating reign of critic as expert judge, it seems apposite to expand the spaces from which to mount critical challenges. For we must surely avoid the danger—common where critique is marginalised—of allowing governmental rationales and programmes to be launched as if absolutely necessary, as if governors have no choice. After all, in the murky recesses of history where critical dissent is suppressed, one often finds the breeding ground of totalitarian governmental subjections (for example, fascism, apartheid, Stalinism). In light of such catastrophes, and in witness to unarticulated injustices that surround us today, this chapter describes a vision of critique designed to enunciate problematic effects associated with advanced liberal governmental patterns (see Rose 1996b). However, I shall not emulate critical theory's penchant to associate criticism with visions of founded judgement, or its concomitant quest to distinguish ideology from truth. Rather, the faltering plight of critique requires a wholly different approach, one which focuses on an image of critique beyond judgement, though without deferring exclusively to notions of genealogy (see Dean 1994: 117–19; Owen 1995; Visker 1995; O'Malley, Weir and Shearing 1997). This takes seriously that:

> "There are many styles of critique, and critique can be directed to a range of subject matters. But a thread running through the styles of critique is an oppositional attitude that highlights the disparity between what is taken as given and what should be. Critique always presupposes some idea in the name of which we engage in critique—however we conceive of this idea and whatever status we claim for it" (Bernstein 1988: 257).

Although I would replace "should" for "could" in the above quotation, its main point—that judgement constitutes one amongst many genres of critique—is apposite.

The following narrative proceeds thus. To begin, I focus on the etymology of the terms "critique" and "criticism" to suggest how, over centuries, judgement has informed dominant genres of political critique. The privilege granted to "critique as judgement" in modern social thinking, however, loses its mooring within the uncertain knowledge-producing arenas facing us nowadays. This realisation prefaces an attempt to redefine critique by (re-)associating it with previously popular images of "separation" and "discernment", rather than judgement. Deferring to Foucault's work on governmentality and critique, the chapter then traces an alternate genre of critique, one that might enunciate injustices within current patterns of governance. Such a genre emerged alongside the "art of government", which focused on the question of "how to govern"; it constantly confronted challenges directed at "how not to be governed thus". Such challenges contain the seeds of a non-judgemental art of critique that could be mobilised within governmental arenas. The final sections of the chapter explore such critique, echoing other attempts to conceptualise resistance to contemporary governance (Ransom 1997; O'Malley 1996c), exploiting the contradictions (Valverde 1996) and failures (Malpas and Wickham 1995) within.

CRITICISM AS JUDGEMENT FOUNDED IN REASON

The words "criticism", "crisis", and "critique" derive from the Greek word *krinein*, to judge, separate, discern, select, differentiate and decide (Koselleck 1988: 103 at note 15). Over time, critique has been associated with at least three spheres of activity: medical diagnoses of crisis stages for a given illness (for example, when someone is in a "critical" condition); judicial decision making; and (Hellenistic) philology directed at literary texts (see Connerton 1980). Criticism has been respectively associated with notions of crisis, judgement or authenticity (Con Davis and Schleifer 1991). Koselleck indicates that the word criticism then "moved away from the originally corresponding word 'crisis' and continues to refer to the art of judging" (Koselleck 1988: 104).

This trend was developed during the Renaissance where both judicial and philological institutions deferred to criticism as a vehicle for judging the truth. The main task of criticism then "consisted in a return to an original condition, and in a determination to reconstruct the authenticity of a source" (Connerton 1980: 17). The older "truth by revelation" is gradually overshadowed by critical practices charged with judging truth on the basis of reason:

> "Critique came to be seen no longer as a symptom of the sharpening opposition between reason and revelation. It was viewed as itself the activity which separated the two spheres. It was the essential activity of reason" (Connerton 1980: 18).

The posture of critique as reasoned judgement was transposed to governmental arenas through such works as Bayle's *Dictionnaire Historique et Critique* (1697/1965). Here, one detects a reliance on reason to judge the truth behind the injustices of political techniques. Through such developments, complemented by the rising number of "critiques" issued from an emerging public domain, the idea of criticism became almost indistinguishable from concepts of founded judgement (see Con Davis and Schleifer 1991: 3–5).

The link between founded judgement and critique is consolidated throughout the nineteenth century with the development of what Con Davis and Schleifer describe as two "modes" of critique. On the one hand, there is a Kantian-inspired mode that "subjects the actual to relentless questioning in order to discover sufficient reason why it should be so and not otherwise" (Con Davis and Schleifer 1991: 23). The point of such critique is to establish the unshakeable grounds of given actualities. On the other hand, there is a Hegelian (and later Marxist) "transformative" critique which "aims to make something happen, to assert that things could be otherwise, that what exists is not necessary" and that critique can allow us to imagine "a narrative in which things could be different from what they are" (Con Davis and Schleifer 1991: 25). Interestingly, Foucault (1994: 147–48) discerns both these modes of criticism within Kant's thinking. The point I wish to emphasise here, however, is that each consolidates an image of critique as judgement. Both modes, it seems to me, embrace versions of critique as judgement.

For instance, Kant's influential investigations into the auspices of critique try to overcome the "pre-critical" approaches of either dogmatic absolutism or anarchic relativism (see Hutchings 1996; Goetschel 1994). It is noteworthy that traces of the distinction remain intact in more recent formulations of a debate between Habermas and Foucault on their different approaches to critical theory (Habermas 1987; Foucault 1982; 1988a; see also Hoy and McCarthy 1996; Kelly 1994; Bernstein 1994). Kant sought reasons for accepting particular criteria as universally valid, Archimedean points of reference from which to judge. His reflexive project mobilised critique to identify its own limits; he supposed that understanding such limits would isolate foundations based on pure reason. In a related approach, Habermas' (1984; 1987) neo-Kantian thinking isolates communicative reason designed to yield universal criteria for critical judgements. By contrast, Hegelian and Marxist approaches that endorse judgemental critique do not seek apodictic foundations for criteria; rather, they rely on dialectical reason to develop immanently formulated criteria that might be used to judge a given social being, and allude to progressive alternatives. As Benhabib explains, Marx distinguishes (Kantian) criticism from critique because:

> "Criticism privileges an Archimedean standpoint, be it freedom or reason, and proceeds to show the unfreedom or unreasonableness of the world when measured against this ideal paradigm. By privileging this Archimedean point, criticism becomes dogmatism, it leaves its own standpoint unexplained, or it assumes the validity of its standpoint prior to engaging in the task of criticism" (Benhabib 1986: 33).

By alluding to a version of Hegel's dialectic, Marx offers an historicised version of critique (see also Dean 1994: 117–19). He wrests criteria from contradictions within existing social conditions to outline emancipatory possibilities (see Benhabib 1986).

Despite differences between these genres of critique, each relies on judgement based on reason—be it pure, communicative or dialectical—as a guide to social progress. Subsequent elaborations of the theme by critical theorists emulate the tendency:

> "Within the terms of critical theory, 'critique' stands for that process by which the pathological processes of rationalisation can be judged from the perspective of universal values and in the name of 'emancipation' " (Dean 1994: 129–30).

There is, no doubt, a comforting element to these formulations, but such comfort has done little to prevent social disasters, wars or expunged social, economic and political injustice. The point is not to assign blame; perhaps the self-enunciated brief was too ambitious in the first place. In any case, the grammar of this critique has proved difficult to sustain in an epistemological ethos wracked by uncertainty (Bauman 1997). Hence, one might fruitfully consider genres of critique that do not defer to founded judgement (for example, Dean 1994; Owen 1995; O'Malley, Weir and Shearing 1997; Ransom 1997).

FOUNDED JUDGEMENT AND UNCERTAINTY

The brief discussion above indicates how critique as founded judgement has been appropriated by quite different legacies of critique. Yet the approach falls on hard times when confronting an uncertain ethos not committed to a (modern) faith in universally valid foundations (Bauman 1997; Pavlich 1998). Lyotard (1984) argues that postmodern conditions licence knowledge production practices different from those previously evident. In particular, claims to knowledge are no longer made on the basis of putative "metanarratives" (for example, philosophical speculation, emancipation). The belief that philosophy (science) can yield eternally valid truths, or lead the way to universal emancipation, has at best waned; at worst, it has fallen into disrepute (Lyotard 1984: 37 *et seq*). For instance, in light of the diverse political claims staked by very different identities (for example, based on gender, sexuality, race, ethnicity, age, culture, etc.), the promise of one progressive social order, or that universal emancipation can liberate all identities, is difficult to validate. Can an overarching metanarrative really address the diverse oppressions within and between contexts, or a universal response be mounted to overcome them all? Baldly asserting faith in some or other universal reason, or capitalist revolution, as a necessary response resounds a hollow echo within the uncertain dystopias that have followed the collapse communist states (Walton 1998).

Yet by holding onto critique as judgement, many critics have failed to take account of the shifting epistemological horizons within which they seek to legitimate their claims. Indeed, the business-as-usual approach has limited the impact of critical challenges and spread the technocratic approaches noted before. Without legitimate critical challenges, statements claiming to increase the technical efficiency or performance of systems (for example, the criminal justice system) enjoy a privileged status (see Lyotard 1984). Questions directed at the foundations of systems (for example, is there such a thing as crime requiring criminal justice systems?) are sidelined, or simply relegated to the realm of idealistic irrelevance. If nothing else, this suggests the value of developing alternative critical genres capable of wresting legitimacy by contesting the limits of contemporary knowledge-producing arenas.

Furthermore, the notion that critique involves judgement predicated on universally valid foundations demands critics to be legislating experts. The latter implies privileged access to reason-based criteria for judgement, and a pundit capable of judging conditions against these. Such legislating practices find a home in modern contexts hell-bent on ordering and advancing the putative chaos of history. However, as Bauman (1992) notes, in an uncertain ethos where the very assumption of a unified order, of progress, is held in abeyance, where knowledge does not appear capable of decoding one essential order, the generation of knowledge is less likely to involve legislation than to licence multiple interpretations (see also Canguilhem 1998). If the condition requires a different image of critique, it also implies the limited value of holding fast to notions of critique as founded judgement. Barthes puts the matter thus:

> "So long as criticism had the traditional function of judging, it could not but be conformist, that is to say in conformity with the interests of the judges. However, the true *criticism* of institutions and languages does not consist in judging them, but in perceiving, in separating, in dividing" (Barthes 1987: 33, emphasis in original).

Although I have reservations about this "true criticism", the statement usefully alludes to critique beyond the language of judgement. It alerts us to an etymological lineage other than judgement and allows us to consider critique as an activity of separating, discerning and dividing. Here, the "grammar" of critique as necessarily requiring a normative basis ("measure or standard") from which to judge is questioned (Bernstein 1994: 213). Our epistemological horizons may no longer countenance necessary standards, or experts to define them; but this does not mean the intelligibility of critique is at stake. It does, however, indicate the limits of judgemental genres, and may even suggest the value of framing an alternative opposition attitude for a "politics of resistance" (Pickett 1996), or, indeed, a "post-social politics that is the successor to socialism" (O'Malley, Weir and Shearing 1997: 508).

In this light, let us turn our attention to reconceiving critique beyond judgement, specifically by returning to etymological traces of critique as separating, discerning, etc. Here, I echo the spirit of Foucault's dream:

> "I can't help but dream about a kind of criticism that would try not to judge but to bring an oeuvre, a book, a sentence, an idea to life; it would light fires, watch the grass grow, listen to the wind, and catch the sea foam in the breeze and scatter it. It would multiply not judgements but signs of existence; it would summon them, drag them from their sleep. Perhaps it would invent them sometimes—all the better" (Foucault 1994: 323).

The following section attempts to explore an alternative genre of critique in the spirit of problematising governing truths.

A GENEALOGY OF GOVERNMENTAL CRITIQUE

Phrased thus, our discussion could usefully draw on Foucault's (1997b) formulations of critique as a "limit attitude" that emerged alongside a certain "governmentality" (Foucault 1991; see also Schmidt and Wartenberg 1994, for a summary and discussion of Foucault's analysis of critique). This is not the place to canvas the numerous discussions interpreting his neologism, but we might refer to its concern with "mentalities of rule" that arose beyond, but with the aim of strengthening, medieval state formations (see, for instance, Allen 1991; Rose and Miller 1992; Burchell, Gordon and Miller 1991; Hunter 1993; Dean 1994; Curtis 1995; Valverde 1996). These mentalities of rule intimate visions of what it is to govern subjects, who is governed, by whom and so on (Gordon 1991). Here we find a certain "art of government" that since the fifteenth century has concerned itself with the question of how to govern individual subjects and their identities. Classical liberal governmentality offered a particularly important conception of how to govern by enticing individual subjects to develop themselves according to a so-called true, autonomous human nature (Burchell 1991; 1993). This political logic recognised the value of governing subjects invisibly, efficiently and continuously (Foucault 1997b: 27), and postulated various objects of singular (for example, individuals) and collective (for example, population, society) governance. For Foucault, such liberal governmentality fuses two previous political rationalities. On the one hand, it defers to the pastoral power of Christian rule which had appropriated the metaphor of a shepherd leading a flock. This political logic seeks governing techniques directed at each member to secure the entire flock's well-being (Foucault 1981; 1982). The well-being of each political entity is deemed crucial to the well-being of all; the singular subject is isolated as an important target for governing the whole. On the other hand, Foucault notes the city-citizen model of the *polis* as a political entity comprising many individuals capable of choosing their future directions. The modern state fuses these political logics, and encourages a "governmentalisation" of the state, techniques of governing singular entities for the good of a collective create the freedom inherent in the notion of the democratic state (Foucault 1991).

At the same time, Foucault consistently argues (in response to various critiques) that all forms of power are deployed only with the permanent possibility of resistance. That is, power relations always "open up a space in the middle of which the struggles develop" (Foucault 1989: 187). Intrinsic to this understanding is his view that power is possible only through the "recalcitrance of freedom". Thus, resistance is endemic to power relations: "Where there is power, there is resistance" (Foucault 1977: 95). Applying this insight in context, it seems that mentalities of how to govern are deployed in the face of struggles directed at an opposing quest, how not to be governed thus. In Foucault's words, facing visions of how to govern:

> "head on and as compensation, or rather, as both partner and adversary to the arts of governing as a challenge, as a way of limiting these arts of governing and transforming them there would have been something born in Europe at that time—which I would very simply call the art of not being governed like that and at that cost" (Foucault 1997b: 28–9).

So, governmentalities are constitutively related to the resistance provided by "adversary" attitudes directed at their limits.

Now, the many different instances of this counter-mentality which focus on "how not to be governed thus" do not always take the form of judgemental critique. One can derive alternative genres of critique from diffuse challenges to governmental power. Foucault (1997b) describes, for example, how an attitude of critique emerges out of resistance to government in three "historical anchoring points" (1997b: 29). First, he points to the church's pastoral governance where the mentalities (soul) of each church member is shaped through prescriptions that claim to derive from authentic scriptures. This way of governing was challenged by various critics, from Wycliffe to Bayle, who questioned the authority of particular church institutions, as well as interpretations of the scriptures. In contemplating how not to be governed thus, these critics reflected a particular attitude towards the limits of their times.

Secondly, Foucault points to the increasing reliance on legal institutions in sixteenth century medieval governance and notes the associated critical challenges directed at specific laws. Such affronts mostly assumed a legal form, and focused on universal rights, or the "limits of the right to govern" (Foucault 1997b: 31). While the problem of natural law looms prominent in these challenges, indicating overlaps with judgemental forms of critique, there is also a prominent (liberal) limit-attitude directed at proper restrictions on government (see Burchell 1993).

For Foucault, the third anchoring point for this alternative critique is reflected by an enlightenment "problem of certainty in its confrontation with authority" (Foucault 1997b: 31). In experiments with secular visions of governance, many critics questioned any general claim to speak with authority. This spawned a critical attitude which refused to accept authoritative declarations of truth unless valid reasons could be offered for the truth of any claim. Foucault extracts from Kant's text "What is Enlightenment?" a clear example of such an attitude. In this essay, Kant *inter alia* contrasts the Enlightenment to a state of tutelage (too much government) in which subjects blindly follow the dictates of an authority (for example, the church). This prevents them from grasping their real conditions. Kant invites subjects to have the courage to embrace their natural autonomy by using an innate reason to achieve political maturity. Here, Foucault detects one version of critique as a response to a modern governmentalisation of medieval state control. That is, Kant's work sets the stage for an interplay between government and critique in the nineteenth and twentieth centuries, and encourages a relentless critique of authority.

Through each of these historical anchors, or lines of descent, Foucault identifies examples of an ongoing tension between the mechanisms of governance (that is, how to govern in this or that way) and resistance offered through a critical attitude which contemplates how not to be governed thus. It is important to stress, however, that critique does not contest governance as a whole; rather it voices the excesses, limitations and perverse effects of locally deployed governmental techniques. No doubt, this critique can (and often does) enunciate visions of injustice, unfairness, dissent, etc. (Pavlich 1998). Overall, it involves a counter-mentality that opposes specific governing truths, and could also be viewed as:

> "the movement by which the subject gives himself [sic] the right to question truth on its effects of power and question power on its discourses of truth" (Foucault 1997b: 32).

This critique contests specific power-knowledge relations that govern subjects. Yet, and this is the point I would emphasise, it does not necessarily do so through founded judgement. Rather, another view of critique is that of a counter-mentality which questions, separates, discerns and divides the truths used to govern subjects in this or that way. Clearly, the practices of reflecting on the limits of specific power-knowledge formations are likely to assume diverse local forms, rendering any static definition redundant. Rather than proposing any ontology of critique, one could appropriate a Derridean (Derrida 1994) "hautology" that grapples with the "spirit" of an art centred around the issue of how not to be governed in this way.

THE ART OF GOVERNMENTAL CRITIQUE

The spirit of a political critique not contained by judgement attends to relations where subjects contest and define specific governmental patterns as problematic (unjust, harmful, unequal, etc.). We might describe this critique as a counter-mentality which contests and stands apart from given mentalities of rule (I shall here draw on various aspects of Foucault 1997b: Part I, a set of influential analyses of critique, Enlightenment and revolution). There are various ways in which subjects detach themselves—however partially, successfully or incompletely—to problematise the limits that constitute them as subjects of particular governmental formations. This critique could contain elements of a genealogy that disrupts by pointing both to the emergence and lines of descent of given "ontologies"; but it might also encourage deconstructive practices that gesture towards alternative possibilities beyond (here, Visker's 1995 image of "genealogy as critique" may be useful; so too may Owen's 1995 formulation, though this formulation runs counter to the "hautology" at hand and begins to look suspiciously like renewing the role of critic as legislating expert). In Foucault's parlance, such an activity implies a "limit attitude" that problematises governmental practices and the limits these impose. It is disruptive when it debunks the taken-for-granted, and opens the present to that which lies beyond its limits (Ransom 1997: 1–9; Falzon 1998). Such a counter-mentality assumes that:

> "the things which seem most evident to us are always formed in the confluence of encounters and chances, during the course of a precarious and fragile history" (Foucault 1988a: 37) .

In trying to evoke the mentality of this critical genre, I am reminded of (haunted by?) a formative event in my mid-teenage years. In South Africa, I recall a newspaper article decrying the resistance generated by the Soweto riots. The report was, for me at least, completely overshadowed by a photograph of a youth poised to throw a stone at an oncoming troop carrier. His eyes divulged a commitment to stand out from, defy and rupture present relations. I now see his stance as an extreme example of the critical genre at hand; a subject opting for the possibility of sanction (for example, injury and even death) over the certainty of continuing to be subjected to apartheid governmental techniques. One need not deny judgement to indicate that experiencing governmental limits as unjust can sometimes propel subjects to adopt a mentality counter to the governmentality of the time. If this case indicates the force of injustice, and the courageous resistance it can sometimes inspire, let us nevertheless be clear: what is most significant for our purposes here is the presence of a critical mentality that is also—no doubt more often—found in much less graphic, everyday oppositions. The possibility of this counter-mentality emerging is permanent within any power relation, and its expressions are diverse.

In any case, the counter-mentality suggested by these examples is not a matter of arbitrary opinion; it emerges through the force of the negative effects as experienced, and conceived, by the subjects of specific governmental practices. As such, critique:

> "is no longer going to be practised in the search for formal structures with universal value, but rather as a historical investigation into the events that have led us to constitute ourselves and to recognize ourselves as subjects of what we are doing, thinking, saying" (Foucault 1997b: 125).

This genre of critique involves an historical analysis of present limits, of governmental processes which produce particular forms of existence. As an "historical investigation", it is likely to include procedures that: (1) problematise the present by reminding us of its contingency; (2) uncouple subjects from the limits of governmental forms; and, (3) trace possible transgressions.

Recovering the contingent

As a counter-mentality of rule, critique often emerges when subjects experience governmental limits as unjust, unequal, unfair, and so on. Discontent can help to articulate dissent, and spawn a counter-mentality that contests prevalent governmental rationales and techniques. In trying to assume a counter-governmentality, critics problematise existing patterns of government and claims to instate necessary truths. Critical subjects are entwined within a given governmentality, but they aim to thwart its historical force and glimpse possibilities beyond. However, contemplating other governmental possibilities means diluting the force of claims that given instances of governance are necessary. The dilution implies contesting governing truths, and seeking to recover the contingent struggles through which governmental rationalities and practices come to be. The point of such a counter-governmentality is to show that political practices assembled through the vicissitudes of historical struggle can equally be dismantled and replaced through further struggle.

No doubt, in developing this critical counter-mentality, subjects cannot regard present patterns of existence as essential, natural or necessary. The latter betrays an *a priori* commitment to existing limits, to a unified conception of its present(s). By contrast, counter-mentalities expressly evoke experiences that dissociate, open, welcome and include; they are not concerned with attempts to gather, entrench, defend or exclude on the basis of defining the "essence" of the present. Their focus on dissociation, on opening up to contingent otherness, contrasts with attempts to stamp out rigid limits:

> "Once you grant some privilege to gathering and not to dissociating, then you leave no room for the other, for the radical otherness of the other, for the radical singularity of the other . . . separation, dissociation is not an obstacle to society, to community, but the condition . . . of any unity as such" (Derrida 1997: 14–15).

By emphasising dissociation, the critic permanently opens him/herself up to the contingent other, through which contested governmental techniques are deployed. Etymologically, such a posture gestures towards a spirit of separation, dividing and opening rather than of founded judgement.

Desubjectification and insubordination

In recovering the contingent, critics problematise aspects of a present to extricate themselves (partially at least) from specific limits. Here one might say, as does Foucault, that:

> "Critique will be the art of voluntary insubordination, that of reflected intractability. Critique would essentially insure the desubjugation of the subject in the context of what we would call, in a word, the politics of truth" (Foucault 1997b: 32).

That is, focusing on limits involves subjects challenging, rather than following, particular governmental forms. This involves an "insubordination" which addresses the question of how not to be governed in this or that way. Moreover, the counter-mentality implies a certain "intractability" *vis-a-vis* limits that constitute particular sorts of subjects. In so doing, they engage in complex processes of "desubjectification"; for example, of refusing (rather than trying to achieve) the patterns of subjectivity encouraged by liberal conceptions of individual selfhood (Foucault 1982; Pavlich 1996b). But critics do not thereby escape governance *per se*. Instead, they encounter and challenge specific governmental limits; they address, in other words, the issue of how not to be governed in this or that way.

For instance, as noted, governmentality involves a power which operates through "truth". In the "advanced liberal" societies of which Rose (1996b) speaks, power relations defer to scientific truths about, say, the population, crime, or housing, and perhaps philosophical truths about individuals, selves, democracy, ethics and freedom. Governance operates, that is, by inscribing its subjects in realms of discourse, and requiring them to recognise themselves in the mirrors of truth that it holds out (Pavlich 1996a). In the process, subjects are all too often governed through power relations claiming to preserve necessary truths and realities (for example, the various economic "realities" and "necessities" upon which different neo-liberal platforms have been built; see Derrida 1994). Subjects who contest the truths that enunciate particular identities embrace degrees of insubordination and desubjectification. Thus, particular subjects may detach themselves from liberal governance by refusing the (consuming) free selves nurtured by (neo-) liberal discourses (Rose 1990). Such actions would recognise that nowadays we are governed far more through liberal truths about freedom than through openly coercive and constraining practices. In any case, critical opposition to the limits of governance enters a politics of truth precisely when it contests specific truths about subjects (singular or collective), especially when such knowledge is used to deploy "necessary" patterns of rule.

Tracing possible transgressions

Nietzsche suggests another dimension to a counter-mentality of governance:

> "When we criticise something, this is no arbitrary and impersonal event; it is, at least very often, evidence of vital energies in us that are growing and shedding a skin. We negate and must negate because something in us wants to live and affirm—something that we perhaps do not know or see as yet. This is said in favour of criticism" (Nietzsche 1974: Book 4, 307).

Negating in order to affirm another existence—the pain of birth?—implies transgressing specific limits to a given being. From this vantage, critique involves not only degrees of insubordination and desubjectification, but also tracing possibilities beyond present limits. Echoing a previously discussed line of descent as discerning and dividing, this critique "will separate out, from the contingency that has made us what we are, the possibility of no longer being, doing, thinking what we are, do, or think" (Foucault 1997b: 125).
It involves:

> "an attitude, an ethos, a philosophic life in which the critique of what is at one and the same time the historical analysis of the limits that are imposed on us and an experiment with the possibility of going beyond these" (Foucault 1997b: 132).

Critical work is "experimental" in the sense that it constantly searches to extend, or to exit from, limits. But it does so without certainty, without metaphysical maps to point us assuredly on the road to social progress (Bauman 1997; Canguilhem 1998).

Tracing possible transgressions is directed at finding an exit, a way out from present limits, and making overtures towards possibilities beyond. There is an endlessness about the prospect, for any transgression yields further limits; yet the promise of escaping, or exiting, particular governmental limits is itself endless. Perhaps one might describe the promise as an incalculable idea relentlessly calculated within limits; Derrida (1992) gives this idea various names, such as justice. Our ongoing openness to justice portends a "gesture of fidelity" to the "spirit" rather than the letter of Marx's work; it also implies the relentless search for justice as a promise of escaping what is. As Derrida puts it:

"A deconstructive thinking has always pointed out the irreducibility of affirmation and therefore of the promise, as well as the undeconstructability of a certain idea of justice. Such a thinking cannot operate without justifying the principle of a radical and interminable, infinite (both theoretical and practical, as one used to say) critique. This critique belongs to the movement of an experience open to the absolute future of what is coming, that is to say, a necessarily indeterminate, abstract, desert-like experience that is confided, exposed, given up to its waiting for the other and for the event" (Derrida 1994: 90).

Tracing possible transgressions, then, is an historically-situated posture which leans out towards the future; it does not seek absolute and certain knowledge of what is, preferring to open up, dissociate existing limits. Critique is without end, because no governmental limits are entirely devoid of danger, of potential excesses. Any guarantees promised in the name of progress, the end of history, or perpetual peace, do little more than privilege particular governmental formations. Seeking an exit from the problematic aspects of a present entails adopting an openness to the future, to the promise of the idea of justice that forever eludes any historical calculations that bear its name. The promise of justice, that is, most often motivates us to contemplate how not to be governed thus.

CONCLUSION: ALLUSIONS

This chapter has explored an image of critique appropriate to the (post-social?) political arenas that constitute how we are presently governed. Eschewing the idea that founded judgement is essential to the grammar of critique, I have proffered an alternative, deriving etymologically from notions of separation, division, discernment and differentiation. This provides a line of descent for understanding critique as an attitude, or mentality, that emerged alongside governmentality. However, instead of being a mentality of rule focusing on questions of "how to govern", critique addresses the issue of "how not to be governed thus". Drawing on Foucault, the discussion then described critique as an attitude attendant upon those moments where subjects confront and contest the ways in which they are governed. It embraces at least three processes (for example, recovering contingency, insubordinate desubjectification, tracing possible transgressions), involving a mentality that dissociates existing limits and gestures towards alternative patterns of governance; indeed, as Hoy and McCarthy note, Foucault's approach provides an "internal critique because it interprets and criticizes contingent social formations from the inside, without positing a transcendent perspective or transcendentally necessary universal standards" (Hoy and McCarthy 1996: 173). Through such images one senses a different grammar of critique from founded judgement, one that aims to disrupt governmental certainties by problematising horizons of governance, leaning always towards the voids beyond.

The local and historically-situated character of this conception will perturb those who see critique as necessarily based on founded judgement. There will, no doubt, be ongoing calls to provide grounds for entertaining critique, or for specifying which paths of action to take (for example, Fraser 1997). As to the former, let us note the wide diversity of opposition frameworks that could count themselves within the realms of critique. It would reverse the spirit of critique as local counter-mentality, mobilised against specific patterns of governance, to suggest uniform grounds for engaging in critique. These are matters that will be, and are, worked out in context. There is a certain historically-located pragmatism implied in such work (see Mouffe 1996). But to ascribe one moral framework as the basis of all critical work is to reverse a critical spirit that does not spring from universal criteria and which tries to limit judgemental postures.

As to the matter of prescribing paths, let us again ponder the interpretative role implied by a critique of limits. It is perhaps appropriate here to reiterate Bauman's (1987: 194) realisation that: "The very activity of prescription-writing has been discredited, not just the individual prescriptions". I take seriously the view that the critic as legislating expert is no longer tenable. Not a judge who prescribes, the critic as local interpreter could separate out, discern and trace possible alternatives to mentalities of rule. The point is to highlight the unjust, unequal or otherwise problematic effects of governmental truths and to allude to the contingent (and thus reversible) decisions that have produced these. In political arenas that claim technocratic truths as essential and necessary, such a counter-mentality may be urgently required; but its urgency should not blind us to this recognition, there are no guarantees, no certainties. There is, however, the permanent possibility of calculating alternate patterns of subjection; the promise of justice forever remains at the horizon of what is. Its elusive shadow beckons us to calculate alternative governmental forms and entices us to exit from problematic ones that already exist. Mobilising an art of critique implies multiplying moments of opposition that discern the contingency of governmental limits, dissociate subjects from problematic subjugations and contemplate possible transgressions. Instead of requiring universally valid prescriptions, we might call for the critic to evoke, again and again, the possibility of not being governed thus.

Bibliography

ADAM, BARBARA. 1996. "Detraditionalization and the Certainty of Uncertain Futures" in P Heelas, S Lash and P Morris (eds) *Detraditionalization* (Oxford: Blackwell)

ALEXANDER, CHRISTOPHER. 1964. *Notes on the Synthesis of Form* (Cambridge, Mass.: Harvard University Press)

ALLEN, BARRY. 1991. "Government in Foucault" (1991) 21 *Canadian Journal of Philosophy* 421–40

ANNAS, JULIA and JONATHAN BARNES. 1994. "Introduction" in Sextus Empiricus *Outlines of Scepticism* (translated by J Annas and J Barnes, Cambridge: Cambridge University Press)

APPLETON, J W. 1879. *Genius: What It Is, and What It Has Accomplished* (London: S.W. Partridge and Co)

ARMSTRONG, DAVID. Undated. "Public Health Spaces and the Fabrication of Identity" unpublished paper presented to a History of the Present seminar, London

Australian Journal of Family Law (institutional author). 1995. "Domestic Relationships Legislation in the ACT" (1995) 9 *Australian Journal of Family Law* 10–11

BAIN, ALEXANDER. 1855. *The Senses and the Intellect* (London: John Parker and Sons)

BAKER, CAROLYN. 1997. "Membership Categorization and Interview Accounts" in D Silverman (ed) *Qualitative Research: Theory, Method and Practice* (London: Sage)

BANDINI, MICHA. 1984. "Typology as a Form of Convention" (1984) 6 *AA Files* 73–82

BARENBRUG, A. 1955. *Psychrometry and Psychrometric Charts* (Johannesburg: Transvaal and Orange Free State Chamber of Mines)

BARRY, ANDREW, VICKI BELL, and NIKOLAS ROSE. 1995. "Special Issue: Alternative Political Imaginations: —Introduction" (1995) 24 *Economy and Society* 485–8

——, THOMAS OSBORNE and NIKOLAS ROSE. 1993. "Liberalism, Neo-Liberalism and Governmentality: An Introduction" (1993) 22 *Economy and Society* 265–6

——, THOMAS OSBORNE and NIKOLAS ROSE (eds). 1996. *Foucault and Political Reason: Liberalism, Neo-liberalism and Rationalities of Government* (London: UCL Press)

BARTHES, ROLAND. 1987. *Criticism and Truth* (translated by K P Keuneman, Minneapolis: University of Minnesota Press)

BAUDRILLARD, JEAN. 1983. *In the Shadow of the Silent Majorities, or, the End of the Social, and Other Essays* (New York: Semiotext(e))

BAUMAN, ZYGMUNT. 1987. *Legislators and Interpreters* (Oxford: Blackwell)

——. 1988. *Freedom* (Milton Keynes: Open University Press)

——. 1992. *Intimations of Postmodernity* (London: Routledge)

——. 1997. *Postmodernity and Its Discontents* (Oxford: Polity)

BAYLE, PIERRE. 1965 [1697]. *Historical and Critical Dictionary: Selections* (translated by R H Popkin, with the assistance of C Brush, New York: Bobbs-Merrill)

BECK, ULRICH. 1992. *The Risk Society: Towards a New Modernity* (translated by Mark Ritter, London: Sage)

BECK, ULRICH and ELISABETH BECK-GERNSHEIM. 1995. *The Normal Chaos of Love* (translated by M Ritter and J Wiebel, Oxford: Polity Press)

BECK, ULRICH and ELISABETH BECK-GERNSHEIM. 1996. "Individualization and 'Precarious Freedoms': Perspectives and Controversies of a Subject-orientated Sociology" in P Heelas, S Lash and P Morris (eds) *Detraditionalization* (Oxford: Blackwell)

BENHABIB, SEYLA. 1986. *Critique, Norm, and Utopia: A Study of the Foundations of Critical Theory* (New York: Columbia University Press)

BERNSTEIN, RICHARD. 1988. "Metaphysics, Critique and Utopia" (1988) 42 *Review of Metaphysics* 255–73

——. 1994. "Foucault: Critique as Philosophic Ethos" in M Kelly (ed) *Critique and Power: Recasting the Foucault/Habermas Debate* (Cambridge Mass.: MIT Press)

BEVERIDGE, WILLIAM. 1909. *Unemployment: A Problem of Industry* (London: Longmans, Green & Co)

BLAIR, TONY. 1998. *The Third Way: New Politics for the New Century* (London: Fabian Society)

BLUNKETT, DAVID. 1997. Department for Education and Employment Press Release 261/97

BOBBIO, NORBERTO. 1987. *The Future of Democracy* (translated by R Griffin, Cambridge: Polity)

BOGGS, CARL. 1976. *Gramsci's Marxism* (London: Pluto Press)

BOTTOMLEY, STEPHEN and STEPHEN PARKER. 1997. *Law in Context*, 2nd edition (Sydney: The Federation Press)

BOTTOMS, ANTHONY and PAUL WILES. 1996. "Crime and Policing in a Changing Social Context" in W Saulsbury, J Mott and T Newburn (eds) *Themes in Contemporary Policing London* (London: Policy Studies Institute)

BOWLING, B. 1993. "Policing Violent Racism: Policy and Practice in an East London Locality" unpublished PhD thesis, London School of Economics

BRAKE, MIKE and CHRIS HALE. 1991. *Public Order and Private Lives: Politics of Law and Order* (London: Routledge)

BRIGHT, JOHN. 1998. "Preventing Youth Crime" (1998) 33 *Criminal Justice Matters* 15–17

BRITTAN, SAMUEL. 1975. *Second Thoughts on Full Employment Policy* (London: Centre for Policy Studies)

BUCHANAN, CATHY and PETER HARTLEY. 1992. *Criminal Choice: The Economic Theory of Crime and Its Implications for Crime Control* (Canberra: Centre for Independent Studies)

BURCHELL, GRAHAM. 1991. "Peculiar Interests: Civil Society and Governing 'The System of Natural Liberty" in G Burchell, C Gordon and P Miller (eds) *The Foucault Effect: Studies in Governmentality* (London: Harvester-Wheatsheaf)

——. 1993. "Liberal Government and Techniques of the Self" (1993) 22 *Economy and Society* 267–82

——, COLIN GORDON, and PETER MILLER (eds). 1991. *The Foucault Effect: Studies in Governmentality* (London: Harvester-Wheatsheaf)

BURROWS, ROGER and BRIAN LOADER. 1994. *Towards a Post-Fordist Welfare State* (London: Routledge)

BURTON JACKSON, JANICE L. 1982. *Not An Idle Man* (Fremantle: M. B. Roe)

COMACK, ELIZABETH and STEPHEN BRICKEY. 1991. *The Social Basis of Law: Critical Readings in the Sociology of Law* (Halifax: Garamond Press)

COTTERRELL, Roger. 1984. *The Sociology of Law* (London: Butterworths)

CANGUILHEM, GEORGES. 1998. "The Decline of the Idea of Progress" (1998) 27 *Economy and Society* 313–29

CARNOY, MARTIN and MANUEL CASTELLS. 1997. *Sustainable Flexibility: A Prospective Study on Work, Family and Society in the Information Age* (Paris: OECD)

CARRIER, WILLIS, REALTO CHERNE and WALTER GRANT. 1940. *Modern Air Conditioning, Heating and Ventilating* (New York: Pitman)

CARTER, PAUL. 1987. *The Road to Botany Bay* (London: Faber and Faber)

CASTELLS, MANUEL. 1997. *The Power of Identity in the Information Age: Economy, Society and Culture*, Volume Two (Oxford: Blackwell)

CHAPMAN, BRIAN. 1970. *Police State* (London: Macmillan)

CHRISTIE, E. 1992. "Toxic Tort Disputes: Distinctive Characteristics Require Special Preparation for Trial" (1992) 22 *Queensland Law Society Journal* 279–93

CHRISTIE, NILS. 1994. *Crime Control as Industry* (London: Routledge)

CHURCHILL, WINSTON. 1973 [1919]. *Liberalism and the Social Problem* (London: Hodder and Stoughton)

CLARKE, JOHN and NEWMAN, JANET. 1997. *The New Managerial State* (London: Sage)

COHEN, Stan. 1985. *Visions of Social Control* (Oxford: Polity Press)

——. 1996. "Crime and Politics: Spot the Difference" (1996) 41 *British Journal of Sociology* 1–21

COLEMAN, ROY and JOE SIM. 1996. "From the Dockyards to the Disney Store: Surveillance, Risk and Security in Liverpool City Centre" unpublished paper presented to the Law and Society Association Annual Conference, University of Strathclyde, Glasgow, July

COLLINI, STEPHAN. 1979. *Liberalism and Sociology: L. T. Hobhouse and Political Argument in England, 1880–1914* (Cambridge: Cambridge University Press)

COLQUHOUN, ALAN. 1981. *Essays in Architectural Criticism* (Cambridge, Mass.: MIT Press)

COMACK, ELIZABETH and STEPHEN L BRICKEY. 1991. *The Social Basis of Law: Critical Readings in the Sociology of Law* (Halifax: Garamond Press)

CON DAVIS, ROBERT, and RONALD SCHLEIFER. 1991. *Criticism and Culture: The Role of Critique in Modern Literary Theory* (London: Longmans)

CONAGHAN, JOANNE, and WADE MANSELL. 1993. *The Wrongs of Tort* (London: Pluto Press)

CONNERTON, PAUL. 1980. *The Tragedy of Enlightenment: An Essay on the Frankfurt School* (Cambridge: Cambridge University Press)

COOK, DEE and BARBARA HUDSON (eds). 1993. *Racism and Criminology* (London: Sage)

COTTERRELL, ROGER. 1984. *The Sociology of Law: an Introduction* (London: Butterworths)

COWARD, ROSALIND and JOHN ELLIS. 1977. *Language and Materialism* (London: Routledge and Kegan Paul)

CRAWFORD, ADAM. 1997. *The Local Governance of Crime: Appeals to Community and Partnership* (Oxford: Clarendon)

CROWTHER, CHRIS. 1999. *Policing the Underclass* (London: Macmillan)

CRUIKSHANK, BARBARA. 1994. "The Will to Empower: Technologies of Citizenship and the War on Poverty" (1994) 23 *Socialist Review* 29–55

CURNOW, HEATHER. 1980. *William Strutt* (Sydney: Australian Gallery Directors' Council)

CURRIE, ELLIOTT. 1997. "Market, Crime and Community: Towards a Mid-Range Theory of Post-Industrial Violence" (1997) 1 *Theoretical Criminology* 147–72

CURTIS, BRUCE. 1995. "Taking the State Back Out: Rose and Miller on Political Power" (1995) 46 *British Journal of Sociology* 575–89

CURTIS, LEWIS. 1968. *Anglo-Saxons and Celts: A Study of Anti-Irish Prejudice in Victorian England* (Bridgeport: Conference on British Studies at the University of Bridgeport)

DALE, ROGER. 1997. "The State and the Governance of Education: An Analysis of the Restructuring of the State-Education Relationship" in AH Halsey, H Lauder, P Brown and A Wells (eds) *Education: Culture, Economy, Society* (Oxford: Oxford University Press)

DAVIES, NICK. 1997. *Dark Heart* (London: Chatto and Windus)

DAVIS, MIKE. 1992. *City of Quartz* (London: Vintage)

——. 1993. *Beyond Blade Runner: Urban Control, the Ecology of Fear* (New York: The Free Press)

DEAKIN, NICHOLAS and JOHN EDWARDS. 1993. *The Enterprise Culture and the Inner City* (London: Routledge)

DEAN, MITCHELL. 1994. *Critical and Effective Histories: Foucault's Methods and Historical Sociology* (London: Routledge)

——. 1995. "Governing the Unemployed Self in an Active Society" (1995) 24 *Economy and Society* 559–83

——. 1998. "Administering Asceticism: Reworking the Ethical Life of the Unemployed Citizen" in M Dean and B Hindess *Governing Australia: Studies in Contemporary Rationalities of Government* (Cambridge: Cambridge University Press)

——. 1999. *Governmentality: Power and Rule in Modern Society* (London: Sage Publications)

DERRIDA, JACQUES. 1992. "Force of Law: The 'Mystical Foundations of Authority' " in D Cornell, M Rosenfeld and D Carlson (eds) *Deconstruction and the Possibility of Justice* (New York: Routledge)

——. 1994. *Spectres of Marx: The State of the Debt, the Work of Mourning and the New International* (London: Routledge)

——. 1997. *Deconstruction in a Nutshell: A Conversation with Jacques Derrida* (edited by J D Caputo, New York: Fordham University Press)

DERRINGTON, THE HON. MR JUSTICE DONALD. 1992. "The Effects of Insurance on the Law of Damages" in P Finn (ed) *Essays on Damages* (Sydney: Law Book Company)

DONZELOT, JACQUES. 1979. *The Policing of Families* (New York: Pantheon Books)

——. 1980. *The Policing of Families: Welfare Versus the State* (translated by R Hurley (London: Hutchinson)

——. 1991. "The Mobilisation of Society" in G Burchell, C Gordon and P Miller (eds) *The Foucault Effect: Studies in Governmentality* (London: Harvester-Wheatsheaf)

DOORDAN, DENNIS (ed). 1995. *Design History: An Anthology* (Cambridge, Mass.: MIT Press)

DOUGLAS, MARY. 1992. *Risk and Blame: Essays in Cultural Theory* (London: Routledge)

DOWNES, DAVID. 1998. From Labour Opposition to Labour Government, unpublished paper delivered to the Renewal of Criminal Justice Conference, University of Hull, 22 September

DRIVER, STEPHEN and LUKE MARTELL. 1997. "New Labour's Communitarianisms" (1997) 52 *Critical Social Policy* 27–46

DUNBAR, IAN and ANTHONY LANGDON. 1998. *Tough Justice* (London: Blackstone Press)

DURKHEIM, EMILE. 1964. *The Rules of Sociological Method* (translated by S A Solovay and J H Mueller, New York: Free Press)

EATWELL, JOHN. 1995. "The International Origins of Unemployment" in Jonathon Michie and John Grieve Smith (eds) *Managing the Global Economy* (Oxford: Oxford University Press)

EHRENREICH, BARBARA, ELIZABETH HESS and GLORIA JACOBS. 1986. *Re-making Love: The Feminization of Sex* (Glasgow: Fontana/Collins)

ELIAS, NORBERT. 1978. *The Civilizing Process, Volume One: The History of Manners* (translated by E Jephcott, Oxford: Blackwell)

ELLIOTT, LARRY and SEAMUS MILNE. 1999. "Labour's election slogan was 'education' but it could have been 'work' " *The Guardian* 4 January

ETZIONI, AMITAI. 1993. *The Spirit of Community: Rights, Responsibilities, and the Communitarian Agenda* (New York: Crown)

European Commission. 1994. *Growth, Competitiveness, Employment: The Challenges and Ways Forward into the 21st Century* (Luxembourg: Office for Official Publications of the European Communities)

European Commission. 1996. *Immigrant Delinquency: Social Construction of Deviant Behaviour and Criminality of Immigrants in Europe* (Brussels: European Commission)

European Forum for Urban Security. 1994. *Security and Democracy* (Paris: European Forum For Urban Security)

European Forum for Urban Security. 1996. *Urban Security and the Elderly* (Paris: European Forum For Urban Security)

EWALD, FRANCOIS. 1991. "Insurance and Risk" in G Burchell, C Gordon and P Miller (eds) *The Foucault Effect: Studies in Governmentality* (London: Harvester-Wheatsheaf)

FAIRCLOUGH, NORMAN. 1995. *Critical Discourse Analysis: The Critical Study of Language* (London: Routledge)

FALZON, CHRISTOPHER. 1998. *Foucault and Social Dialogue: Beyond Fragmentation* (London, Routledge)

FEELEY, M. and J SIMON. 1994. "Actuarial Justice: the Emerging New Criminal Law" in D Nelken (ed) *The Futures of Criminology* (London: Sage Publications)

FERRELL, JEFF. 1996. *"Crimes of Style: Urban Graffitti and the Politics of Criminality"* (Boston: North East University Press)

FIELDING, NIGEL. 1991. *The Police and Social Conflict* (London: The Athalone Press)

FINN, DAN. 1997. "Labour's New Deal for the Unemployed" (1997) 12 *Local Economy* 247–58

FINNANE, MARK. 1994. *Police and Government* (Melbourne: Oxford University Press)

——. 1996. "Comment on Pat O'Malley, 'Post-Social Criminologies' " (1996) 8 *Current Issues in Criminal Justice* 39–42

FITZPATRICK, PETER. 1988. "The Rise and Rise of Informalism" in Roger Matthews (ed) *Informal Justice?* (London: Sage)

FITZROY, ROBERT. 1839. *Narrative of the Surveying Voyages of His Majesty's Ships Adventure and Beagle* (London: H. Colburn)

FLANAGAN, RICHARD. 1991. *"Parish-Fed Bastards": A History of the Politics of the Unemployed in Britain 1994–1939* (Westport: Greenwood)

FLEMING, JOHN. 1992. *The Law of Torts*, 9th edition (Sydney: Law Book Company)

FOUCAULT, MICHEL. 1966. *Les Mots et les Choses: Une Archéologie des Sciences Humaines* (Paris: Gallimard)

——. 1973. *The Order of Things: An Archaeology of the Human Sciences* (New York: Vantage Press)

——. 1977. *Discipline and Punish: The Birth of the Prison* (translated by A Sheridan, New York: Vintage Books)

——. 1980. *Power/Knowledge: Selected Interviews and Other Writings 1972–1977* (edited by C Gordon, New York: Pantheon Books)

——. 1981. "Omnes et Singulatim" in S McMurrin (ed) *The Tanner Lectures on Human Values*, Volume Two (Cambridge: Cambridge University Press)

FOUCAULT, MICHEL. 1982. "The Subject and Power" in H L Dreyfus and P Rabinow (eds) *Michel Foucault: Beyond Structuralism and Hermeneutics* (Chicago: University of Chicago Press)

——. 1986. *The Care of the Self* (translated by R Hurley, New York: Pantheon)

——. 1988a. *Politics, Philosophy, Culture: Interviews and Other Writings, 1977–1984* (edited by L D Kritzman, New York: Routledge)

——. 1988b. "Technologies of the Self" in L H Martin, H Gutman and P H Hutton (eds) *Technologies of the Self: A Seminar with Michel Foucault* (Amherst: University of Massachusetts Press)

——. 1989. *Foucault Live (Interviews, 1961–1984)* (New York: Semiotext(e))

——. 1991 [1978]. "Governmentality" in G Burchell, C Gordon and P Miller (eds) *The Foucault Effect: Studies in Governmentality* (London: Harvester-Wheatsheaf)

——. 1994. "Genealogy and Social Criticism" in S Seidman (ed) *The Postmodern Turn: New Perspectives on Social Theory* (Cambridge: Cambridge University Press)

——. 1997a. "Ethics, Subjectivity and Truth" in P Rabinow (ed) *Michel Foucault: Ethics, The Essential Works 1* (translated by R Hurley and others, New York: The New Press)

——. 1997b. *The Politics of Truth* (New York: Semiotext(e))

FRANKEL, BORIS. 1997. "Confronting Neoliberal Regimes: The Post-Marxist Embrace of Populism and Realpolitik" (1997) 226 *New Left Review* 57–92

FRASER, NANCY. 1997. *Justice Interruptus: Critical Reflections on the 'Postsocialist' Condition* (London: Routledge)

FRIEDMAN, MILTON and ROSE FRIEDMAN. 1984. *The Tyranny of the Status Quo* (London: Secker and Warburg)

GAMBLE, ANDREW. 1988. *The Free Economy and the Strong State* (London: Macmillan)

——. 1994. *The Free Economy and the Strong State: The Politics of Thatcherism*, 2nd edition (London: Macmillan)

GARLAND, DAVID. 1983. "Philosophical Argument and Ideological Effect: An Essay Review" (1983) 7 *Contemporary Crises* 79

——. 1985. *Punishment and Welfare: A History of Penal Strategies* (Aldershot: Gower)

——. 1996. "The Limits of the Sovereign State: Strategies of Crime Control in Contemporary Society" (1996) 36 *British Journal Of Criminology* 445–71

——. 1997. " 'Governmentality' and the Problem of Crime" (1997) 1 *Theoretical Criminology* 173–215

GARLAND, DAVID and PETER YOUNG. 1983. *The Power to Punish* (London: Heinemann)

GIDDENS, ANTHONY. 1992. *Transformation of Intimacy* (Cambridge: Polity)

——. 1994. *Beyond Left and Right: The Future of Radical Politics* (Cambridge: Polity)

GOETSCHEL, WILLI. 1994. *Constituting Critique: Kant's Writing as Critical Praxis* (Durham: Duke University Press)

GOODALL, HEATHER. 1996. *Invasion to Embassy: Land in Aboriginal Politics in New South Wales, 1770–1972* (Sydney: Allen and Unwin)

GORDON, COLIN. 1991. "Governmental Rationality: An Introduction" in G Burchell, C Gordon and P Miller (eds) *The Foucault Effect: Studies in Governmentality* (London: Harvester-Wheatsheaf)

GORNICK, VIVIAN. 1997. *The End of the Novel of Love* (Boston: Beacon Press)

GOWING, LAWRENCE. 1987. *Paintings in the Louvre* (New York: Stewart, Tabori and Chang)

GRAHAM, JOHN and TREVOR BENNETT. 1995. *Crime Prevention Strategies in Europe and North America* (Helsinki: European Institute for Crime Prevention and Control)

GRAMSCI, ANTONIO. 1997. *Selections from The Prison Notebooks of Antonio Gramsci* (edited by Q Hoare and G Nowell-Smith, translated by Q Hoare and G Nowell-Smith, New York: International Publishers)

GRUNCHEC, PHILLIP. 1982. *Géricault's Horses* (Lausanne: Sotheby's Publications)

GUNNINGHAM, NEIL. 1994. "Beyond Compliance: Management of Environmental Risk" in B Boer, R Fowler and N Gunningham (eds) *Environmental Outlook: Law and Policy* (Sydney: The Federation Press)

HABERMAS, JURGEN. 1984. *The Theory of Communicative Action, Reason and Rationalization of Society,* Volume One (Boston: Beacon Press)

——. 1987. *Philosophical Discourses of Modernity* (Cambridge, Mass.: MIT Pres).

HACKING, IAN. 1986. "Making Up People" in T C Heller, M Sosna and D E Wellbery (eds) *Reconstructing Individualism, Autonomy, Individuality and the Self in Western Thought* (Stanford: Stanford University Press)

——. 1995. *Rewriting the Soul* (Princeton: Princeton University Press)

——. 1999. *The Social Construction of What?* (Cambridge, Mass.: Harvard University Press)

HADOT, PIERRE. 1987. *Exercices Spirituels et Philosophie Antique* (Paris: Etudes Augustiniennes) English trans. 1995. *Philosophy as a Way of Life: Spiritual Exercises from Socrates to Foucault* (edited by Arnold Davidson, translated by Michael Chase, New York: Blackwell)

HALDANE, ROBERT. 1986. *The People's Force* (Melbourne: Melbourne University Press)

HALL, STUART, CHARLES CRITCHER, TONY JEFFERSON, JOHN CLARKE and BRIAN ROBERTS. 1978. *Policing the Crisis* (London: Macmillan)

HALL, STUART and PAUL DU GAY. (eds). 1996. *Questions of Cultural Identity* (London: Sage)

HANKINSON, RJ. 1995. *The Sceptics* (London: Routledge)

HARPHAM, GEOFFREY G. 1987. *The Ascetic Imperative in Culture and Criticism* (Chicago: University of Chicago Press)

HARRIS, JOSE. 1972. *Unemployment and Politics* (Oxford: Clarendon Press)

HARTIN, WARWICK. 1993. "Human Relationships and Parenting" in *National Family Summit Report* (Parliament House, Canberra) 51–61

HARTZ, LOUIS. 1964. *The Founding of New Societies: Studies in the History of the United States, Latin America, South Africa, Canada and Australia* (New York: Harbinger)

HAUFFE, THOMAS. 1998. *Design: A Concise History* (London: Lawrence King)

HAWKES, GAIL. 1996. *A Sociology of Sex and Sexuality* (Milton Keynes: Open University Press)

HAY, COLIN. 1996. *Re-stating Social and Political Change* (Milton Keynes: Open University Press)

HAYDON, ARTHUR L. 1911. *The Trooper Police of Australia* (London: Andrew Melrose)

HAYES, MARTIN. 1994. *The New Right in Britain* (London: Pluto Press)

HEELAS, PAUL. 1996. "Introduction: Detraditionalization and its Rivals" in P Heelas, S Lash and P Morris (eds) *Detraditionalization* (Oxford: Blackwell)

HEIDEGGER, MARTIN. 1957. *Der Satz vom Grund* (Pfullingen: Günther Neske)

——. 1976. "Brief über Humanismus" in *Gesamtausgabe,* Volume Nine: *Wegmarken* (Frankfurt-am-Main: Vittorio Klostermann) 145–94

——. 1991 [1929]. *Kant und das Problem der Metaphysik,* 5th edition, enlarged (Frankfurt-am-Main: Vittorio Klostermann)

——. 1993 [1927]. *Sein und Zeit,* 17th edition (Tübingen: Max Niemeyer)

HILEY, DAVID. 1988. *Philosophy in Question: Essays on a Pyrrhonian Theme* (Chicago: University of Chicago Press)

HILL KAY, HERMA. 1990. "Private Choices and Public Policy: Confronting the Limitations of Marriage" (1990) 5 *Australian Journal of Family Law* 69–85

HILL, MICHAEL. 1996. *Social Policy: A Comparative Perspective* (London: Harvester-Wheatsheaf)

HILL, WILLIAM R O. 1907. *Forty-Five Year's Experience in North Queensland, 1861 to 1905* (Brisbane: H. Pole and Co)

HINDESS, BARRY. 1998. "Neo-liberalism and the National Economy" in *Governing Australia: Studies in Contemporary Rationalities of Government* (edited by M Dean and B Hindess, Melbourne: Cambridge University Press)

HIRST, JOHN B. 1988. *The Strange Birth of Colonial Democracy* (Sydney: Allen and Unwin)

HIRST, PAUL. 1986. *Law, Socialism and Democracy* (London: Collins)

——. 1994. *Associative Democracy: New Forms of Economic and Social Governance* (Cambridge: Polity)

—— and PENNY WOOLLEY. 1985. "Nature and Culture in Social Science: the Demarcation of Domains of Being in Eighteenth Century and Modern Discourses" (1985) 16 *Geoforum* 151–61

HOGG, RUSSELL. 1983. "Perspectives on the Criminal Justice System" in M Findlay, S Egger, and J Sutton (eds) *Issues in Criminal Justice Administration* (Sydney: Allen and Unwin)

——. 1996. "Criminological Failure and Governmental Effect" (19967) 8 *Current Issues in Criminal Justice* 43–59

—— and DAVID BROWN. 1998. *Rethinking Law and Order* (Sydney: Pluto)

—— and KERRY CARRINGTON. 1998. "Crime, Rurality and Community" (1998) 31 *Australian and New Zealand Journal of Criminology* 160–81

HOLSTEIN, JAMES A and JABER F GUBRIUM. 1997. "Active Interviewing" in D Silverman (ed) *Qualitative Research: Theory, Method and Practice* (London: Sage)

HOOD, CHRISTOPHER. 1991. "A Public Management for All Seasons" (1991) 69 *Public Administration* 3–19

HOPE, TIM. 1998. "Preventing Crime in the Community: Community Crime Prevention" in P Goldblatt and C Lewis (eds) *Reducing Offending: An Assessment of Research Evidence on Ways of Dealing with Offending Behaviour* (Home Office Research Study 187, London: Home Office)

HOROWITZ, M. 1982. "The Doctrine of Objective Causation" in D Kairys (ed) *The Politics of Law: A Progressive Critique* (New York: Pantheon)

HOY, DAVID COUZENS and THOMAS MCCARTHY. 1996. *Critical Theory* (Oxford: Blackwell)

HUGHES, GORDON. 1996. "Strategies of Multi-Agency Crime Prevention and Community Safety in Britain" (1996) 5 *Studies On Crime and Crime Prevention* 221–44

——. 1998. *Understanding Crime Prevention: Social Control, Risk and Late Modernity* (Milton Keynes: Open University Press)

HUNTER, IAN. Undated. "Michel Foucault: Discourse versus Language", unpublished manuscript (Griffith University, Brisbane)

——. 1993. "Subjectivity and Government" (1993) 22 *Economy and Society* 123–34

HUTCHINGS, KIMBERLEY. 1996. *Kant, Critique and Politics* (London: Routledge)

HUTTON, P H. 1988. "Foucault, Freud, and the Technology of the Self" in L H Martin, H Gutman and P H Hutton (eds) *Technologies of the Self: A Seminar with Michel Foucault* (Amherst: University of Massachusetts Press)

International Labour Office. 1996. *World Employment Report 1995* (Geneva: International Labour Office)

JEFFERSON, TONY. 1990. *The Case Against Paramilitary Policing* (Milton Keynes: Open University Press)

JESSOP, BOB. 1994. "The Transition to Post-Fordism and the Schumpeterian Workfare State" in R Burrows and B Lauder (eds) *Towards a Post-Fordist Welfare State?* (London: Routledge)

——. 1995. "The Regulation Approach: Governance and Post-Fordism—Alternative Perspectives on Economic and Political Change" (1995) 24 *Economy and Society* 307–33

JOHNSTON, LES. 1992. *The Rebirth of Private Policing* (London: Routledge)

——. 1999. *Policing Britain: Risk, Security and Governance* (London: Longman)

JONES, GARETH STEDMAN. 1984 [1971]. *Outcast* (London: Penguin)

KANT, IMMANUEL. 1781/1787. *Kritik der Reinen Vernunft.* First (A) edition/second (B) edition (Riga: Johann Friedrich Hartknoch) English trans. 1933. *Critique of Pure Reason* (translated by Norman Kemp Smith, London: Macmillan)

——. 1958. *Critique of Pure Reason* (New York: Modern Library)

KELLY, MICHAEL. (ed). 1994. *Critique and Power: Recasting the Foucault/Habermas Debate* (Cambridge, Mass.: MIT Press)

KELSEY, JANE. 1993. *Rolling Back the State: Privatisation of Power in Aotearoa/New Zealand* (Wellington: Bridget Williams Books)

KENDALL, GAVIN and GARY WICKHAM. 1999. *Using Foucault's Methods* (London: Sage)

KEYNES, JOHN MAYNARD. 1936. *The General Theory of Employment, Interest and Money* (London: Macmillan)

KING, DESMOND. 1993. "The Conservatives and Training Policy 1979–1992: From a Tripartite to a Neoliberal Regime" (1993) 41 *Political Studies* 214–35

KING, MICHAEL. 1991. "The Political Construction of Crime Prevention: A Contrast Between the French and British Experience" in K Stenson and D Cowell (eds) *The Politics of Crime Control* (London: Sage)

KOSELLECK, REINHART. 1988. *Critique and Crisis: Enlightenment and the Pathogenesis of Modern Society* (Oxford: Berg)

LACEY, NICOLA and LUCIA ZEDNER. 1995. "Discourse of Community in Criminal Justice" (1995) 22 *Journal of Law and Society* 301–25

LAMBERT, BRYAN and BERYL MASON. 1996. "Justice, Welfare or a New Direction?: An Examination of the Juvenile Justice Act 1996 (Qld)" (1996) 12 *Queensland University of Technology Law Journal* 99–114

LARSEN, ANN-CLAIRE. 1995. "The Child Health Service: A Means of Regulating Western Australian Families of Pre-School Children", unpublished PhD thesis, University of Western Australia

LATOUR, BRUNO. 1993. *We Have Never Been Modern* (Cambridge, Mass.: Harvard University Press)

LEA, JOHN. 1997. "The Return of the Dangerous Classes", unpublished Inaugural Professorial Lecture, presented at Middlesex University, 10 December

LEVITAS, RUTH. 1986. "Competition and Compliance: The Utopias of the New Right" in R Levitas (ed) *The Ideology of the New Right* (Oxford: Blackwell)

——. 1996. "The Concept of Exclusion and the New Durkheimian Hegemony" (1996) 16 *Critical Social Policy* 5–20

LIANG, HSI-HUEY. 1992. *The Rise of Modern Policing and the European State System from Metternich to the Second World War* (Cambridge: Cambridge University Press)

LISTER, RUTH. (ed). 1996. *Charles Murray and the Underclass* (London: Institute of Economic Affairs)

LOCKE, JOHN. 1964 [1690]. *An Essay Concerning Human Understanding* (Oxford: Oxford University Press)

LOMBROSO, CESARE. 1891. *The Man of Genius* (London: Walter Scott)

LOW, M. 1999. " 'Their Masters' Voice': Communitarianism, Civic Order, and Political Representation" (1999) 31 *Environment and Planning A* 87–111

LUHMANN, NIKLAS. 1986. *Love as Passion: The Codification of Intimacy* (translated by J Gaines and D L Jones (Cambridge: Polity)

LUNTZ, HAROLD, and DAVID HAMBLY. 1995. *Torts: Cases and Commentary* (Sydney: Butterworths)

LUPTON, DEBORAH. 1993. "Risk as Moral Danger: The Social and Political Functions of Risk Disclosure in Public Health" (1993) 23 *The International Journal of Health Sciences* 425–35

LYOTARD, JEAN-FRANCOIS. 1984. *The Postmodern Condition: A Report on Knowledge* (Minneapolis: University of Minnesota Press)

——. 1988. *The Differend: Phrases in Dispute* (Minneapolis: University of Minnesota Press)

MACGREGOR, SUZANNE. 1998. "A New Deal For Britain" in H Jones and S MacGregor (eds) *Social Issues and Social Politics* (London: Routledge)

MACHIAVELLI, NICCOLO. 1996. *The Prince* (translated by P Sonnio, Atlantic City: Humanities Press)

Macquarie Library. 1984. *The Macquarie Illustrated World Atlas* (Sydney: Macquarie Library)

MAIER, CHARLES. 1987. *In Search of Stability: Explorations in Historical Political Economy* (Cambridge: Cambridge University Press)

MALDONADO, TOMAS. 1995. "The Idea of Comfort" in V Margolin and R Buchanan (eds) *The Idea of Design* (Cambridge, Mass.: MIT Press)

MALPAS, JEFF. 1992. *Donald Davidson and the Mirror of Meaning* (Cambridge: Cambridge University Press)

——. 1996. "Speaking the Truth" (1996) 25 *Economy and Society* 156–77

—— and GARY WICKHAM. 1995. "Governance and Failure: On the Limits of Sociology" (1995) 31 *Australian and New Zealand Journal of Sociology* 37–50

—— and GARY WICKHAM. 1997. "Governance and the World: From Joe DiMaggio to Michel Foucault" (1997) 3 *The UTS Review* 91–108

MARKS, GARY, FRITZ SCHARPF, PHILIPPE SCHMITTER and WOLFGANG STREECK. 1996. *Governance in the European Union* (London: Sage)

MARSLAND, DAVID. 1991. *Understanding Youth* (London: Institute of Economic Affairs)

MARX, KARL. 1971. *Frühe Schriften, Werke*, Volume Two (Darmstadt: Wissenschaftliche Buchgesellschaft)

MAWBY, ROB. 1990. *Comparative Policing Issues: The British and American Experience in International Perspective* (London: Unwin Hyman)

MCGRATH, ANN (ed). 1995. *Contested Ground: Australian Aborigines Under the British Crown* (Sydney: Allen and Unwin)

MCLAUGHLIN, EUGENE and JOHN MUNCIE. 1994. "Managing the Criminal Justice System" in J Clarke, A Cochrane and E McLaughlin (eds) *Managing Social Policy* (London: Sage)

McQuilton, John. 1987. "Police in Rural Victoria: A Regional Example" in M Finnane (ed) *Policing in Australia: Historical Perspectives* (Sydney: University of New South Wales Press)

Mead, Lawrence. 1986. *Beyond Entitlement: The Social Obligations of Citizenship* (New York: Free Press)

Michael, Alun. 1998. "Towards a Radical Century", speech presented at New Statesman and London School of Economics Annual Conference, London

Miller, Gale and David Silverman. 1995. "Troubles Talk and Counselling Discourse: A Comparative Study" (1995) 36 *The Sociological Quarterly* 725–47

Miller, Peter and Nikolas Rose. 1990. "Governing Economic Life" (1990) 19 *Economy and Society* 1–31

Milovanovic, Dragan. 1988. *A Primer in the Sociology of Law* (New York: Harrow and Heston)

Milte, Kerry. 1977. *Police in Australia* (Melbourne: Butterworths)

Minford, Patrick. 1991. *The Supply-Side Revolution in Britain* (London: Edward Elgar)

Minson, Jeffrey. 1993. *Questions of Conduct: Sexual Harassment, Citizenship, Government* (London: Macmillan)

Monk, Ray. 1990. *Ludwig Wittgenstein: The Duty of Genius* (New York: Free Press)

Mouffe, Chantal (ed). 1996. *Deconstruction and Pragmatism* (London: Routledge)

Mulgan, Geoff. 1997. *Connexity: How to Live in a Connected World* (London: Chatto and Windus)

Muncie, John, Garry Coventry and R Walters. 1995. "The Politics of Youth Crime Prevention: Developments in Australia and England and Wales" in L Noakes *et al* (eds) *Contemporary Issues in Criminology* (Cardiff: University of Wales Press)

Nagle, John F. 1996. *Collins, the Courts and the Colony* (Sydney: University of New South Wales Press)

National Inquiry into the Separation of Aboriginal and Torres Strait Islander Children from their Families. 1997. *Bringing Them Home* (Sydney: Human Rights and Equal Opportunity Commission)

Nietzsche, Friedrich. 1974. *The Gay Science* (New York: Vintage Books)

Novak, Tony. 1997. "Hounding Delinquents: the Introduction of the Jobseekers' Allowance" (1997) 17 *Critical Social Policy* 99–109

O'Malley, Pat. 1992. "Risk, Power and Crime Prevention" (1992) 21 *Economy and Society* 252–75

——. 1994. "Neo-liberal Crime Control: Political Agendas and the Future of Crime Prevention in Australia" in D Chappell and P Wilson (eds) *The Australian Criminal Justice System: The Mid 1990s*, 4th edition (Sydney: Butterworths)

——. 1996a. "Indigenous Governance" (1996) 25 *Economy and Society* 310–26. (Also published in 1998 in M Dean and B Hindess (eds) *Governing Australia: Studies in Contemporary Rationalities of Government* (Melbourne: Cambridge University Press))

——. 1996b. "Criminology and the New Liberalism", the 1996 John Edwards Memorial Lecture, unpublished lecture delivered at Center of Criminology, University of Toronto

——. 1996c. "Post-Social Criminologies: Some Implications of Current Political Trends for Criminological Theory and Practice" (1996) 8 *Current Issues in Criminal Justice* 26–38

——. 1998. "Risk, Power and Crime Prevention" in P O'Malley (ed) *Crime and the Risk Society* (Aldershot: Ashgate/Dartmouth)

O'MALLEY, PAT. 1999. "Volatile Punishment" (1999) 3 *Theoretical Criminology* 175–96
——. 2000. "Uncertain Subjects: Risks, Liberalism and Contract" (2000) 29 *Economy and Society* 460–84
——. PAT and DARREN PALMER. 1996. "Post-Keynesian Policing" (1996) 25 *Economy and Society* 137–55
——, LORNA WEIR and CLIFFORD SHEARING. 1997. "Governmentality, Criticism, Politics" (1997) 26 *Economy and Society* 501–17
OECD. 1990. *Annual Report for 1989* (Paris: OECD)
OECD. 1994. *The OECD Jobs Study: Facts, Analysis, Strategy* (Paris: OECD)
OECD. 1997. "Preface" in Martin Carnoy and Manuel Castells *Sustainable Flexibility: A Prospective Study on Work, Family and Society in the Information Age* (Paris: OECD)
OFFE, CLAUS. 1996. *Modernity and the State: East, West* (Cambridge: Polity)
OWEN, DAVID. 1995. "Genealogy as Exemplary Critique: Reflections on Foucault and the Imagination of the Political" (1995) 24 *Economy and Society* 489–506
PALMER, STANLEY. 1988. *Police and Protest in England and Ireland 1780–1850* (Cambridge: Cambridge University Press)
Parliament of Victoria, Law Reform Committee. 1993. *Restitution for Victims of Crime* (Melbourne: Government Printer)
PARSONS, WAYNE. 1988. *The Political Economy of British Regional Policy* (London: Routledge)
PAVLICH, GEORGE. 1995. "Contemplating a Postmodern Sociology: Genealogy, Limits and Critique" (1995) 43 *The Sociological Review* 548–67
——. 1996a. *Justice Fragmented: Mediating Community Disputes Under Postmodern Conditions* (London: Routledge)
——. 1996b. "The Power Of Community Mediation: Government and Formation of Self-Identity" (1996) 30 *Law and Society Review* 707–33
——. 1998. "Phrasing Injustice: Critique in an Ethos of Uncertainty" (1998) 18 *Studies in Law, Politics and Society* 245–69
——. 2000. *Critique and Radical Discourses on Crime* (Aldershot: Ashgate/Dartmouth)
PETERSEN, ALAN and DEBORAH LUPTON. 1996. *The Public Health: Health and Self in the Age of Risk* (London: Sage)
PICKETT, BRENT L. 1996. "Foucault and the Politics Of Resistance" (1996) 28 *Polity* 445–66
PIERSON, PAUL. 1994. *Dismantling the Welfare State: Reagan, Thatcher, and the Politics of Retrenchment* (Cambridge: Cambridge University Press)
PLATO. 1963. *Republic* In *Collected Dialogues of Plato* (edited by E Hamilton and H Cairns, Princeton: Princeton University Press)
POWER, MICHAEL. 1994. *The Audit Explosion* (London: Demos)
PRATT, JOHN. 1989. "Corporatism: The Third Model of Juvenile Justice" (1989) 29 *British Journal of Criminology* 236–54
PRATT, JOHN. 1996. "Governmentality, Neo-liberalism and Dangerousness: Reflections on Recent Trends Toward the Punishment of Persistence", Unpublished paper, Victoria University of Wellington
RABIN, ROBERT. 1993. "Institutional and Historical Perspectives on Tobacco Tort Liability" in R Rabin and S Sugarman (eds) *Smoking Policy: Law, Politics and Culture* (New York: Oxford University Press)
RAEFF, MARC. 1983. *The Well Ordered Police State* (New Haven: Yale University Press)

RANSOM, JOHN S. 1997. *Foucault's Discipline: The Politics of Subjectivity* (Durham: Duke University Press)

RAWLINSON, PADDY. 1997. "A Threat to Europe?" (1997) 27 *Criminal Justice Matters* 10–11

READINGS, BILL. 1996. *The University in Ruins* (Cambridge, Mass.: Harvard University Press)

REINER, ROBERT. 1992 *The Politics of the Police*, 2nd edition (London: Harvester Wheatsheaf)

RHODES, ROD. 1990. "Policy Networks: A British Perspective" (1990) 2 *Journal of Theoretical Politics* 293–317

RORTY, RICHARD. 1998. *Leftist Thought in 20th Century America* (Cambridge: Cambridge University Press)

ROSE, NIKOLAS. 1987. "Beyond the Public/Private Division: Law, Power and the Family" in P Fitzpatrick and A Hunt (eds) *Critical Legal Studies* (Oxford: Blackwell)

——. 1988. "Calculable Minds and the Management of Individuals" (1988) 1 *History of the Human Sciences* 179–200

——. 1989. *Governing the Soul* (London: Routledge)

——. 1990. *Governing the Soul: The Shaping of the Private Self* (London; New York: Routledge)

——. 1992. "Governing the Enterprising Self" in P Heelas and P Morris (eds) *The Values of the Enterprise Culture: The Moral Debate* (London: Routledge)

——. 1993. "Toward a Critical Sociology of Freedom", inaugural lecture, delivered on 5 May 1992 (Goldsmiths' College, University of London: Occasional Paper)

——. 1996a. "Authority and the Genealogy of Subjectivity" in P Heelas, S Lash and P Morris (eds) *Detraditionalization* (Oxford: Blackwell)

——. 1996b. "Governing 'Advanced' Liberal Democracies" in A Barry, T Osborne and N Rose (eds) *Foucault and Political Reason: Liberalism, Neo-liberalism and Rationalities of Government* (London: UCL Press)

——. 1996c. "The Death of the 'Social'?: Refiguring the Territory of Government" (1996) 26 *Economy and Society* 327–46

——. 1999. *Powers of Freedom: Reframing Political Thought* (Cambridge: Cambridge University Press)

—— and PETER MILLER. 1992. "Political Power Beyond the State: Problematics of Government" (1992) 43 *British Journal of Sociology* 173–205

RUGGIERO, VINCENZO, MICK RYAN and JOE SIM (eds). 1995. *West European Penal Systems: A Critical Anatomy* (London: Sage)

RUSSELL, BERTRAND. 1988. *A History of Western Philosophy* (London: Allen and Unwin)

SACKS, HARVEY. 1992. *Lectures on Conversation*, Volumes One and Two (edited by G Jefferson, Oxford: Blackwell)

SADLEIR, JOHN. 1973 [1913]. *Recollections of a Victorian Police Officer* (Melbourne: George Robertson and Company)

SCHAMA, SIMON. 1995. *Landscape and Memory* (London: Harper Collins)

SCHARPF, FRITZ. 1991. *Crisis and Choice in European Social Democracy* (Ithaca: Cornell University Press)

SCHMIDT, JAMES and THOMAS E WARTENBERG. 1994. "Foucault's Enlightenment: Critique, Revolution and the Fashioning of the Self" in M Kelly (ed) *Critique and Power: Recasting the Foucault/Habermas Debate* (Cambridge, Mass.: MIT Press)

SCHON, DONALD. 1985. *The Design Studio: An Exploration of its Traditions and Potentials* (London: RIBA Publications)

SCHUTZ, ALFRED. 1966. *Some Structures of the Life-World in Phenomenology and Sociology: Selected Readings* (edited by Thomas Luckmann, Harmondsworth: Penguin)

SCRATON, PHIL and KATHY CHADWICK. 1991. "The Theoretical and Political Priorities of Critical Criminology" in K Stenson and D Cowell (eds) *The Politics of Crime Control* (London: Sage)

SCRUTON, ROGER. 1984. *The Meaning of Conservatism* (London: Macmillan)

SEXTUS EMPIRICUS. 1994. *Outlines of Scepticism* (translated by J Annas and J Barnes, Cambridge: Cambridge University Press)

SHEARING, CLIFFORD. 1996. "Public and Private Policing" in W Saulsbury, J Mott and T Newburn (eds) *Themes in Contemporary Policing* (London: Policy Studies Institute)

SHEPTYCKI, JAMES. 1995. "Transnational Policing and the Makings of a Postmodern State" (1995) 35 *British Journal of Criminology* 613–35

SILVERMAN, DAVID. 1993. *Interpreting Qualitative Data: Methods for Analysing Talk, Text and Interaction* (London: Sage)

SIMON, JONATHAN. 1995. "They Died with their Boots On: The Boot Camp and the Limits of Modern Penality" (1995) 22 *Social Justice* 25–49

——. 1996. "Criminology and the Recidivist" in D Shichor and D K Sechrest (eds) *Three Strikes and You're Out: Vengeance as Public Policy* (Beverly Hills: Sage)

SINGER, SIMON. 1996. *Recriminalising Delinquency: Violent Juvenile Crime and Juvenile Justice Reform* (Cambridge: Cambridge University Press)

SKOLNICK JEROME and DAVID BAYLEY. 1988. *Community Policing: Issues and Practices Around the World* (Washington: National Institute of Justice)

STAPELTON, JANE. 1995. "Tort, Insurance and Ideology" (1995) 58 *Modern Law Review* 820–45

STENSON, KEVIN. 1991. "Making Sense of Crime Control" in K Stenson and D Cowell (eds) *The Politics of Crime Control* (London: Sage)

——. 1993. "Community Policing as a Governmental Technology" (1993) 22 *Economy and Society* 373–89

——. 1996. "Communal Security as Government: The British Experience" in W Hammerschick, I Karazman-Morawetz and W Stangl (eds) *Jahrbuch fur Rechts und Kriminalsoziologie* (Baden-Baden: Nomos)

——. 1998. "Beyond Histories of the Present" (1998) 29 *Economy and Society* 333–52

——. 1999. "Crime Control, Governmentality and Sovereignty" in R Smandych *Governable Places: Readings in Governmentality and Crime Control* (Aldershot: Darmouth)

—— and FIONA FACTOR. 1994. "Youth Work, Risk and Crime Prevention" (1994) 45 *Youth and Policy* 1–15

—— and FIONA FACTOR. 1995. "Governing Youth: New Directions for the Youth Service" in *The Social Policy Review No. 7* (edited by M May and J Baldock, Canterbury: The Social Policy Association)

—— and PAUL WATT. 1999. "Governmentality and the 'Death of the Social'?: A Discourse Analysis of Local Government Texts in South-East England" (1999) 36 *Urban Studies* 189–201

STERN, VIVIEN. 1997. "A Paradise for Prisoners?" (1997) 27 *Criminal Justice Matters* 5–6

STRUTT, WILLIAM. Undated. Autobiography 1825–1897. Unpublished microfilm record CY Reel 195, MLMSS 867, Original Papers, 7 Volumes, Mitchell Library, Sydney.

——. 1979. *The Australian Journal of William Strutt, 1850–1862* (edited by George Mackaness, Dubbo: Review Publications)

STRUTT, WILLIAM. 1980. *Victoria the Golden* (Melbourne: Parliamentary Library Committee)

——. 1989. *Cooey* (Canberra: National Library of Australia)

SUMNER, COLIN. 1994. *The Sociology of Deviance: An Obituary* (Milton Keynes: Open University Press)

TAME, CHRIS. 1991. "Freedom, Responsibility and Justice: The Criminology of the 'New Right' " in K Stenson and D Cowell (eds) *The Politics of Crime Control* (London: Sage)

Taskforce on Families. 1995. *W.A. Families: Our Future. Report of the Taskforce on Families in Western Australia* (Perth: Government Printer)

TAYLOR, IAN (ed). 1990. *The Social Effects of Free Market Policies: An International Text* (London: Harvester-Wheatsheaf)

——. 1998. "Crime, Market Liberalism and the European Idea" in V Ruggiero, N South and I Taylor *The New European Criminology: Crime and Social Order in Europe* (London: Routledge)

TAYLOR, WILLIAM. 1993. "Building the Invisible City" in J MacArthur *Knowledge and/or/of Experience: The Theory of Space in Art and Architecture* (Brisbane: Institute of Modern Art)

——. 1995. "Living in Glasshouses: Vegetality and the Curvilinear Forcing Houses of the Early Nineteenth Century" (1995) 15 *Journal of Garden History* 207–20

THOMPSON, GRAHAME. 1992. "The Evolution of the Managed Economy in Europe" (1992) 21 *Economy and Society* 2–29

——. 1993. "Causality in Economics: Rhetorical Ethic or Positivist Empiric?" (1993) 27 *Quality & Quantity* 47–71

——. 1998. "Encountering Economics and Accounting: Some Skirmishes and Engagements" (1998) 23 *Accounting, Organizations and Society* 283–323

TURNER, JONATHAN H. 1991. *The Structure of Sociological Theory*, 5th edition (Belmont, California: Wadsworth Publishing)

VALVERDE, MARIANA. 1996. " 'Despotism' and Ethical Liberal Governance" (1996) 25 *Economy and Society* 357–72

VISKER, RUDI. 1995. *Michel Foucault: Genealogy as Critique* (London: Verso)

WACQUANT, LOIC. 1999. "Penal 'Common Sense' comes to Europe" *Le Monde Diplomatique* (English Edition: Monthly Supplement to *The Guardian Weekly*) 6 and 10–11 April

WALKER, JOHN. 1989. *Design History and the History of Design* (London: Pluto)

WALTERS, WILLIAM. 1994. "The Discovery of 'Unemployment': New Forms for the Government of Poverty" (1994) 23 *Economy and Society* 265–90

——. (2000) *Unemployment and Government: Genealogies of the Social* (Cambridge and Melbourne: Cambridge University Press)

WALTON, PAUL. 1998. "Big Science, Dystopia and Utopia" in P Walton and J Young (eds) *The New Criminology Revisited* (London: Macmillan)

WEIR, LORNA. 1996. "Recent Developments in the Governance of Pregnancy" (1996) 25 *Economy and Society* 372–92

Western Lands Commission. 1990. *Western Lands* (Sydney: Department of Lands)

WHITE, ROB. 1994. "Shame and Reintegration Strategies: Individual, State Power and Social Interests" in C Alder and J Wundersitz (eds) *Family Conferencing and Juvenile Justice* (Canberra: Australian Institute of Criminology)

WILLIAMS, KAREL and JOHN WILLIAMS. 1987. *A Beveridge Reader* (London: Allen and Unwin)

WITTGENSTEIN, LUDWIG. 1979. *On Certainty* (edited by G E M Anscombe and G H von Wright, translated by D Paul and G E M Anscombe, Oxford: Blackwell)

WORSTHORNE, PEREGRINE. 1988. *The Politics of Manners and the Uses of Inequality* (London: Centre for Policy Studies)

YATES, FRANCES. 1984. *The Art of Memory* (London: Routledge)

ZEDNER, LUCIA. 1995. "In Pursuit of the Vernacular: Comparing Law and Order Discourse in Britain and Germany" (1995) 4 *Social and Legal Studies* 517–34

Index